WASHINGTON IS WONDERFUL

To Those Who Came—and Stayed and Stayed:
The Native Washingtonians

WASHINGTON IS WONDERFUL

By DOROTHEA JONES

Pen and Ink Drawings by Pietro Lazzari

Harper & Brothers Publishers New York

Library of Congress catalog card number: 55–8057

CONTENTS

PART II

Ten Tours for Easy Sight-seeing

A group of photographs will be found following p. 22.

PREFACE

In writing this book I hope to give you a special gift—a city. With it goes a full set of instructions for peering behind the scenes and finding the Washington that makes people want to stay. Welcome to Washington!

Here you will discover a warm, spacious, charming city which, despite its place as a leading world capital, never outgrew its country accents, its take-it-easy manner. Two hundred and sixty-three thousand native Washingtonians—a complacent, quietly proud breed whose members you seldom meet—form the solid-gold nucleus of the population. Be warned, then, that the balance are "assimilated tourists" who came to look and stayed, or who completed assignments here, departed, and returned to enjoy the delights of a permanent attachment.

"They never go back to Pocatello!" So goes the old saw, applied to those who grumble about Washington's climate and other real or fancied hardships but who somehow contrive to stay on, or, having gone away, hasten back at the earliest opportunity.

Seldom were truer words spoken. The reasons they never go back to Pocatello are as pleasantly satisfying, as spicily tantalizing, as a bowl of the crab soup that near-by Chesapeake Bay has contributed to Washington cuisine.

In essence, Washington is an international city. Parisians fall in love with it because it is the living dream of their countryman, Major Pierre Charles L'Enfant, designer-extraordinary of the city. Amid the seedy grandeur of Capitol Hill and the quiet elegance of George-town, Londoners find reminders of their beloved mews. If you're a Scot, be at home: Pennsylvania Avenue was a bit late in opening because one David Burnes, whose farm extended over that way from the Potomac, had left his corn in the ground. If you're a Moslem, be at peace: builders of the exquisite Islamic Center on Massachusetts Avenue called on top cartographers to orient the mosque precisely, indisputably toward Mecca. If you're an Episcopalian, welcome: the Cathedral Church of Saints Peter and Paul waits in Gothic magnificence atop Mount St. Alban; or, in demure little St. John's, the Church of Presidents on Lafayette Square, you may worship where Dolley Madison was baptized in that faith. (If you're a French Protestant, St. John's would like to see you between October and June at *Service Français Dimanche à 4 heures*.)

The air is thick with history, if you care—with reasons why the Declaration of Independence happened.

But it's useless to tell a bone-weary tourist who has just collapsed on a bench at the foot of the Monument that seeing Washington is a gay business, full of unforgettable moments. The hope is to find you earlier, to help plan your day, so that right now you can be sipping a cool drink on the Hotel Washington roof, or studying a menu at the Occidental ("where statesmen dine"), with a pocketful of mementos to show for your morning.

One half, the first part, of this book is for your easy reading and concerns the broad picture of Washington. The latter portion is for down-to-business sight-seeing.

The *real* point of these paragraphs is this: Those expecting you home on the first of next month, to see about the storm windows, put in the soybeans, or get Junior back in school, may receive only a postcard saying "Having wonderful time, etc.," followed by silence. The following pages could be called a kind of indoctrination, because through them you might hear the city's elusive call and be unable to turn away.

You may never leave Washington.

ACKNOWLEDGMENTS

The preparation of such a book as this would be quite impossible were it not for the good-humored assistance of hundreds of people who have taken the time and trouble to answer innumerable questions and shed much light upon the subject. There are those to whom I am indebted, like Emma B. Hawks and Frank Edgington, who glanced back for lively reminiscences. There are others out of whose sheer enthusiasm for their own fields came my own spark of understanding. To name only a few: William L. Brown, Benjamin Lawless, Jr., and Dr. William Mann, all of the Smithsonian Institution; Frederick R. Goff, of the Library of Congress; Karl L. Trever, of the National Archives; Gretchen Feiker, of the Young Women's Christian Association; Jane Brewer Amann-Jones, of the Special Libraries Association, and Katharine McCook Knox, art historian.

I am indebted to Dr. Elizabeth McPherson of the Library of Congress for guiding me to valuable source materials relating to the early Capital. The Manuscript Division also made available Dolley Madison's signature, verifying the name, Dolley, as authentic, and spelling it with the "e."

Woven into the fabric of the book are the thoughts and feelings of interesting people I encountered everywhere: taxi drivers, next-door neighbors, friends, and strangers who queued up beside me at the monuments. Then, too, there was the steady help of all those, long gone, who, like one John Sessford, kept meticulous records of the early days in this Capital City.

To that distinguished artist Pietro Lazzari, I am most grateful, for he magically captured on the tip of his pen the grace and charm of Washington. My warm thanks go, too, to all those who patiently helped me check my facts—even the gracious lady who returned some corrected copy and called to say that the two spots on page 6 were made by some tomato aspic she had had for lunch.

For careful reading of the manuscript and valuable critical suggestions I am grateful to Horace W. Peaslee and Margaret G. Bledsoe. Most of all I am indebted to my husband, Stuart E. Jones, for editorial counsel, unfailing understanding, and aid above and beyond the call of duty.

PART I

Behind the Scenes in the Capital

I

Stop, Look—and Listen

PICTURE YOURSELF AT SOME PLACE OUTSIDE WASH-
ington. You are not yet knocking on the gates of the city, but in
about twenty minutes some view of the Capitol will open before
you, whether you come by automobile, by plane, or by train.

So there's time for a word.

Getting under Washington's skin calls for much energy, careful
listening, and some luck. Involved, too, are scraps of American history you've almost forgotten; that biography of Lincoln you read last
winter, even your fondness for those pewter spoons Aunt Bessie left
you, plus every news item you've read under a Washington date line,
or magazine article on the Capital scene. And really to succeed you
must be interested, expectant—and at the right place at the right
time. Wherever you are, take time to listen. Of course, things have
changed since President Ulysses S. Grant's day. Grant, encountering
a Government official one day, looked him in the eye and uttered
the single word, "Resign!" Even so, those two men you see convers-
ing in a Capitol corridor may be exchanging words of international
importance.

It may even call for standing off by yourself, away from the tourist
tide, to ensure that you aren't roaming about in a manufactured
climate that is less realistic than one you could get on your TV set
at cherry-blossom time. Invite a kind of latent receptivity, the happy
spongelike quality that changes a rank tourist into an observer.

3

But when you queue up at the Washington Monument, take the one-minute, ten-second elevator trip all the way to the highest landing of the 555-foot shaft, and then peek through elbows for a glimpse, this too must be part of your experience. (One recent April day over 5,300 people went up to the top.)

That smooth ride, to which the pleasantly recorded welcome of the National Capital Parks is expertly geared, in no way illustrates how the Monument reached its now cherished and unique place on the local skyline. Like many another shrine and the Capitol Building itself (which was left for years looking as though its hat had blown off), the Monument suffered growing pains and many indignities before it was opened to the public in 1888. During the Civil War it was left unfinished to weather in sun and rain; today you'll detect a slight variation in the color of the upper marble which, though the same white Maryland marble as below, marks the period of neglect and indecision—when the obelisk was even captured by a political party.

Red lights come on at nightfall to warn planes, but often, during spring and fall migrations, birds crash into the dark form and are found lifeless at its base in the morning.

Tomorrow you may find yourself standing beside a European visitor who utters an exclamation in any one of a dozen languages. Whatever it sounds like, translated it probably means, "You call this old?"

Yes, we admit it. There isn't a pre-Roman ruin anywhere around. Of course, Captain John Smith, that seafaring Englishman, did sail up the Potomac River a few hundred years ago and discover Indians; you'll see, in the Smithsonian Institution, exhibits of objects excavated in this area. Luckily, the Capital is young enough to remember where she's been and old enough to look back and value every step along the way.

This Capital, as capitals go, is pretty modern. You don't have to boil your drinking water, or get your money changed into anything more baffling than dollars and cents. The plumbing is dependable; so is the weather. In fact, it's so dependable that a large part of conversation about Washington weather doesn't mention the word at all: it runs on endlessly about humidity, and stops only when the phrase "air-conditioned" crops up.

If you are here on a high-humidity day, look about. Perhaps you'll be like a local artist who minds the heat but goes out to see the houses panting. "They have asthma," he says.

Geologically, of course, we are venerable. As you stroll through the lobby of the Mayflower Hotel it may give you a sense of deep roots to know that a prehistoric cypress swamp once shared this site. Or on your trip to Great Falls, you'll see a wild, winding stream, the Potomac, churning through rocks that have held firm for a billion years.

Two hundred years ago Washington didn't exist at all. But you'll be turning up names of people who made their mark over that sweep of time: red men, white men, Negroes, brave generals, brilliant lawyers, dreamers with plans, patriots, names that trip from every Independence Day orator's tongue.

For this city from its start was as planned as any modern blueprint Suburbia today. It was mapped on paper, despite the fact that more than a dozen firmly settled cities dearly wanted to be the Capital of this young country. This moment you might well be outside the Capital City of Alexandria, Virginia, or Kingston, New York. Congress was wooed by these dollar-conscious towns, even before armed soldiers insulted the legislators in Philadelphia, and they hastily switched in a body to Princeton. In 1789 New York City had ready its Federal Hall, specially remodeled for the first Congress and the work of the same gifted French engineer who was, in two short years, to plan the city of Washington. By Act of Congress on July 16, 1790, "a district . . . not exceeding ten miles square" was authorized to be the permanent seat of the government.

On March 29, 1791, a handful of mounted men, including George Washington and Major Pierre Charles L'Enfant, reined in on hilltop vantage points and gazed at the chosen site for the Federal City. History draws a graphic picture of the ardent Frenchman riding slowly over the heavily wooded area days before, hampered greatly by a dense fog, but determined to learn the land's contours and report on his plans. Soon to put on paper his ideas for a great Congress House, grand avenues, cascades, columns, and a President's House, L'Enfant must have foreseen it almost as you, driving in from the south or west onto the Potomac bridges, can see it now.

Ideally for that first view, let your arrival be by night from Virginia. Shining before your eyes, Washington is the dramatic, sensitive pulse of democracy. The glowing Capitol dome dominates the scene, not pale nor overbright, but of a soft translucence. A trail of lights follows the shore and bridges, and the dark Potomac holds the picture in quivering image. The story is told of a young Congressman, who, nearing the city, caught this first night glimpse of the Capitol and was gripped with the sense of destiny and high duty symbolized there, a feeling that never left him during his stay.

If your approach is from points north, such as New York or New England, you will probably use the new Baltimore-Washington Parkway, bringing you into the Capital through some of the city's less beautiful sections. Before you leave, plan a circle tour some evening, going southwest over the Francis Scott Key bridge, south on the George Washington Memorial Parkway, returning to Washington on the Arlington Memorial Bridge.

About 750 airplanes land and take off at the Washington National Airport each twenty-four hours. Seen from the air, the Capital is a breathing, life-size jewel. The best times for this view are at night or before noon. But some think the motor approach has the edge, perhaps because you can hold it longer—providing, of course, you aren't siphoned off your traffic lane into a Virginia cloverleaf that could deposit you in a Pentagon parking lot or send you halfway to Richmond.

Some 230 trains thunder in and out of Union Station each day (one crashed partly through it in 1953), and there local cab drivers are ready to share their cabs and personal history with you in the best tradition. You may pop into the taxi of one graying Negro who is writing a book.

"It's all about what happens here," he says. "Do a little every day.

Once I picked up a Vice President—saw him comin' out the side door of a big house on Massachusetts Avenue. It wasn't Nickerson—it was Garnet."

Even cab drivers get lost here. One prominent Washingtonian used the "Letters" column of a newspaper to tell cabmen, once and

Capitol of the United States, West Front

for always, how to find his house. But do get lost yourself, a few times. L'Enfant must have had this in mind when he disarmingly described his street plan "to connect each part of the city with more efficacy by, if I may so express, making the real distance less from place to place."

The tall Paris-born architect is once again the man you'll want to know better. His chief defect was also his greatest quality: all his projects he saw in such magnificent dimensions, on such scale, and at such expense, as to shock his associates. After enlisting and fighting for our cause against the British, he was engaged by General Washington to plan the Capital. (That Washington could see a great architect in this soldier-artist, as well as a great city in the wilderness, speaks for his own wisdom and foresight.) But L'Enfant felt he had only one boss, the President. City Commissioners and others, some perhaps with personal axes to grind, soon found it increasingly difficult to work with him.

Six feet of commanding personality, L'Enfant was a familiar sight in his enveloping greatcoat and bell-crowned hat, going to and from his Georgetown office. When wealthy landowner Daniel Carroll built a house that intruded upon an avenue planned on paper, the Frenchman promptly and imperiously had it torn down. This incident added to his disfavor and more surely brought an end to his services in 1792. He was almost forgotten when he died thirty-four years later.

His grave in Prince Georges County, Maryland, was left quite unnoticed until 1901. Then, the McMillan Commission, created to provide for further development of the Capital, acclaimed L'Enfant's plan for "having stood the test of a century." The following year, President William Howard Taft headed a group of statesmen and admirers who honored the man in a fashion of which even he would have been proud, and moved his remains to a place altogether fitting. High on a Virginia hill, a few yards from the Custis-Lee Mansion, where a tablet is inscribed with a chiseled reproduction of his plan, L'Enfant rests, free to watch the city fulfill the promise he saw in it. (But even his admirers fell short in honoring him; an error crept in and L'Enfant's birth date is shown on the monument as August 2, 1755. The correct year is 1754.) An interesting postscript to history happened only a few years ago. A lady appeared on the Washington scene with the statement that she was a direct descendant of L'Enfant. The gentleman, though ever courtly to the ladies, was a bachelor.

It is apparent that L'Enfant lived long before his time. Confronted with hills and hollows, did he level the hills to fill up the valleys? Never. He adapted the plan to the site. His ideas were uniquely suited to the plotting of a city, the hub of which would capitalize on the eighty-eight-foot height of Jenkins Hill, now known as Capitol Hill.

That L'Enfant's name does not appear on his celebrated plan has prompted all sorts of skepticism. Inadvertently, a marginal note adds confusion when it states that "in order to execute the above plan, Mr. Ellicott drew a true meridional line," thus mentioning his surveyor-assistant. Lancaster, Pennsylvania, believes that its citizen, Andrew Ellicott, and not L'Enfant, was the real planner, and has gone so far as to publish a small tract saying so. Although Ellicott carried on after L'Enfant's dismissal, George Washington in 1792 gave his opinion in a letter to Thomas Jefferson: "The plan I think ought to appear as the work of L'Enfant."

It won't take you long to realize that Washington today is a city on two levels. There's the L'Enfant-planned city visitors see: the "Nation's Capital," pictured world-wide, beautiful, rivaling European capitals, but with much still to be done. Perhaps the rightful ruler might be this year's cherry-blossom princess, with an assist from the Washington Board of Trade. Inextricably involved with all this is the second largest industry in Washington: the care, feeding, and entertainment of tourists. This accounts for some five million people going to and fro annually between hotels, restaurants, and the famed sight-seeing attractions. (Mount Vernon "passed" the Statue of Liberty in 1952, joining those national shrines which draw a million or more visitors a year.) Add some 300,000 convention-goers, such as the American Federation of Astrologers or the Society for the Preservation and Encouragement of Barbershop Quartet Singing.

The other Washington is equally historic, yet modern; grimy, yet beautiful. Within its confines are wild, wooded areas that flank embassy neighborhoods thick with civilized protocol; red-brick row houses and a few Federal homes, *circa* 1800; unbelievable slums, due to be wiped out by 1965; plus distinguished residential areas. Eighteen hundred acres of Rock Creek Park in the heart of the Capital beckon to city dwellers and harbor small animals and many birds. (Not long ago a ragged gray fox tied up traffic in Dupont Circle.)

This Washington (more rightfully called the District of Columbia) has been likened to a lusty, healthy youngster—noisy, demanding, struggling to give voice to his needs and problems. Some think he can only bawl and wave his arms distractingly; that until some form of self-expression is achieved he must go on screaming to his three commissioner-nurses and his guardian, Congress, for attention. (Those interested bystanders anxious for the boy's welfare are representatives of many citizen groups and the appointed Citizens' Advisory Committee.)

It all goes back to 1878 when the Organic Act ended seventy years of political rights for the people of the District. Into the hands of Congress were placed the making of the District's laws, the levying of taxes, and the important decision of how much the Congress shall pay toward the Capital's upkeep. Some say the drastic action was provoked by a runaway spending program that paved streets, created parks, and planted thousands of trees, but which kept the city in debt for fifty years. Others insist that the change in government was influenced by political forces involving many factors, not the least of which was the existence of equal suffrage in the District, regardless of race or color, and granted in 1867 by Congress. But whatever the cause, the record shows that while the division of financial responsibility began on a 50–50 basis, it shifted to a 60–40 basis, with the District bearing the greater amount; gradually Congress has spent less and less here. In 1954, the Federal Government's share of the District's budget dropped to a slim 8.52 per cent; in 1955 it amounted to about 15 per cent.

For years, amendments to the Constitution have been discussed, and home-rule bills have been drafted, endorsed, revised, criticized, and batted back and forth between the Houses of Congress and the District. Groups of Washingtonians work doggedly toward this goal. Just as persistently, anti-home-rule groups have defended their stand that the commissioner form of government is both clean and constitutional. Others would hold out for national representation, while still others urge the right to vote for delegates to Presidential conventions.

In 1955, Congress passed a law which authorized the first citywide election in more than eighty years, a kind of primary, to elect from the District officials of political parties, including those who help to choose party candidates for President and Vice President.

Home rulers cry, "We don't want to be second-class citizens. This is taxation without representation." Opponents in Congress and elsewhere answer, "Washington is the city of all the people of the country—a small local group can't rule it . . ."

Paradoxically, Washington's major industry is government. One in every three gainfully employed persons in the Metropolitan Area goes to work five days a week somewhere in the sprawling congeries of departments and agencies. On January 1, 1956, the Washington Board of Trade estimated the total metropolitan population as 1,872,000, all of whom you suspect drive home to Virginia and Maryland in separate cars if you are in town about five o'clock on weekdays.

Some rock-ribbed realists insist that for many life in Washington is pretty humdrum, just "home town," that you can't expect to meet, informally or otherwise, any of its more distinguished residents.

But I say, what about the time I ran into an Attorney General going with his ten-year-old to an F Street movie? Or eavesdropped on the sari-robed wife of an Ambassador as she shopped for her family in Hecht's at Seventh and F? Or sympathized with the agitation of the girl across the street who wanted to throw away all her furniture and get new because Mamie Eisenhower was coming that afternoon for bridge?

Or the time on upper Connecticut Avenue when an elderly man darted across the rain-slick street in mid-block? That jaywalker was Alben Barkley, Senator and former Vice President.

Yes, it's home town, but with a magic difference.

Only some 263,000 native Washingtonians live here today; almost as many have wandered away to some of the forty-eight States. This is our sad lack, because often the most important friend or stranger you can meet is a native Washingtonian.

Ten minutes with a remembering native is better than a full conducted tour. Casually, one long-time resident recounted how her grandfather and his friend—both young men of nineteen—were in Ford's Theater the night Lincoln was shot, a story she had heard many times in her family circle. Their boyish fear as they waited at the house across the street . . . the doctor's appearance at the door . . . his request for a penknife . . . the young friend offering his . . . the pressing of the crowd . . . It was a brief sidelight on history, which sometimes can touch a historic place or an incident with life.

Here history is always at your elbow. I myself discovered that the little man who was reupholstering a love seat for me in the newest nylon fabric was using a venerable Davis sewing machine like those that had stitched Civil War uniforms in the early 1860's.

Perhaps it can be summed up best by the high school boy who, on his first trip to the Capital, shook his head, and said, "I feel I've seen it all before."

II

Remember It's a River City

At night, from the roof deck of my apartment house high above the streets of Northwest Washington, I can see the shining dome of the Capitol of the United States. The bright glitter of Connecticut Avenue traffic feeds around Dupont Circle; the red gnat-eyes of planes wheel over the airport. When I show this sight to out-of-town visitors, up crop names of streets and places, some still used, others all but forgotten. The words are pleasant to say.

There's Foggy Bottom—the lingering early name for that once swampy downtown area extending from the Potomac to about the Lincoln Memorial and north to H Street. It was named for the thick morning haze that hung over this bottomland.

Cabin John and Glen Echo are favorite names, too. Cabin John is a village, a creek, and a bridge in near-by Maryland. A trolley with that name meanders along Pennsylvania Avenue into Georgetown and then almost flies to Glen Echo Park near the Little Falls of the Potomac. Clara Barton, founder of the American Red Cross, lived out that way. Cabin John Creek is believed to have been named from Captain John's Branch, mentioned in early court records.

Early holdings in the area around Washington had such names as the Widow's Mite, Poor Tom's Last Shift, and Beall's Levels, but they have gone, along with Clean Drinking Manor and Girl's Por-

13

tion. Indian names you may not run across are Pomonkey, Piscat-away, and Nanjemoy, still found along the Potomac.

To locate Washington properly, remember it's a river city. On the corner of an old Form 57 (handy for filing for Government employment) draw a big "Y." The long left line is the Potomac River; the small right line forming the V midway is the Anacostia River. Around the area of the V the city is located.

Here also is a highly simplified way of solving the Washington street puzzle; at least on paper. First draw a simple plus sign, marking the ends of the lines with the cardinal points of the compass— the north and south line, and east and west line. Where the two lines cross, put a circle. That is the Capitol dome.

You now have the basic bones of the city, with the Capitol representing its geographical heart. To name these basic 'bones,' the north-south line is North Capitol and South Capitol streets; the east line is East Capitol Street, and the west line follows The Mall, that green rectangle stretching between the Capitol and the Washington Monument. Thus, fanning out from the Capitol are four sections, into which the city is divided: Northeast, Northwest, Southeast, and Southwest. Over this simple arrangement has been placed a grid of streets and avenues, which has become more and more confusing over the years since L'Enfant first conceived his grand idea.

The important thing to remember is that each of these sections has its own street system and that the systems in all four are identical. When you give an address to a cab driver, or ask directions of a policeman, each will assume your goal is in Northwest (probably your area of chief interest) unless you say otherwise. The most important avenues are those named for States; they run diagonally across the city, seeming to plunge boldly through such edifices as the White House, the Treasury, the Capitol, and the Library of Congress.

About the numbered streets, remember that they run north and south—the lowest numbers being closest to the Capitol, of course. Alphabetical streets go east and west, running from A to W, with J omitted. After these come streets with one-syllable names beginning with A, B, etc., and continuing to two-, three-, and four-syllable names in the same fashion. Scattered among these are many roads and places. Roads meander aimlessly with no regard for the rules, and places are simply short streets within blocks.

Having absorbed this explanation, you may have decided that the street plan is simplicity itself. And so it would be, were it not for the tricks played by city fathers after Washington, Jefferson, and L'Enfant. Some of the changes made by these worthies were dictated by the real needs of a growing city. Others appear to have been born of personal whim, sheer idiocy, or even downright meanness.

Let us suppose, for example, that you are sauntering eastward on Pennsylvania Avenue, past the White House, with nothing more on your mind than a continuation of your stroll on that famous thoroughfare. You pass the Treasury Building and come to the busy corner of Pennsylvania Avenue and Fifteenth Street. This is easy, you say to yourself as you cross Fifteenth and strike out along a broad avenue which, though it veers slightly to the north, couldn't possibly be anything but the way.

Are you on Pennsylvania Avenue? You are not. You are on New York Avenue. You should have turned right at Fifteenth Street and walked two blocks southward; then you would have seen Pennsylvania Avenue, the famous route of parades and conquering heroes, of incoming and outgoing Presidents, stretching before you to the Capitol. For this discouraging dog-leg, and also the fact that the Treasury blocks L'Enfant's Pennsylvania Avenue vista from White House to Capitol, we may blame the prickly impatience of President Andrew Jackson. Old Hickory, fed up with a committee's delay in choosing a site, or so the story goes, stormed out of the White House with a group of underlings one day, thrust his cane into the ground, and barked, "I want the cornerstone right here!" "Right here" is the present northeast corner of the Treasury.

Remember about streets running due east and west bearing alphabetical designations? Even in this simple scheme there are deceptions. Let's say you are at Connecticut Avenue and K Street, NW, and want to get to M Street. K, L, M . . . what could be easier? So, confidently, you head north on Connecticut. Sure enough, the next street above K is L . . . so far, so good. You press on, perhaps pausing to admire the lobsters in Harvey's window. When you reach the next street, is it M? Not quite. It is DeSales Street. M Street lies another half-block north. You may notice that DeSales is only a block long, running from Connecticut to Seventeenth Street beside the Mayflower Hotel. You remember reading that short streets within blocks are properly called places. Why, then, isn't DeSales a place instead of a street? Well, that's Washington. Everywhere there are traps for the unwary. Alertness is the watchword.

Even present-day builders seem to go out of their way to compound the confusion. A case in point is a spanking new office building with frontage on K Street, Connecticut Avenue, and Seventeenth Street. The main entrance and frontage are on K Street. But the owners, apparently preferring a tony address to geographical accuracy, chose to call the edifice "1001 Connecticut Avenue."

And now for the circles, those extraordinary street arrangements which have caused strong motorists to weep and wonder why they ever left Blue Eye, North Dakota. Here is good news: the circles are not as bad as they used to be. In recent years underpasses have been built at the three most notorious ones—Dupont, Scott, and Thomas—so that many cars dive underground and reduce confusion on the surface. Also, the system of marking streets and principal motor routes has been greatly improved. A circle consists of a landscaped plot, usually with a Civil War hero's statue in the middle, girdled by a roadway. Consider the center of the circle as the hub of a wheel. The spokes are avenues and streets radiating outward from the hub. Most motorists, upon first encountering a circle, make a wrong turn. The best approach is a slow, careful one, with an alert eye on the direction signs. One motorist, driving into Washington for the first time, parked his car when the first circle loomed up, and then walked around it to get his bearings. His is a sure-fire system (if you can find a place to park), and there's only one better for the anxious ones: store your car as soon as you arrive in Washington, and get about by taxi, sight-seeing bus, public transportation, or on foot.

A current, easy-to-read map of the District of Columbia is valuable to you. Here are several ways to get one:

A very adequate map is available free from the Greater National Capital Committee of the Washington Board of Trade, 1616 K Street, NW. It shows all the sight-seeing high spots along The Mall, and will get you back to your hotel with reasonable directness.

An excellent pocket map of Washington and its environs is on sale at the National Geographic Society, Sixteenth and M streets, NW, for fifty cents. It shows all important buildings with complete index.

The Esso Tour Service at 261 Constitution Avenue has a sight-seeing map, and Gulf Oil Company also puts out a Washington map for tourists; both are free.

III

Through This Door Went Washington, Jefferson—and Now You!

LATELY, EACH SPRING, A KIND OF MAGIC DUST RISES over the Potomac lowlands, sweeps up Pennsylvania Avenue, and swirls around Capitol Hill. Straight-thinking Washingtonians, who should be facing up to taxes and crab grass, go on a spree into past splendor. This is no fly-by-night happenstance, but a masterfully planned and skillfully staged eight-week performance officially billed as the House and Garden Tours. Call it a Grand Tour of History.

So, welcome to one of Washington's more pleasant diversions, and be ready for these signs: snarled traffic, big-name receiving lines, long queues that curl around corners and pile up dollars—all for sweet charity's sake.

Most important of all, it will get *you* behind the scenes. After the friendly gaiety of the Georgetown Garden Tour, or an international cup of tea on Embassy Row, this city throws off its mantle of chilly white marble. For the price of a ticket, about three dollars, you can see where busy and prominent Washingtonians do their worrying (indeed, the cushions seem still warm); but they have bundled up their small fry, admonished the cat to stay in hiding, and disappeared for four or five hours to let the public troop (or snoop) through.

Along with your ticket comes lively mention of famous points, architecturally, plus human-interest notes about early occupants. For most of these dwellings are famous for yesteryear's occupants, for romances, intrigues, and scandals upon which the passing of time has laid a glamorous patina.

Each spring (the other seasons have them, too) at least five official tours in and about the Capital fill the calendar. If you take in all five, you'll see about forty historic and show-place homes plus a dozen lovely gardens. Almost any week end in April and May you can pick yourself a tour or two. Add to these more distant journeys to Annapolis, to Alexandria, and deeper into Maryland and Virginia. You can stroll by candlelight through Woodlawn's gracious rooms, or travel by shanks' mare all over Washington.

This pleasant practice started years ago in the hospitable Deep South—in New Orleans, Charleston, and Natchez, and has spread to a number of history-conscious cities. But in Washington each year more clever women discover that people will gladly pay to turn back the clock and walk through rooms once familiar to long-gone heroes and heroines. So a worthy cause gets a sponsor, a committee sets to work, a mountain of detail is conquered, publicity peppers the papers, and another tour is born.

Lucky agencies or activities that benefit by these fantastically successful tours include neighborhood houses, the Goodwill Industries, orphanages, and historic buildings. While some of these groups get support from organized drives, it is these additional tour-raised funds that enable them to reach goals and fulfill programs.

One reason, surely, why each tour succeeds is because wives of Congressmen, long-time residents, and other women, imbued with the dream of aiding the cause closest to their hearts, supply ideas, energy, and time unlimited. (One day soon, Madison Avenue may send down some of its brainy lads to study the careful, detail-perfect unfolding of this springtime laboratory in money-raising and public relations. It goes beyond snob appeal to trade on that universal trait: curiosity.)

Another reason enters in. Washingtonians and visitors alike have rediscovered history; what's more, they like it.

For many visitors, half the fun of tours is the receiving line where Cabinet wives, many in picture hats and elegant gowns, manage to be radiant for hours as they murmur your name and hand you graciously along. When the First Lady comes she is of course the drawing card. Mamie Eisenhower and Bess Truman before her have brought out tremendous crowds. If you wonder how they maintain that welcoming smile, as women and more women and an occasional man stream by, it must come down to this: official wives help earn their husbands' salaries. (For a while one spring, I answered to Mrs. Earl Warren's pleasant "How-d'ye-do" so many times in receiving lines that I began to feel like a California cousin.)

An old regular among tours is the House and Embassy Tour, benefiting the Washington Home for Incurables. One year 3,500 ticket holders paid $11,000 into the Home's funds. The First Lady greeted long lines at the Admiral's House, official residence of the Chief of Naval Operations, on the Naval Observatory grounds.

In a class by itself is the annual Phantom Dinner, another kind of benefit; the subscription covers a dinner which you never attend—you don't even taste the fruit cocktail—because it never takes place. The whole amount subscribed is set aside for the House of Mercy, a home for unwed mothers and their babies, and is under the Episcopal Diocese of Washington.

Another is the Embassy Tour and Tea sponsored annually by the Goodwill Guild of the Davis Memorial Goodwill Industries. Mrs. Richard M. Nixon, wife of the Vice President, shook hands tirelessly for three hours one cloudy spring day at the Embassy of the Dominican Republic. The cause: that of rehabilitating the handicapped. Near by, chartered buses were stacked up on Massachusetts Avenue; and competing that same afternoon in another part of town, the Georgetown Garden Tour was a complete sellout!

These official Embassy Tours held each spring offer you a warm welcome spelled out in many languages. All year impressive homes of foreign diplomats remain private residences despite longing glances from visitors with no official business. But at tour time doors are thrown wide. Ticket holders watch for such treasures as the palatial marble stairway with its hand-carved rosewood altar rails from Bahia, Brazil, in the entrance hall of the Brazilian Embassy; for scenic wallpaper of Italy, said to be three hundred years old, in the dining room of the Embassy of the Dominican Republic.

Even as you cross the threshold of a famous show place, you may be sure that long before this moment has arrived, much has been done to bring plans, publicity, and people to this fruitful point. So it was when a very special tour was held one January day and a thousand determined people not only paid three dollars each, but braved snow, slush, and bitter cold to meet Mamie Eisenhower in the Marine Commandant's House, and wander through a dozen others. One old lady did it all on crutches. That was up on old Capitol Hill, when the eighteen portraits in the 150-year-old quarters of the Marine Commandant had a last-minute straightening, and near by, a group of "official" homes, all lived in, got their final polishing and were thrown open.

How did this tour start? First came the need, then the idea. The institution in need was Friendship House, the beautiful and busy neighborhood center of the Capitol Hill area, where a fight was on to end slums in the shadow of the Capitol. A Community Chest agency, Friendship House had suffered a budget cut which threatened to curtail some of its most helpful services, such as the nursery to aid working mothers and classes for teen-agers.

Everyone associated with it felt this was critically important, but particularly did those who had moved lately into the Hill's historic houses, some a century or more old. Their affection for Friendship House was real because of its fine service record, but the house itself inspired a special kind of faith. Its history is rich and varied, going back beyond an entry in General Washington's diary calling it "the house in the woods." These recent settlers fervently believed that slums could be wiped out, that early planners knew what they were doing when they faced the Capitol to the east, thus benignly tapping this area of red-brick Civil War homes and a few lingering Federal houses, too, for Number One residential honors. (As for

L'Enfant, he was probably more restless than usual on his Potomac hillside.)

Then came the idea, born perhaps in more than one fertile feminine brain, but caught up and vitalized by Mrs. Richard Bolling, wife of a Democratic Congressman from Missouri. Living on pleasant, tree-lined streets east, north, and south of the Capitol were Senators, Congressmen, and many professional people in Washington life. Why not, she asked, invite people to see Capitol Hill's official restored homes, for a price—in a big-name, gilt-edged tour? It would aid Friendship's slender budget, and win new friends for the area. (St. Peter's Sodality had sponsored tours of Capitol Hill homes for several years to benefit rural Catholic schools, so it was not an untried idea.)

But what drawing card, that primary ingredient? Mamie Eisenhower, of course, but how to persuade her to lend her prestige? It would have to be a different kind of request, to set it apart from the hundreds of others seeking her sponsorship and time. Then came the angle: surely if there were one place where the First Lady would feel completely "at home," where her natural interest would be spontaneous, it would somehow involve the military. Why not, then, a receiving line at the distinguished Marine Commandant's House, the oldest "continuously lived-in" official house in Washington?

"In the old days I could just call NAtional 8–1414, and ask for Mrs. Truman. The White House operator would say, 'Who's calling?' and the next voice would be Bess Truman's. No more!" Many a comment like this follows an administration change.

It was finally the gracious invitation issued by Mrs. Lemuel C. Shepherd, Jr., wife of the Commandant, that accomplished the coup. The First Lady accepted. So did the Cabinet ladies.

Details—"one million and ten is a good round number"—piled up. Committees blossomed and orders for posters, invitations, and announcements went out. Three thousand names were carefully selected to receive pairs of subscription tickets. Right then the hand-wringing section might have grown, but the cool voice in command,

C. H. Severance

LINCOLN MEMORIAL

Photo by Abbie Rowe—Courtesy National Park Service

JEFFERSON MEMORIAL

Photo by Abbie Rowe—Courtesy National Park Service

MOUNT VERNON

Photo by Abbie Rowe—Courtesy National Park Service

Canal Clipper IN GEORGETOWN

NATIONAL ARCHIVES BUILDING

Photo by Abbie Rowe—Courtesy National Park Service

SOUTH PORTICO OF THE WHITE HOUSE

Photo by Abbie Rowe—Courtesy National Park Service

THE CAPITOL

AIR VIEW OF THE PENTAGON

Photo by Abbie Rowe—Courtesy National Park Service

WASHINGTON MONUMENT

unruffled and confident, always said, "Of course you can do it. I know you can."

More committees were born, covering publicity, tour plan and transportation, receiving line, tickets and telephoning, invitations and printing, local clubs and associations, tea hostesses, tea chairmen, church co-ordination, posters and maps, historical societies, booklet descriptions of houses, state societies, advertising, house hostesses, junior hostesses, houses, flowers, and so on. Off in the upper reaches of the Library of Congress a committee member wallowed elbow-deep in old documents. For the moment, husband, children, and PTA were forgotten as she carefully searched out the history behind a house to be written up for the tour.

Delightful stories came to light and went into the tour booklet, such as the one about Commandant Archibald Henderson, who served the longest tour as head of the United States Marine Corps. "One day persons calling at his headquarters found the place closed tight as a drum and this sign on the door: 'Have gone to Florida to fight the Indians. Back when war is over.'"

The girls always tried for an angle. In publicity, a durable Capitol Hill grandmother with a twinkle in her eye and a hundred-year-old cookie recipe went far. She baked 'em and baked 'em (the photographers came to expect samples) and on tour day, a bare half-hour before closing, every single one was gone. Newsworthy names with pictures, prepared knowingly and continuously around committee ladies, formed an almost daily design for getting tour statistics not only in the three big dailies but in outlying papers in Maryland and Virginia. No mention was too small to be courted, whether in transit news on buses or in shopping papers.

Like a giant snowball it rolled up to the big day. And literally—it snowed and sleeted. Builders' paper made heavy-duty paths to save fine rugs from wet footprints; florists donated stately bouquets; Congressmen, temporarily dispossessed, became chauffeurs and drove many a soggy-soled tourist to the next house. Indoors, housewives who would have disappeared in favor of hostesses stayed on to keep cheerful hearth fires crackling a warm welcome as more visitors burst in on every gust of air.

Despite the weather, the tour was a resounding success; Mrs. Eisenhower not only came, but stayed past her expected thirty minutes, and Friendship House thankfully shored up its sagging budget that year and again the next spring as the affair was happily repeated. If you want to browse through old rooms where Washington and Jefferson gathered, or find the broad slope of New Jersey Avenue where L'Enfant pulled down Daniel Carroll's house, it's all up on old Capitol Hill.

Now and then, local sight-seers fall heir to a once-in-a-lifetime tour. Decatur House on Lafayette Square was one of the houses shown in a history-packed four hours when famous dwellings of the Federal Period were opened to benefit the National Trust for Historic Preservation.

On this same tour was Blair House, the State Department's guest house, along with The Octagon, the Arts Club, and John Marshall House, which had long been on every knowing resident's list of "This I must see." (As I stood in line at Decatur House that fair April afternoon, three Saturday shoppers on their way across the Square saw the line and fell in behind me. "Well, this *is* something. Mother used to say this house was haunted, and it really looked it then." A native was summing it up.)

Any day sitting across the street you can glance over to the corner of H Street and Jackson Place, and it's likely the green shutters will be closed. It has a simple Georgian façade of handmade rosy brick and white trim. You may say it's too plain, or that it doesn't look as though anybody lives there. But if you should happen along on the winter evening of the White House Diplomatic Reception you would see that the handsome carriage lights in front have been lighted with candles and the shutters thrown back. Filtering through the exquisite lace curtains are lights, voices, and gaiety as Mrs. Truxtun Beale's traditional supper party for Ambassadors and their wives gets under way.

Entering this house is an excursion into history. The moment you step inside you feel the 1820's close about you. I, for one, could easily have come out, climbed into a carriage at the door, and rolled off into the dusty sunshine of another day.

On gold-toned walls of the roomy library hang dozens of pictures, some dark oil paintings in heavy frames, some photographs of bygone queens and handsome soldiers, with fading personal inscrip-

Jackson Statue, Lafayette Square

tions. In a wall case is a pair of pistols, which might have been those used in the Barron-Decatur duel. Along one book-filled wall *Horace Walpole Letters* in six fat leather-bound volumes stand out. This is the room in which young Commodore Stephen Decatur lay when he died that unhappy March day in 1820.

Built barely more than a year before Decatur's death, the house was the first private residence on the Square. The architect, Benjamin H. Latrobe (you'll meet Benjamin many times), planned it to suit the tastes of Decatur and his young bride, who looked ahead to many seasons of brilliant balls and distinguished guests. The Commodore had just returned from his highly successful naval exploits; it was the prize money he won in the War of 1812 that paid for the house. For a brief time, carriages bearing lovely ladies and great men rolled to what is now 748 Jackson Place; dozens of wax tapers burned low around the upstairs drawing rooms in a single night. Decatur, handsome, daring, and wealthy, was at the peak of his career. Then, in an early morning hour on the dueling ground at Bladensburg, Maryland, he was mortally wounded by Commodore James Barron.

Since then, Decatur House has added many famous names to its history. Among those to live here were Henry Clay, Secretary of State under John Quincy Adams; Martin Van Buren and Edward Livingston, succeeding Secretaries of State under President Andrew Jackson. (On the roof in those days were "lookouts" where slaves watched for wigwag signals from similar posts on the White House roof, until Alexander Graham Bell put that communication system out of business.)

Edward Fitzgerald Beale, of a Virginia family and grandson of Commodore Truxtun, bought the house after the Civil War; his son Truxtun Beale, formerly U.S. Minister to Persia and to Greece, inherited it. Today Decatur House is the private residence of his widow, Mrs. Truxtun Beale.

On the second floor are spacious drawing rooms. In the excellent restoration of the house, great crystal chandeliers seem ready today to spring into jets of gaslight, so tiny are the electric bulbs. Decorating the ceiling of the large drawing room, overlooking the Square, rosy-toned grapes intertwine with green leaves, and the floors are laid in patterns of pale and dark woods.

A special highlight of this tour was the unique display of Latrobe's original plans of Decatur House, all pen-drawn with carefully worded directions. They are dated 1818, signed Benjamin H. Latrobe, and addressed to Commodore Stephen Decatur, Navy Commissioner's Office, Washington City. The package came by stage, with the word "Baltimore" printed by hand, and Decatur paid for it by weight.

Mrs. Beale, well aware of the ageless values in her home and their link with the Capital's past, has announced her intention to place Decatur House in the future care and protection of the National Trust. One day, through a planned endowment, the dwelling with many of its contents will be a national monument for all to enjoy.

Blair House is quite another story. In the memory of Mrs. Victoria Geaney, now hostess-manager and formerly housekeeper for the Blairs, this is only the third time in thirty years that the house has been opened to the public. If another opportunity should come along, prepare to see a gleaming masterpiece of good housekeeping which, after the nostalgic accumulations in some tour houses, is suddenly refreshing. But this is as it should be, for you'll be looking in on the State Department's best front bedrooms for company, and, since 1942, United States property.

It is virtually unchanged, from family portraits to furniture arrangement. "The Government didn't have to buy a dish towel," recalls Mrs. Geaney.

Here, recently, important foreign visitors have unpacked, been feted, packed up, and hardly rolled off to the airport before another official visitor and staff mount the steps. (As we waited to get in, our line was far shorter than the queue which would form if we could single-file the kings, Presidents, and their entourages who have been entertained in a single year—particularly a full one like 1954.)

When you have climbed to the third floor, leaned as far as the silk cords will permit into the pleasant suite used by Margaret Truman, and earlier by Mrs. Montgomery Blair; gone on to yearn over the early American Sandwich, luster, and Steigel glass glowing under cabinet lights; admired the rich red carpeting and graceful white mantels in the library below—you may want to label this your dream house for contemporary living. It is a town house to end all looking.

Yet it has more than 130 years of history in it. Newspaper advertisements for its sale in 1836 after the death of the Joseph Lovells, first owners, described the house as "a spacious two story brick building, with a basement; was built under the eye of the late proprietor for his permanent residence, and has every convenience for a family in and about it; a well of excellent water is in the yard; brick stable and carriage house adjoining the alley; flower and fruit garden tastefully laid out and highly cultivated."

Francis Preston Blair bought the house for $6,500, and from his ownership stems its present name.

Many historic figures stayed here. President Andrew Jackson, with his pipe and forthright ways, was a close friend and frequent visitor. No doubt Peggy O'Neale Eaton's name cropped up often in the conversation. The beautiful Peggy precipitated social and political bitterness which almost dissolved the Cabinet. Old Hickory was urged to stay at Blair House after his defeat by Van Buren, until spring brought milder weather for the journey homeward to Tennessee, but he declined. For a brief period the house was rented to political leaders. George Bancroft, who was Secretary of the Navy during his time in the house, laid the foundation for the United States Naval Academy at Annapolis while here. A wedding in 1850 brought such illustrious guests as President Zachary Taylor, Daniel Webster, and Henry Clay. That was Ellen Ewing's marriage to William Tecumseh Sherman, later a major general in the Civil War.

It was at Blair House that Robert E. Lee met with the elder Francis Preston Blair as the latter "sounded him out" on taking command of Union forces. Abraham Lincoln during the war years stopped in at Blair House occasionally.

President Harry Truman, aroused from his nap by gunfire one afternoon in 1950, appeared briefly at a window while guards and would-be assassins shot it out at the front door. The Truman family moved into Blair House late in 1948 and stayed until 1952, while the White House was being reconstructed.

Although it is quite unlikely that this tour will be repeated, other equally famous homes may turn up for a first time on a tour while you're in town, so watch for them.

IV

Historic Tours in and Around the Capital

THE STORY GOES THAT A VACATIONING FAMILY, returning to their home in near-by Virginia, walked in on several appreciative strangers wandering through the rooms. It seemed there was a tour in the neighborhood, and the house looked so inviting.

Starting in April about cherry-blossom time (one of the prettiest free spectacles in the world) or even late March, house and garden tours start piling up. But in any season, watch for them in the newspapers, at the American Automobile Association, 1712 G Street, NW, or listed in the District of Columbia Recreation Department's free monthly bulletin *Do You Know*, made available by the Washington Board of Trade, 1616 K Street, NW.

Transportation for in-town tours is no problem. Almost all houses on Embassy Tours are found along bus lines on Massachusetts Avenue, NW, or on Sixteenth Street, NW. Walking from one house to the next is usually the best way. Maps of the tour layout may appear with your ticket, or in the daily papers, along with shuttle bus schedules between far points.

Admission price is usually three dollars or less, but an occasional Embassy Tour runs to four dollars. If you are in a group, investigate group rates. Tickets may be purchased at the individual houses, wherever you start your tour. Starting time is usually early afternoon, closing about five or six o'clock. You will find one show place designated for the reception or tea; hostesses will tell you when the "star" will head up the receiving line. If the First Lady is the drawing card, it's unlikely that she will stay a full hour, and then the line forms early. But official greeters will be on hand all during teatime to receive you.

Here are some of the in-town spring tours you can expect:

Tours	*To Benefit*
House and Embassy Tour	Washington Home for Incurables
Official Homes for Friendship Tour	Friendship House
Goodwill Embassy Tour and Tea	Goodwill Industries
Georgetown House Tour	Old St. John's Church
Georgetown Garden Tour	Georgetown Neighborhood House

You won't be alone or feel unfamiliar long in this atmosphere. Just plan to get there, and you'll find a gay crowd sharing a sense of expectancy. After all, it isn't just every day you're able to inspect such historic housekeeping from garden to boudoir. (Your booklet will tell you that the beautiful table in that dining room was designed by Thomas Jefferson and was used in the Morning Room at Monticello—and comes to this house by inheritance; that the window shutters in this living room [a Congressman's home] were taken from the Ulysses S. Grant home when it stood near Seventeenth and K streets.)

Everybody talks to you or around you. You'll hear comments like: "Awfully cluttered! . . . Now why would anybody want to save that dust-catcher?" and the knowing answer: "But, my dear, that's Georgetown—it's an heirloom."

Or overhear two cave dwellers shaking out a few ghosts: "Why she wasn't anybody till she married him . . . then her old friends weren't good enough." Too, it's always possible you'll be standing alongside a Jeffersonian scholar on holiday from the Library of Congress, or an interior decorator down from New York looking for an authentic little print.

FLOWER MART. (No admission charge.) Of course, if it turns out you won't arrive until later in the spring, and you must miss the early tours, you are still in luck if you're here the first Friday in May. That's the annual date of the Flower Mart of the Washington Cathedral—and it has nothing to do with historic homes or classic doorways.

But it *is* a firsthand glimpse into one of the city's most successful community enterprises. Held rain or shine from 11:00 A.M. to 5:00 P.M. in beautiful Oak Grove on the Cathedral grounds, this yearly money-maker is sponsored by the ladies of All Hallows Guild for care and maintenance of the Bishop's Garden and Cathedral Close. It attracts projects from a dozen area-wide garden clubs, competing for prizes.

Basically, it resembles an old-fashioned church social, with booths, band, flowers, bake sale, and many special features—but this is the Capital's more glamorous version. Since the Mart began in 1940, the "committee ladies" each year with much imagination and skill adapt such permanent features of the grounds as the quaint Herb Cottage to their plans. One year it was a French theme; another year, British Isles overtones successfully created a village green and country fair complete with English park, even to a "nanny" with perambulator. (Where but in Washington could you count on the wife of the Ambassador to cut the ribbon and award the grand prize?) A favorite place of children, too.

BISHOP'S GARDEN AND HERB COTTAGE. (No admission charge.) No matter when you come here, do plan to visit the Bishop's Garden and sweet-smelling Herb Cottage, on the Cathedral grounds. Open weekdays from 9:00 to 5:00, but closed Sundays. (The Cathedral itself is open from 9:00 to 5:00 every day and until 6:00 in summer; pilgrimages conducted daily every hour on the half-hour; Sunday after 11:00 A.M. and 4:00 P.M. services.)

Herbs, dried and packaged, or plants and seedlings are on sale at the Herb Cottage, or will be sent to any place in the world for you. Look for stone walks dividing the Garden, where on one side grow herbs mentioned in the Bible; on the other, those mentioned by Shakespeare—assistants will quote you chapter and verse.

Souvenir suggestions: ambrosia to flavor a fireside cup of tea next winter; myrrh for the children's crèche at Christmas, or a packet of mugwort to sprinkle in your shoes—the Pilgrims did it, they say, to ease aching arches.

DUMBARTON OAKS PARK. (No admission charge.) Hours: 9:00 A.M. to 5:00 P.M., Saturdays, Sundays, and holidays, April through October. A fantastically beautiful sight which you must see is found in Georgetown's Dumbarton Oaks Park each spring, when yellow forsythia, massed on bank and terrace, bursts into bloom. This breath-taking display creates the lovely, impossible illusion of clothing you in splendid golden light, and you go away entranced. The naturalistically landscaped valley comprises the twenty-seven-acre park presented to the District of Columbia by Mr. and Mrs. Robert Woods Bliss. After the forsythia passes, bluebells, primroses, and a succession of spring flowers bloom here, and are followed by summer blossoms. The entrance is at Lover's Lane, located one block east of Wisconsin Avenue on R Street, NW, just past Thirtieth. The park is to the left through a wire gate, at the bottom of this sloping, cobbled lane.

Adjacent, but separate, are the formal gardens of Dumbarton Oaks, which now, with the house, library, and rich collection of Byzantine art, by gift of Mr. and Mrs. Bliss, are the property of Harvard University. It is a research center for Byzantine and medieval studies. (No admission charge. Garden hours: 9:00 A.M. to 4:45 P.M., Monday through Friday, and 2:00 to 4:45 P.M. on week ends; the collection is open from 2:00 to 5:00 P.M. daily except Monday.)

This land is all part of the early Rock of Dunbarton holdings of onetime landowner Ninian Beall. The mansion, dating from 1801, later came into the Calhoun family and its most famous member, John C. Calhoun, resided here during his terms as Cabinet officer, Vice President, and Senator.

SUNSET PARADE, United States Marine Corps. (No admission charge.) On any Friday at about 5:00 P.M. during Daylight Saving Time, a brilliantly colorful ceremony takes place at the Marine Barracks at Eighth and I streets, SE, up on old Capitol Hill. (Entrance on Eighth Street.) The Commandant of the Marine Corps, or often a distinguished guest, reviews the troops as they pass up and down the Quadrangle, within the grounds. You'll see and hear the Drum and Bugle Corps and the famed Marine Band, in scarlet and white. You'll watch the "March on the Colors," stand at attention while the Stars and Stripes on its tall white standard is ceremoniously lowered. Stirring Fourth-of-July marches fill the air, and all in all, it's an exciting forty-five minutes.

The Marine Commandant's House faces on G Street. President Thomas Jefferson selected the site for the Barracks, after riding on horseback in the area, because "it lay near the Navy Yard and within easy marching distance of the Capitol."

FRANCISCAN MONASTERY. (No admission charge.) Each spring thousands make this pilgrimage to Fourteenth and Quincy in Northeast Washington to see the magnificent rose gardens. At their peak from May to the first of July, the display extends all around the portico. Tours of the gardens, which include the shrines and replicas of Holy Places in Palestine, are held year round, 8:00 A.M. to 5:00 P.M.

If you are a local resident with the special privilege of introducing foreign guests to this Capital City, do take them along when you do your week end buying at the supermarket. (It will be like taking your visitors through the pages of a modern woman's magazine.) No matter if they come from the west of Ireland, where such convenience is pure fantasy, or from cosmopolitan Paris, the first experience of seeing, touching, and buying any of the thousands of beautifully packaged foods is thrilling, indeed. Do pick one with soft music, where children wheel tiny carts with their own selections, or where there is a kind of nursery section fortified with story books, and all around acres of eye-appealing greens, oranges, berries, corn-on-the-cob are year-round staples. One English visitor who never could quite tear himself away from the cellophane-wrapped steaks and rolled roasts just kept returning to the meat section.

Your visitors will find a drugstore worth visiting, too. The merry juxtaposition of whisk brooms, face cream, ham sandwiches, and an entire set of dishes offers an endless "what next" delight.

Another step along this line, if your timing permits, is to escort your guests on the Fall Festival of Homes, where in town house or suburban hillside dwelling he may see the newest in floor plan, furnishings—and all elbow-to-elbow with the American consumer herself.

The NATIONAL HOUSING CENTER at 1625 L Street, NW, (open from 10:00 A.M. to 6:00 P.M.; guide service available) is another place of interest to domestic and foreign visitors. Here are five solid floors of exhibits expressing the latest ideas and designs for the American home. Complete kitchens, dramatized in color or wood, in unit installations; full bathrooms with luxury features such as vanities and wood panelings; and a host of separate exhibits make for tempting browsing.

OUT-OF-TOWN TOURS

As a kind of orientation course in our own beginnings, plan at least one trip out to the near Virginia and Maryland countryside when flowering dogwood and redbud present a spring picture at every turn. If yours is an autumn visit, that same view is a blend of flaming reds and mellow gold, and the wandering is equally rewarding.

A car, of course, is necessary to get around (buses, because of their size, are not allowed into many of the estates). If this means you can't go, call on any of the local car rental services and *give* yourself one of these trips. The current rate for car rental is eight cents per mile plus the standard charge of eight dollars for the car, gas and oil included. In other words, in one day you can go fifty miles—spin across the Potomac to Mount Vernon, Arlington Cemetery, Alexandria, and do a bit of sight-seeing around Washington—for about twelve dollars.

Here are some of the out-of-town tours to watch for in Virginia:
>Historic Garden Week in Virginia
>Historic Garden Week in Alexandria District
>Alexandria Tour of Old Homes

Historic Garden Week always falls in the last week of April. The Garden Club of Virginia, which sponsors the tour, offers much more than buds and bowers. You'll find it hard to stay on the District side of the Potomac as several hundred private homes, gardens, shrines, old churches, and public buildings go on exhibition.

Francis Scott Key Bridge, from Virginia Shore

Admission prices range from fifty cents for a house or garden, to a dollar and a half for a very few other sights. (Tickets, if sold in blocks or groups, may be purchased in the area in which the houses or gardens are on view; separate admissions are paid at individual places as the visitor enters.) And if you should find yourself down in Tidewater Virginia or far from a restaurant around lunchtime, never fear—provision has been made. The ladies of the church are expecting you, for in almost every section of the State they prepare and serve food for the convenience of tour guests.

Dollars thus added to Garden Club coffers go to pay for authentic restorations. Even now you may be admiring some of these as you trip about the State. There's Thomas Jefferson's garden and wall at Monticello in Charlottesville, Bruton Parish Churchyard in Williamsburg, and the garden of Stratford Hall, birthplace of Robert E. Lee, to salute only a few. Time and neglect deal unkindly with historic landmarks, often losing them for years in crumbling brick and thick overgrowth. Expert exploration and painstaking care recreate the plantings as they were, and time adds the mellowing illusion.

Special maps showing where private homes are located are available from the American Automobile Association and the Virginia State Travel Bureau, both in Washington; or direct from Garden Club headquarters in Richmond. A guidebook giving detailed information is ready early in February. Co-ordinated tours, such as at Alexandria, make it possible for you to concentrate your Garden Week explorations around one historic area.

So take this pleasant way to discover the leisurely grace of early American living. You'll marvel at formal gardens, at serpentine walls, and at holly tree hedges with a timeless air. There'll be original garden patterns, such as the "Mary" garden, modeled after the medieval practice of planting only flowers bearing the name of Mary or of Biblical reference, as Rosemary, or Madonna lilies. In the city, you'll find old town houses graced by eighteenth-century gardens hardly larger than an old-fashioned nosegay, and just as charming.

But do remember that, quite independent of the tours, and apart from Mount Vernon and the Custis-Lee Mansion, you can visit these Virginia showplaces almost any day:

GUNSTON HALL. (Admission charge: 50 cents. Members of the Armed Forces in uniform and children under 12 admitted free. Open 9:30 A.M. to 5:00 P.M. every day except Christmas.)

On a five-hundred-acre tract of rolling land on the Virginia shore located fifteen miles south of Alexandria, is the two-century-old home of the Virginia statesman, George Mason. Your first view of this Georgian brick home—graceful, yet compactly set into the landscape—opens from the road. You'll be unprepared for the ample rooms inside, the distinguished workmanship and rich furnishings which create an air of simple elegance. Architects call Gunston Hall a gem or "one of the great jewels of American architecture." (Historians more and more are recognizing Mason as an able, if unsung, figure who made a great and lasting contribution to his country.)

Walk into the great hall, over wide pine flooring—most of it original—and stand at the threshold of each room. The Queen Anne table and two Chinese Chippendale chairs in the hall belong to the Mason family now and were here originally.

To the right is the green-and-ivory Chippendale Room where long ago dinner was served by candlelight before the blazing fireplace. Perhaps the table is set for four today, but George Mason was the father of nine and a man who enjoyed his family and fireside. History knows him as good friend of George Washington and creator of the Virginia Bill of Rights. Mason's influence through this single document was far-reaching, for he tersely set forth for the first time for any State the foundation of the American way of life. On it other States based their constitutions, and many historians believe Jefferson drew on it for several truly notable passages in the Declaration of Independence. (Drafts of both these famous documents are on permanent display at the Library of Congress.)

In the Palladian drawing room, look for the exquisite Adam mantel, the Masons' silver tea set, and an original handsomely carved door. The companion portrait of Mason's young wife hangs here. This is thought to be the most beautiful room in the house. But the study, also on the first floor, especially reflects the cultivated taste of this wealthy planter. On the table in this room, Mason wrote his famous document. That ladder propped against the bookshelves was given to Mason by Thomas Jefferson, and is like one Jefferson ingeniously designed for his own use at Monticello. When folded together, it becomes again the single long pole from which it was fashioned.

Upstairs in the room set aside as a museum you'll find a photostat of a document, the indenture of William Buckland to George Mason's brother, Thomson, dated August 4, 1755. This is one of the few clues to the young architect who came over from England as an indentured servant; Buckland not only designed Gunston Hall, but performed much of the actual labor as well. Mystery cloaks the early history of this gifted craftsman. Before coming to Virginia at the age of twenty-one, he was apprenticed when he was fourteen to an uncle in London who was a "joyner." Little is known of how he acquired his skill. But he went on to become America's leading designer of interiors in Colonial times.

From upstairs, also, is your best view of the hedges and formal gardens. But you sniffed the spicy fragrance of English boxwood as soon as you entered the grounds.

This two-hundred-year-old boxwood is often called the finest in the country, much of it surviving from original plantings by George Mason. Gaps were filled by great bushes of similar parentage from Rockbridge County, Virginia, when the Garden Club of Virginia undertook restoration work at Gunston Hall. The length of the 250-foot walk to the Potomac overlook takes you between two towering green walls, clipped table-smooth, reaching to twelve feet. Formal gardens, stretching on either side, are divided into four sections or parterres, each a distinct area with paths and flower beds of unique design.

Gunston Hall, a three-hundred-slave tobacco plantation, remained in the Mason family until just after the Civil War. Deprived of slave labor, the owner was forced to sell outside the family. The last of four such owners, Mr. Louis Hertle, conveyed the title of Gunston Hall to the Commonwealth of Virginia, and restoration was undertaken by the Colonial Dames of America. In 1952 the home was opened to the public not only as a notable achievement in architecture, but for historical significance as the home of Virginia statesman Mason and his family.

POHICK CHURCH. (No admission charge.) At Gunston Hall, you're just five miles from old Pohick Church, parish church of Mount Vernon, Woodlawn, and Gunston Hall. Truro Parish dates from 1732, but the little gemlike church you find today was begun nearly forty years later and designed by George Washington. Pews 28 and 29 were Washington's; he was a vestryman for more than two decades and his father before him. George Mason completed the building; he, also, was a vestryman and held two pews. That old friend of the hatchet and cherry tree story, Mason Locke (Parson) Weems, once occupied the pulpit.

As you approach the church, you'll see bullet-pocked bricks, crudely carved dates and initials—many are mementos of the Civil War. The interior with gallery is pure white; the box pews and striking red cushions are reminiscent of some of the old English churches. Originally the pews were built very high to keep icy drafts out and the heat of footwarmers in during winter months. From his perch on the high wineglass pulpit, the preacher could easily see all his parishioners. An interesting example of restoration problems is that of a baluster taken as a souvenir in 1861 and returned in time to serve as a model for the missing balusters. A plate marks it in the communion rail today.

Not only is Pohick an active parish church with Sunday services and a busy community life, but it is a national shrine of the oldest military order, the Order of the Purple Heart (combat wounded). This order was founded by General Washington and reactivated in 1932 by order of the President of the United States.

A stroll in the historic churchyard on a summer afternoon gives one the feeling of having escaped to a peaceful island, despite the traffic roaring past on U.S. 1, a few yards away.

WOODLAWN PLANTATION. (Admission charge: 50 cents; groups of 20 or more, half price; children under 14 years, free. Open from 10:00 A.M. to 5:00 P.M. every day.) Thirteen miles south of Washington and four miles from Mount Vernon is Woodlawn Plantation, George Washington's wedding gift to his beloved foster daughter, Eleanor Parke (Nelly) Custis. The legacy of two thousand acres, including a grist mill and distillery, was mentioned in his will shortly after Nelly married the General's nephew, Lawrence Lewis, at Mount Vernon on Washington's last birthday. Dr. William Thornton, first architect of the Capitol, provided plans for the house.

The Plantation has weathered 150 years of sun and rain. Less than a decade after Major Lewis died, the house passed to strangers, and,

until 1900, barely survived periods of total neglect. The mansion
finally came to public attention through the tireless efforts of interested citizens, among them many local people, even school children.
Woodlawn Public Foundation, Inc., was the result, and the property
was purchased for the public in 1948 to take its place as one of the
national shrines of the Capital area. Woodlawn Plantation is now
administered by the National Trust for Historic Preservation.

Garden Club of Virginia archaeologists and landscape architects
searched long for old driveways, flower beds, and walls to serve as
models for authentic restoration of grounds and gardens. That great
encircling hedge in front was there from the first, and Nelly had
yellow jasmine on one wing of the mansion, and roses—florabunda,
multiflora, and damask varieties.

Inside the house, the story is equally interesting. Piece by piece
the elegant interior has taken shape. That yellow French Empire
sofa in the hall and the Duncan Phyfe dining room chairs were probably purchased by Nelly between 1810 and 1820. Restoration problems were many, for Nelly and Lawrence inherited Mount Vernon's
pieces when Martha Washington died. When Mount Vernon was
restored, these were returned to their rightful home. For example,
the harpsichord on which Nelly played is not at Woodlawn, but at
Mount Vernon, where she grew up. However, to supplement the
missing pieces, only authentic antiques prior to 1839 have been used.

Yet all around you'll see reminders of the gay personality of the
young and beautiful mistress, in family portraits and needlework.
You can almost imagine her in the drawing room at the pianoforte
playing an old tune like "The Yellow Hair'd Laddie with VARIATIONS
by the late Mr. BACH."

Upstairs look for the charming water colors known as the Gage-
Ingersoll courtship pictures hanging in the young son Lorenzo's
room. In a guest room, too, Nelly's skill with the needle is shown in
the framed piece called "Spaniard on a Jack-ass," probably one
Sancho Panza. Her embroidery frame is in the hall room.

A most unusual way to visit Woodlawn is by night when candlelight tours are held. So watch the papers for announcements, or

write to Woodlawn Plantation, Lorton, Virginia, for information.

STRATFORD HALL. (Admission charge: 50 cents for adults, 25 cents for children; open 9:00 A.M. to 5:00 P.M. every day except Christmas Day.) About ninety miles from Washington via Fredericksburg, and seventy by the Potomac River Bridge, this ancestral plantation home of the Lees stands guard above the Potomac. This mansion dates back 230 years, when Thomas Lee built Stratford among the sweeping meadows and great stands of trees on the Virginia shore.

The eighteenth-century gardens have been restored by the Garden Club of Virginia. Stratford Hall was purchased in 1929 by the Robert E. Lee Memorial Foundation, Inc., and is operated as a national shrine by the Foundation.

You will see the "mother's room" where Robert E. Lee was born and, before him, Richard Henry Lee and Francis Lightfoot Lee, two of the "five patriot sons," and both signers of the Declaration of Independence.

From the surrounding land, which is a thriving farm, come such products as hams, slabs of bacon, and water ground corn meal. Some of these are on sale to the public.

WATERFORD FAIR. (Admission charge: $1, children free; tickets on sale near the parking lot in Waterford, Virginia. About forty miles from Washington, D.C., via Chain Bridge, through McLean, Tyson's Corner, and Leesburg.) For a real change of pace and some very pleasant hours in the Virginia countryside, plan to visit the three-day Waterford Fair usually held the first week end in October, on Friday, Saturday, and Sunday. Activities start in midmorning and go on until 5:00 P.M.

This tiny mill town, some 220 years old, was once a Quaker settlement. The steep main street winds down to a big red barn, and, on a crisp week end in fall, visitors swarm into town to see the many handicraft exhibits and savor the country atmosphere. Funds raised are used by the Waterford Foundation, Inc., for improvements.

You'll pass the empty old jailhouse, yearn perhaps over a great bubbling kettle of spicy apple butter cooking out of doors, and hear a program of Negro spirituals. In the Old Mill you can stroll about, watching weaving, spinning, rug hooking, pottery making, lamp making—as the good ladies of the town demonstrate these skills. (And don't miss the ironmongering!) The Corner Store has homemade preserves, jewel-toned jellies, home-churned butter, and country cheese to tempt you. One year I came away happily with a huge armful of magnificent zinnias, a jar of crisp watermelon pickle, and a loaf of home-baked bread.

If you have an eye for antiques, you can hardly fail to recognize authentic pieces in the few restored houses usually opened to the public during the fair. But for the Annual Waterford Antiques Show, you'd better come back about the middle of May, when dealers from the surrounding country rent space and sell their wares in the Red Barn, under sponsorship of the Citizens Association of Waterford.

Coming back across the Potomac, tours can take you near and far in the Free State of Maryland. Here are several you may want to take:

Annapolis—to benefit Historic Annapolis, Inc.
Maryland House and Garden Pilgrimage

ANNAPOLIS, State Capital. It's thirty-six miles from Washington to this historic town of fine Georgian homes, brick sidewalks, crabs and oysters, sailing ships, and Naval Academy midshipmen strolling to the movies on a Saturday.

To aid the carless, there's bus service via Greyhound, which costs about two dollars round-trip. Most of the landmarks are within five blocks of the bus station, but a hired car would be of great service, particularly for a drive through the spacious United States Naval Academy grounds, or across the Severn River bridges for a view of that lovely stream, or to Spa Creek where hundreds of sailboats are tied up.

Street names in this charming early State capital are a story in themselves: King George, Duke of Gloucester, Compromise, Cornhill, and Shipwright.

Be sure to ask about the famous Carroll-Davis House which was literally picked up and moved from the town's busy Main Street to the St. John's College campus in 1955.

Among the finest sights here are the Hammond-Harwood House, 19 Maryland Avenue (admission charge: 50 cents), and the Chase-Lloyd House, 22 Maryland Avenue (admission: 25 cents). Both houses bear the master touch of colonial architect William Buckland in their design. These are always included in the official Annapolis Open House, which is held once a year, usually in October. In addition, costumed hostesses welcome you to fine old drawing rooms, not otherwise open.

But a year-round schedule of tours makes historic sight-seeing possible whenever you happen to visit Annapolis. It offers personally guided tours for groups every day but Sunday, and a "non-conducted" tour for individuals, who can set out with map and Tour Book. Another arrangement has been worked out for student groups. (Advance notice is necessary for groups.) Prices vary, so write for details to Historic Annapolis, Inc., 64 State Circle, Annapolis, Maryland.

While you are in this pleasant capital, of course you will want to walk through the Naval Academy grounds, and visit buildings and sights open to tourists. These include the impressive Chapel, wherein lie the remains of John Paul Jones; Memorial Hall, where visitors may see the flag flown by Commodore Oliver Hazard Perry at the Battle of Lake Erie; and the Academy Museum, with ship models, swords, and foreign battle flags. High spot of the year is June Week (first week in June). Then four-year men receive their commissions, toss away their midshipman caps, and pretty girls are as numerous as cameras.

MARYLAND HOUSE AND GARDEN PILGRIMAGE. In late April or early May, the Maryland Pilgrimage beckons visitors to many of its famous counties, to see the great estates that began when first colonists settled, prospered, and built here. Admission prices for a day's tour run about $3.50 each, or $1.00 for a single admission to a house. Transportation is by private or rented car. Tickets, maps, and information may be obtained from the American Automobile Association, 1712 G Street, NW, Washington.

The tour, covering a fortnight, focuses on different history-rich sections, taking you to rolling meadowlands, rich tobacco country, and Tidewater estates. You'll see homes marked uniquely with massive chimneys placed in perfect balance at each end; with decorative brickwork patterns. You'll discover the "telescope house"; additions, each slightly higher and wider than the last, grow out of one end of the house.

In St. Marys County, for example, where the original settlers landed from the *Ark* and the *Dove,* famous private homes such as Mulberry Fields, Cremona, and Sotterley may open their doors to the tour. Tulip Hill, in Anne Arundel County, is another private dwelling sometimes included. Exquisitely restored, it is situated overlooking the West River and Chesapeake Bay. From the pierced chimneys outside to arched stairway within, this house is completely beautiful. But all are in excellent condition, gleaming with the hand-rubbed perfection which only wealthy ownership can maintain.

Along the roads of southern Maryland you will pass unpainted, weathered buildings with hinged planks that may be opened for ventilation. These are tobacco barns. The air-curing process begins after the crop has been harvested in early fall. Close by in Upper Marlboro, great warehouses hold tobacco auctions in the spring. Stop in and listen as the singsong goes on.

V

These Daily Papers and You Are Making History

You'LL WANT TO READ THE LOCAL NEWSPAPERS—
and not simply because this is the news center of the world.

Mirrored in the Washington *Post and Times Herald,* the *Evening Star,* and the Washington *Daily News* are most of the subtle and not-so-subtle influences that make the Capital what it is. Too, they capture, each in a different way, the pleasant leisurely pattern of living here that makes Northerners say, "This is a Southern city," and Southerners feel at home.

In the Capital's newspapers you'll see what folks here are worrying, hoping, and dreaming about, if you read at least one from headlines to "Lost and Found," from advertisements to editorials—and don't overlook the want ads.

It is altogether characteristic of easygoing Washington that all three dailies eschew the sensational in their handling of news. You're pretty certain never again to read anything like this little shocker: "People [here] eat more, drink more, dress more, cheat more, lie more, steal more, pray more, and preach more, and are more ignorant and indigent." These violent views came from the sharp pen of Mrs. Anne Royall, who as reporter-observer for a quarter of a century made a deep impression on the new Capital.

She was fifty-seven years old and widowed when she published her first book. By 1829 she had won enough displeasure with her outspoken views to be indicted by her enemies as a public scold. But she was not subdued. She went on to write nearly a dozen volumes which she peddled herself, on her travels around the country. In 1831 she started a weekly called *Paul Pry*, later changed to the *Huntress*. A sample of her vigorous prose: "How Thomas, the bookseller, gets his bread is a mystery in such an illiterate place as Georgetown." Even her neighbors must have vowed vengeance when they saw themselves in her nicknames—Miss Dismals, Holy Willy, Hallelujah Holdfork, Sally Smart, and Tom Oystertongs!

At breakfast discover the *Post and Times Herald*. It's the "bright young man" of the three dailies, with penetrating, well-written editorials that elicit approving nods from liberals and angry snorts from conservatives. The *Post's* star performer is Herblock (Herbert L. Block), whose daily cartoons may impale Cabinet officers or puncture political air masses shaped like bureaucrats. Walter Lippmann, Marquis Childs, and Joseph and Stewart Alsop also appear regularly in the *Post*, as does George Dixon with his irreverently madcap treatment of Capital doings.

This is the city where the world's top newspapermen make their headquarters, and this is the city they write about. Here all the newspapers are filled with the same subject: Washington news as it happens and affects the world. The latest headline, a blast in Congress, a statement from the President becomes suddenly personal, because you may be in the Senate gallery or walking through the White House, close enough to sense the movement of history around you.

Don't miss, in the *Post and Times Herald*, the compact "President's Appointment List" and the doings of Congress found facing the editorial page; both are sure to make news later in the day. (That man who disappeared into Congress with those rosy promises, your Congressman, might be mentioned.)

The Scripps-Howard *Daily News*, a sprightly tabloid, reaches the streets well before noon. It features sharp, concise reporting, often with an engaging light touch. In the *Daily News* you'll enjoy the first-class reporting of Martha Strayer, long-time newspaperwoman, and find more of your syndicated favorites—down-to-earth Peter Edson, philosopher-humorist Fred Othman, and others, writing from home base. (This was Ernie Pyle's old newspaper.)

Washington's large Negro population has its own newspaper, the *Afro-American,* which costs twelve cents a copy and is published on Tuesdays and Saturdays. The *Pittsburgh Courier,* another leading representative of the Negro press, also publishes a Washington edition.

Even the most ambitious monument-hopping calls for an hour off in the evening. So take time for the *Star.* Magically, it shares with the city a warm, neighborly quality that, beneath the glamour, is the very essence of Washington. How this is contrived is a century-old mystery, although the *Star's* history-steeped reporters seem ever conscious that Jefferson or Washington nudges their elbows as they write. Other papers come and go, change their names and formats, but the *Star* has been and continues to be a going institution.

Watch "Letters to the Editor" as a special gauge to the city's boiling point. They come from Moose, Wyoming; London, England; and midtown. Just before Congress voted itself a salary raise in early 1955, a fifth-grade girl named Sharon Reilly visited the Capitol with her class and saw Congressmen at work.

"Some of them were sitting around reading a newspaper," she wrote to the *Star.* "This is a fact. I want to know why they should get a pay raise if this is the way they spend their time in the Capitol." In the "Letters" column you may find a Supreme Court Justice warning against destroying the old C. & O. towpath wilderness, amateur and professional engineers arguing for or against a bridge across Roosevelt Island, a road into Rock Creek Park, or a tunnel under the Potomac.

Maybe you're not vitally interested in whether a multimillion-dollar tunnel pokes a highway to Virginia under the river, or another bridge springs up behind the Lincoln Memorial. But your favorite offspring and their children may stand there one day and say, "They

never should have started this." It's your town, you know, as long
as Congress puts Federal money into the District of Columbia.

Let your eyes wander to the *Star's* "Reader's Clearing House," a
women's page feature for exchange of small and great bits of knowledge. In one day's helping have come requests for a "golf club putter
named Paul Bunyan, Little Poison, or Paddle Grip"; a good
cucumber-pickle recipe; the translation of *"colleum tueri"*; calls for
How to Play the Piano and a *Philosophy of History* by Ortega y
Gasset; and an SOS following strange noises in a new split-level
rambler: "a steady crunchy sound . . . when our heads are on the
pillow." The feature reflects the town's transient trend, too, with a
continuous travel service. Queries bring firsthand descriptions of life
in Guam, the Canal Zone, Athens, the Far East, or Sarasota, Florida.

Glance through "Personals," to see the wonderful machinery going
round. Each new Congress or administration brings a crop of charm
schools offering to transform the veriest oafs and wallflowers into
social ornaments. "How to Attain and Hold a Social Position in
Washington" met the Eisenhower ladies. Another ad said: "Winter
semester opens with 84th Congress. Washington's oldest school of
personality development, speech and protocol is prepared to serve
you." Slanted toward the Government girl there's "Capsule Course,
grooming for glamor . . . for the girl on a budget . . . complete
1-month course $20."

What better than a new Congress to link politics to want ads?
There's "Capitol Hill, $250, no shorthand. Good typing. Republican
side." Or "Secretary, Capitol Hill, $3600 up. Prefer W. Va. or Va.
Res[ident] immed."

Close to cherry-blossom time you may see "Wanted: sightseeing
lecture girl, with D.C. and Va. driver's permit, age 25–35. $15
per day."

In the columns of houses and apartments furnished and otherwise, a new Congress is offered town houses off Connecticut Avenue,
ranch houses in the suburbs, and up on restored Capitol Hill: "1
block from Supreme Court, in a newly remodeled building, first floor
apt., charming garden, available immediately."

Almost a hundred years ago, in the *Evening Star* the approach was different. This ad appeared in January, 1860, and ran for weeks:

Senators, Members of Congress—Two splendid suites of ROOMS, elegantly furnished, will be rented during the session of Congress, in the most desirable locality of this city, being within one or two squares of Brown's and the National Hotel. Those in pursuit of such rooms will do well to make early application at No. 379 8th Street between D and Pennsylvania Avenue.

The first edition of the *Star* was eight hundred copies, printed on a hand press on December 16, 1852, set in five columns and four pages. Today, five high-speed presses efficiently print the news. This is a real success story, even before you consider that this vast journalistic graveyard of a city holds the bones of newspapers by the score.

From the start, it seemed that every man's dream was to be an editor in the new Capital, but readers were so scarce that one Georgetown publisher ran an ad in his own journal pleading that he could not stay in business unless more copies were sold.

In the hottest mayoralty campaign in the city's history the *National Intelligencer* refused to publish an article sent to it because its writer praised one candidate and maligned another. Yet that paper prospered. The *National Intelligencer* survived from 1800 to 1870, great boon to historians. It was all dignity, with few social items, and often it let a week elapse before giving notice that the President had issued a message.

Its advertisements in 1814 for J. Milligan's bookstore in Georgetown probably brought in a few hardy tourists for copies of new music received: "Said the Smile to the Tear," "Wood Robin," or "Marche Turque"; or *Lewis and Clarke's Expeditions* in two volumes for $6, and a small book called *Bride of Abydos,* by Lord Byron, for 37½ cents.

That same year, the "Lost and Found" items in the *National Intelligencer* were strangely historic.

"Found, one flea-bitten mare" which probably strayed during the burning of the Capitol or bolted in fright in the hurricane that followed which brought torrents of rain to quench the flames, and literally swept the British back to their ships on the Patuxent. Another advertisement appeared one month and four days after the battle:

A sword was left the evening of the Battle of Bladensburg at some house in Washington—the person in whose possession the sword was left will please send it to this office to be forwarded to the owner. The sword is brass mounted, with a broad red belt attached to it.

This advertisement, written on a scrap of paper and signed with the initials R.C.C., again turned up among some yellowing city documents marked in pencil "run 3 or 4 times—paid $1.00." It makes for endless wondering. Did he ever get the sword? Was he wounded? What could have made a soldier forget his sword?

Out of the *National Intelligencer* came the first official reporting of Congress. Heated floor clashes were written up by Joseph Gales, Jr., and William Winston Seaton, its long-time editors, from their seats near the President of the Senate and the Speaker of the House, where they could share official snuffboxes.

Another famous daily was the *Globe*, founded in 1830 by Francis Preston Blair, whom President Andrew Jackson himself called to the Capital to publish the administration's paper. He next established the *Congressional Globe*, forerunner of the present *Congressional Record*.

Other newspapers, with catchy names, came and went from 1801 to the Civil War: the Washington *Union*, the *Daily Madisonian*, the *Southern Press*, the *Spectator*, the *Daily Bee*, the Washington *Metropolis*, the *Citizen*, the *Spirit of Seventy-six*, the *Capitol*, the *Constitution*, *True Whig*, the *Native American*, Washington *Gazette*, and Washington *Sentinel*. Some did not last a year.

The *National Era* was an antislavery paper. It was in this journal that serialized portions of *Uncle Tom's Cabin; or Life among the Lowly* first appeared. In June, 1851, Chapter I began: "In which the reader is introduced to a man of Humanity." Mrs. Harriet Beecher Stowe continued the sensational story to April, 1852. When published in book form, it sold three thousand copies the first day.

Nearest thing to a social item appeared in an 1814 issue of the *National Intelligencer* when at Charleston "an elegant collation was provided in the rigging loft for the Mechanics who assisted in the building of the U.S.S. *Independence* at which about 300 men assembled." Among the eleven toasts was this rousing one: "Valley Forge Fare: no hats—no blankets—no coats—no stockings—no shoes— no money—no credit—one eye'd salt shad, and dirty water to all the enemies of our country!"

One glance at today's social pages and the change is apparent. Now Washington, socially, is the most thoroughly reported city in the world. Women feature editors are frank to admit that society is their Number One assignment.

This change, gradual at first, but strikingly marked in the past few decades, has kept pace with the Capital's growth and rise to world importance. On the *Star*, four reporters cover social events regularly; but twelve more are ready and able to handle party news along with other women's features.

So don't miss the unique social reporting of as many as twenty women reporters who cover for the three daily papers. Their beat is the eating, drinking, clothes, and conversation of official (that's Government and military), diplomatic (Embassy Row), and residential Washington. It's unique because this world capital goes charmingly countrified right before your eyes.

Do you get tight little paragraphs of names and places, just the careful, conservative facts? Never. Careful facts, yes, but set in lush and lively detail, inch after inch of it. "New York laughs at us," one reporter told me. "Calls us provincial, but here parties are politics— you can't separate them."

Who reads this vast encyclopedia of who's entertaining whom? Everybody in Government. Men read it as carefully as women. That includes new Congressmen and their wives; it's a short course in manners and social patterns.

"Taxi drivers eat it up," one columnist said. Reporters and editors, those responsible for news of politics and international affairs, always run through this airy chitchat in their check of daily papers, looking for straws in the wind. Who is courting what pressure group? Did Senator you-know-who get a White House invitation? And it's not unusual to find social scoops on the front page.

Finally, Washington social reporting can be pretty funny. Descriptions of the ladies' raiment are standard procedure in newspapers almost everywhere, but only in Washington, I submit, do the public prints mention what the *gentlemen* wear to parties. At dressy evening affairs, of course, male finery is limited to either white tie or black tie, leaving the reporters with little to say on the subject. But in an account of an important cocktail party you may be regaled with breathless tidings of an undersecretary's flowered waistcoat, an attaché's lemon-yellow trousers, or a Cabinet officer's extraordinary cuff links. In masculine retreats like the National Press Club and the Cosmos Club it is not uncommon, I'm told by a reliable spy, to hear groups guffawing over such nuggets of prose.

Be on the lookout for brisk little paragraphs like: "Did you know that a member of Washington's 'cave dweller' set, when asked by her ex-husband to send his oil portrait to him, tore it up instead and returned only one finger and one eye?" (Marie McNair in the *Post and Times Herald*.) Or: "One Washington woman's bid for the most expressive eyes I've ever seen goes to the Shah of Iran. The Shah, by the way, wears light ties, white shirts and dark suits." (The Sunday *Star*.)

If parties are big business here, they're big business to the girls who cover them. The girls hear people say, "What a wonderful job —parties all the time, how I envy you!"; but it's often heavy going, with little sleep and a surfeit of rich food.

Marie McNair was pounding her typewriter until the antennae on her smart white hat quivered when I found her on the fifth floor of the *Post and Times Herald* offices on L Street. For twenty-five years a social reporter here, she "broke in" writing weddings and engagements. But that was before the embassies doubled their number and diplomatic parties pyramided.

Mrs. McNair was bound for a State Department reception at Anderson House that evening, and would return to her desk later to write it up for next morning's *Post*. In her schedule book, bulging with social events, she leafed through the remaining blank pages ahead and sighed wistfully, "They won't stay that way."

When several parties fall in one evening, she phones in her story, perhaps from a kitchen crawling with caterers, or from a churning hallway. How to get to the next party is often a problem. Unable to get a taxi one midwinter night, she stepped up to a U.S. mail truck for best advice on the nearest thoroughfare, and agilely accepted a stand-up ride among sacks of mail. Another time, she came out of a hotel reception—no cab in sight—and a police prowl car that was going her way dropped her off at a second event.

As I talked with other social reporters, it was plain that the girls play no favorites or hold no grudges. Betty Beale, in her column, told the old story of a Chief Justice's wife who incurred the total displeasure of Capital reporters in an earlier day. Thereafter, no matter what kind of gown the lady wore, it was always a "dark dress" in the paper.

But it's not hard to ruffle feelings today. "Just fail to mention that Mrs. Bore was there!" one reporter laughed. "Getting invited isn't enough. Some *have* to see their names in the papers." They'll even go so far as to remind the reporter next day, as one did, testily, "I was the best-dressed woman in the room, and you know it. Well, why didn't you say so?" But there's one recent exception. If it's the Soviet Russian Embassy's annual party to celebrate the Great October Revolution, some guests readily accept the invitation but would prefer not to be mentioned at all.

As you read today's social columns, you can safely say that many a reporter got to bed early in the morning after putting in hours of careful listening, gracious smiling, judicious querying, and hard writing to get up the next day and begin again. These tireless newspaperwomen slip from one party to the next, hovering long enough to produce a wonderful sampling, and then off again. Fountains spouting pink champagne, buffets set with a whole stuffed lamb, pheasant *en plumage*, or sculptured ice eagles bearing up bravely over a sea of toothsome fare—they see it all as casual props of this social stage. Details pile up.

"The hors d'oeuvres . . . were stuck on small trees which surrounded a miniature lake that had ducks swimming in it. . . ." "As always at the Turkish Embassy where the table linen is embroidered with gold thread, there were miniature red linen napkins. . . ." "On the buffet will be individual Ozark puddings, made from Bess Truman's own recipe. . . ."

Betty Beale in the *Star* put her finger on a foreign-policy trend toward Far Eastern affairs when she wrote: "The amount of rice with spice dished up in this community is staggering."

For historic impact and insight into today's social picture through keen knowledge of old Washington, there's Evelyn Peyton Gordon, in the *Daily News*. Her column never fails to bring out, and briskly, too, some new-old facet of the party picture. When Secretary Dulles entertained a visiting Prime Minister at a state dinner, she described the two gentlemen seated together "in thronelike chairs. Whence this notion of seating two men, side by side, I don't know. But it sure throws a table out of protocol!" Mrs. Gordon's respect for good victuals creeps in often; she may include an entire menu with mouthwatering comment.

That durable White House social secretary, Mrs. Edith Helm, who skillfully guided the Wilsons, Roosevelts, and Trumans over the social hurdles, cherished this homely definition of protocol: "Since the good God made us so that we cannot all get through the same door at once, there must be precedence." Protocol, the system of rank, or who sits where (and likes it), was thus summed up by a British diplomat, as Mrs. Helm recounts in her book, *The Captains and the Kings*.

Even in the old days, social ingenuity counted for a good bit. The ways of the newcomer were interesting then, protocol notwithstanding. At President Buchanan's reception in pre-Civil War days, the entrance of perhaps the first one-man lobby was recorded in the *Star*:

A stranger in the room attracted considerable attention by the peculiarities of his attire, which consisted of a military uniform with a silk scarf thrown over his shoulders. It is said that he comes to Washington as an applicant for a patent for a steam plough and that his brilliant costume was worn . . . with the advice of some of his boarding house acquaintances, who suggested . . . he must make himself somewhat prominent in Washington society and thus attract the attention of influential politicians.

VI

"Roast Beef Sandwiches Are $20 a Hundred. . . ."

In EARLY WASHINGTON, WHEN PENNSYLVANIA Avenue was a bog that bordered on a marsh, a disturbing number of visitors came to town and promptly died. Rumors that the location might be unhealthy became so widespread that measures were finally taken. The first health officer was appointed to investigate. Soon thereafter, the public prints carried periodic lists of what cut down the hapless victims. It seemed that most of the deceased had one foot well in the grave before ever setting the other in the Capital City.

Today almost the worst disability that can beset a newcomer is one called Potomac fever. No rash accompanies this ailment, because it appears to strike only persons with very thick hides—such as social climbers. If there's a cure or scientific answer to the problem, surely it would have to come from a really disinterested source like the mechanical brain at the National Bureau of Standards. Someday technicians might feed in the following query:

If there are 5,000 cocktail parties this year, and Mrs. X gets invited to 25, tosses 50, and meets 200 of the same people at least 30 times, how long will it take her to be a social success?

Estimates of the number of big-time Washington parties given in a month run as high as four hundred (cocktail parties, dinners, debutante affairs, receptions—all catered!). Add to these the hundreds of similar functions that play the minor social circuits, and you have the pyramiding Washington social picture. Whatever the number, Washington party-giving may well become the town's Number Three industry. It's piling up dollars for caterers, food and drink purveyors, dressmakers, suit-rental houses, long-glove makers, and lemon peel twisters.

Party-giving and party-going merge into the Capital's leading avocation. It's highly likely that every party here has a purpose.

The whole idea might have started with a dinner given by Thomas Jefferson, with a gilt-edged guest list headed by Alexander Hamilton, even before there was a Federal City. It, too, was a party with a purpose.

A deadlock involving the location of the new Capital had suddenly halted all plans. The North wanted it. The South wanted it. In fact, it was just possible that two cities might be considered, to make everybody happy. Quite aside from this, Secretary of the Treasury Hamilton wanted the new Federal Government to pay for the States' war debts and Jefferson's own State, Virginia, objected.

Jefferson wrote later:

Hamilton was in despair. As I was going to the President's one day I met him in the street. He walked me backwards & forwards before the President's door for half an hour. . . . I proposed to him however to dine with me the next day, and I would invite another friend or two, bring them into conference together. . . .

So "consulting together coolly," at the dinner, tempers perhaps mellowed by Madeira and fine fowl, Jefferson and the State of Virginia agreed to Hamilton's plan to let the Government assume the debts, and Hamilton graciously lent his weight to the Potomac River site for the Capital. Successful party-giving was off to a fine start.

"I got more work done in thirty minutes than I could in a week through usual channels," a Congressman was heard to remark after he had spent those thirty minutes at an important Washington func-

tion. That's true, too, of embassy parties. They form the greater share
of all party-giving, probably more than 50 per cent. Here a foreign
diplomat may, for the first time, gain a Senator's ear and in au-
spicious surroundings, after choice food, drink, and perhaps a distinguished musical program have eased the harsh pressures of the
Hill. (Of diplomatic assignments the world over, Washington is now
considered by many to be the favored post.)

Perhaps no diplomatic mission has ever won friends and charmed
the right people with the astonishing success of two "foreigners" who
came as special envoys in 1836. They were two Texans who came
seeking recognition for the hard-won republic just north of the Rio
Grande. From that year forward they managed to win all social
Washington. As one writer put it, "The diplomats from Texas were
the toast of the hour."

Even today the astute embassy chatelaine, well informed and in-
telligent, strives to build good will for her country through her
entertaining. This she sees as an important step toward understanding between nations. She wants her parties relaxing, eminently pleasant, but "different." So, partaking of hospitality that runs from
native dishes to native dances, Congressmen and officials are able to
while away many a supper hour on local "foreign" soil.

Who sets the table and the scene literally for these endless official
functions? Surely not the hostess in her imported gown, her un-
creased brow, and charming smile, who in herself is a successful
production to be described in detail. Most of the time, it's catered.
Even now as you read this, the staffs of Washington's leading society
caterers are busy (unless it's July and August, the slow season).

Someone at a desk is answering jangling phones.

"Yes, Madam, very good, four hundred on the seventh." Or:
"Roast beef open-faced sandwiches—twenty dollars a hundred—the
two-bite size." Or: "The menus are on their way over now." Or if
you could eavesdrop in the warehouse behind the scenes: "But they
can't pass sandwiches on that tray—it's for a whole salmon!" And
along with the jangling phones there is a constant undertone of
adding machines, tapping out "Business is good, business is

good. . . ." A detail-perfect buffet, from dishes to doorman, can cost as much as thirty dollars a person, liquor additional.

Chief difference between Avignone Frères, Hubert, Inc., Ridgewell's Caterers, and one or two others of the ninety-some listed in the yellow pages of the telephone directory is that they usually equip and service diplomatic and official Washington's exclusive parties. Why this neat little hierarchy? Experience, reputation, and vast supplies are the answer.

When the phone rings at any one of these, the caterer may check out an order for two bars, six coat racks, or twelve wedding present tables, or a succulent roast of beef, if it's that kind of party. Under plates and china on his list he may put down one hundred or five hundred soups, dinner plates, and cups and saucers. There are nineteen pieces of flat silver which might turn up at one setting of a formal state dinner. Fish platters, oval platters, round platters, square platters, silver urns, chafing dishes, and hurricane lamps can go rolling on their way. Fourteen kinds of glasses, from punch cups to tumblers to shot glasses, and four kinds of ice—cubes, crushed, block, and snow. If you need a pantry maid, three bartenders, and a babysitter, they'll be right over.

At one Washington party a departing guest was heard to mutter, "The liquor flowed like glue." This is not always so. In fact, liquor costs at most functions (except at embassies, which bring in their own wines and spirits duty-free) cover 15 to 20 per cent of the total. Such hospitality is an old Washington custom, in and out of embassies.

Back in the eighties one reached for egg nog, "cherry-bounce," a liqueur, or Roman Punch, a delicate combination of cognac, lemon, and effervescing champagne. But the problem is still the one noted in the old *Star's* column:

Beware of too much egg-nogg. It is intoxicating after the eighth tumbler; then, if persevered in you will be metamorphosed into a tumbler yourself, and besides have a great big head next day.

One morning in March I watched seventy-two cocktail glasses

and as many highball glasses go in the direction of an embassy. I was at Ridgewell's and Clarence H. Ellis was saying that "there's a personal feeling between caterer and customer. The top hostesses all have their kind of party, and the caterer knows." In his hand was a little book entitled *The Association of Private Waiters,* and he was lining up waiters for May and June. He knew he would need them (he already had them signed up for New Year's Eve next).

As he talked, I gathered that some hostesses are perfectionists who strive for the perfect picture, while others prefer dignity to the point of downright stuffiness. Then there are a few of whom caterers and guests agree, "It's always a good party." Magic ingredients: people, opinions, plus good food on a generous scale. Some parties even gain through gifted amateur entertainers.

When Charles Edison was Secretary of the Navy under President Franklin D. Roosevelt, he would delight friends with the playing of his own composition, "The Orange Symphony." For this he would sit at the piano, hands hidden from the audience, and sound a thunderous bass with his left hand. With his right, he would skillfully roll an orange over the treble keys. The sheer symphonic effect always brought a standing ovation.

Behind the scenes at Avignone Frères is a network of rooms where the supplies, gleaming damask, and padded chests of silver are kept. As I waited for him in the restaurant where French cooking is a specialty, Pietro Orcino, an affable, round little man with a gift for detail, was planning dimensions for a portable steam table. "It must be able to roll on trucks, and keep hot for three or four hours a roast of beef, creamed lobster, or hors d'oeuvres."

First in my introduction to catering came the tour of the kitchen. This was just before Easter, and sleek chocolate roosters, rabbits, and Dutch shoes gleamed fresh from their molds. There were a dozen tiny heartshaped cakes, iced in white and yellow, marked with the name "Florenz" on special order. Tall metal closets fitted with shelves held freshly baked cakes, unfilled patty shells, bite-size cocktail canapés waiting for filling.

In the main kitchen were six chefs and cooks, busy among copper pans and a near-by steam table. A girl was plucking pheasants.

In the great walk-in refrigerator I saw some twenty of these plump birds, wild rice stuffing already tucked inside, with a square of thin fatback lard laid gently over their breasts, ready for the oven. Thirty-five or forty pheasants, all deliciously browned, were to be part of a superlative dinner that evening. As Mr. Orcino described it with sweeping gesture, "A celebration—they say, 'It happen one in a life'— they want, how you speak, the most!"

The next day I watched backstage. Avignone Frères was catering an embassy reception for four hundred at the Pan American Union's beautiful Hall of the Americas. It was, Mr. Orcino said, a "usual reception," one of hundreds he has catered there for Latin-American countries. The long ballroom with twenty furled flags and the Stars and Stripes at each end, the shimmering chandelier from Tiffany, and balconies overlooking the gardens provide the perfect setting for official entertaining by countries in the Organization of American States.

From the moment that the two waiters, Pierre and Charles, unpacked the first carton of snowy linen (cloths eight yards by three) there was no lost movement. In broad white aprons, their spotless sleeves rolled up, they opened racks of cocktail and highball glasses, "treasure chests" of candelabra, gleaming nested spoons, stacks of metal platters, gold-banded china, polished chafing dishes. . . .

The twenty-two-foot table got a first cover of flannel, then the cloth; cups and saucers for coffee were set at the far end. Two bars were set up on corner tables; hundreds of tall glasses clinking together were banked beside high pitchers. The liquor sent over by the embassy was waiting in these proportions: five cases of Scotch, three of bourbon, two of gin, one of vermouth, and a supply of brandy.

South Americans have good appetites and excellent taste, as well. The menus for these affairs are, in Mr. Orcino's own flowery words, "to match any demand, any fantasy in the mind," such as:

Assorted Canapés of Caviar, Paté de Foie Gras,
Smoked Salmon, Filet of Anchovies
Fresh Shrimp and Lobster Served in Ice Blocks,
with Cocktail Sauce

Open Faced Sandwiches   Meat Balls au Jus
Hot Rissole   Hot Pizza   Codfish Cakes, Tartare Sauce
Variety of Miniature French Pastries
Ice Cream Sherbets
Fancy Cakes, Petit Fours
Bonbons, Mints, Nuts

An imposing floral arrangement of snapdragons in pink and rose arrived and took position between the candelabra. Suddenly, it was time for the hot food to go into chafing dishes. I was not sure whether it would be Arroz con Pollo, Patty Shells Financière (a specialty of the house), or Filet de Boeuf Bourguignon. Here was a magnificent platter of cold fresh Columbia salmon decorated by an artist's hand, with platters of cold sliced young turkeys, Smithfield and Virginia hams flanked by Galantine of Capon.

At such affairs, too, there is usually a very large cake beautifully decorated with the national colors and flag of the host nation.

As the next morning's Washington *Post* and *Times Herald* account ran,

In spite of the rain, last night turned out to be a good partying night on both sides of the Potomac. On the East bank Brig. Gen. José Machado Lopes, the new Brazilian Military Attaché . . . and Mrs. Lopes were being introduced to military and diplomatic Washington in the beautiful Hall of Americas room in the Pan American Union. First through the receiving line to meet the Lopeses (she was wearing a stunning black satin with all-over clusters of beading) . . .

Local butlers often switch to the catering business; it gives them more time for their families. The Association of Private Waiters is made up of 125 members, only about 40 of whom are full-time. The others are messengers, Government clerks, or such by day, but by night they are available and listed in the little booklet of membership. The hardest job? The garden parties during late spring months, when the hot sun beats down on their heads as they set up and service countless outdoor receptions and parties.

It was Henry Trilling, native Washingtonian and retired owner of Hubert, Inc., who looked back after a life of catering on the change from afternoon teas to cocktail parties. (Sons Edward and Joseph are carrying on.)

"Before the First World War you never saw a cocktail party in the afternoon; there was sherry on the sideboard, or they would serve champagne or champagne punch in the afternoon, but no hard liquor." Part of the change here he feels has come through the re-linquishing of great old homes. "People just don't have the money now to keep them, what with income tax and inheritance tax, too." He could remember back when he catered vegetarian dinners to famous Mrs. John B. Henderson in her red-turreted "castle" on Six-teenth Street.

That was almost thirty years ago when the thriving and elegant establishment of Rauscher's stood at Connecticut Avenue and L Street. Rauscher's catered only to the exclusive and wealthy, parties, dinners, *thés dansants,* and balls, for such names as Walsh, Town-send, Anderson, Leiter, and McLean. In splendor of equipment and service it had no match in Washington. There were even several ballrooms.

Affairs often took place in the great private homes, however. Anderson House at 2118 Massachusetts Avenue, NW, is one which still stands and is open to the public. Its gracious hospitality, made available by the Society of the Cincinnati for which it is head-quarters, extends to official State Department entertaining. Some of the old mansions have been transformed into embassies, but many more are gone, just as Rauscher's is only a memory. For after prohi-bition and the depression, such lavish catering could not survive.

But Henry Trilling remembers back to the day in 1901 when he joined Rauscher's, and went on, years later, to own his own firm, Hubert, Inc. Then the caterer's horse and wagon left L Street at seven o'clock in the wintry morning bound for Mrs. Evalyn Walsh

McLean's fabulous home uptown to make early preparations for her New Year's Eve ball.

"We wouldn't get there for two or three hours if it snowed—"

If heavy winter weather halted traffic, an old January issue of the *Star* also notes:

The ice dealers of Washington generally are taking advantage of the pending freeze to fill their ice houses from the river. . . . Ice has formed from seven inches in thickness, and as pure and free of pores as any usually received from the colder North.

In those days, too, good waiters were hard to find. When William Howard Taft was inaugurated, Rauscher's prepared dinners for two thousand. A hundred extra waiters were brought from Baltimore. They arrived on time, all wearing Tuxedos, properly enough, but set off by bright yellow shoes. And that's the way they served the dinner.

Ask the veteran caterers and they will tell you the cocktail buffet was unheard of back there.

"Then, an invitation was generally for dinner. Everyone sat down in a civilized way, ate, had perhaps a liqueur; the ladies departed to the drawing room to chat, the gentlemen were busy with their smokes. At eleven o'clock everyone went home."

Now, it is a required social grace to be able to compete with one hundred, or one thousand, other hungry people in filling a plate, cafeteria style, and balancing it neatly while holding gifted conversation with a ranking guest.

"The party breaks up when the bar closes," adds one observer.

The abracadabra that creates an eight o'clock formal State Department dinner in the Hall of the Americas room took about five energy-packed hours one late March day. The occasion was a dinner given by Secretary of State and Mrs. John Foster Dulles in honor of Italy's Prime Minister, Mario Scelba, and Signora Scelba. But in the early hours, long before the guests had even gathered in the tropical patio for cocktails, the principals were Mr. Orcino, the caterer; the florist, the State Department's behind-the-scenes hostess, and many busy hands.

"Hear that siren?" asked Mrs. Victoria Geaney. "There they go to

Mount Vernon and Arlington Cemetery." Mrs. Geaney, as hostess-manager of State Department's Blair House, not only knew where her visitors were going, but since they were living at Blair House during their official stay, she had a chance to really know them.

"But no matter who they are, they like to be treated like human beings," she said. "We try to make our guests happy. We fly the flag of their country. This is their home while they are here. When I left, my girls were pressing the gowns for tonight."

When I walked into the long room that afternoon a sixty-eight-foot horseshoe-shaped table was getting its tablecloth stapled on. Racks of fine glassware, representing a caterer's investment of twelve dollars at each place, were stacked near by.

The caterer and Mrs. Geaney looked down the table. "How many d'you have now?"

"Ninety-one the last I heard. What'd you hear?"

"Eighty-eight." Mr. Orcino smiled. "But I have for a hundred."

A waiter passed between the table and the stream of little gold chairs with an armful of Avignone Frères' best gold-banded china, muttering, "Fifty-six on the outside, thirty-two on the inside." Soon another waiter followed, dropping a big square damask napkin on the plate. Just then Aristides Chaconas, florist, made a dramatic but almost unnoticed entrance up the center of the horseshoe, pulling a small truck crowned with the first of the twenty-six snapdragon-and-rose bouquets he had spent two days creating. Three of the graceful low arrangements, the large ones, he placed at the curve, inside, and twenty down each side at intervals. (Three more filled wall niches.) Ropes of tender green smilax he fastened in loops against the drop of the cloth around the inside of the tables. He worked fast, his mouth full of long pearl-headed pins. He moved a dozen or more potted palms to screen the north anteroom entrance, from where the waiters would serve, then laced shiny smilax through them. "This is the first time in this room," he remarked. "Another time I build a trellis for this."

Through that entrance and into the hall, I passed by a door

marked "GENTLEMEN-CABALLEROS" and on to the areaway where Mr. Orcino had set up against the wall his five gas plates and tall steel cabinets, fitted with trays, all ingeniously connected to a tank of bottled gas. The roast spring lamb, new potatoes, fresh peas, and other hot food on the menu would arrive and be placed in warming ovens before serving. Twenty-seven maroon chests of supplies stood beside cases of liquor. The food would not come over until after seven. (The caterer breaks up such large dinners into units of ten; that is, for a hundred guests, there would be ten units, with two waiters to each unit, indicating the need for ten serving platters, bowls, trays, and such. Tonight there would be twenty waiters, about two to each nine persons. Through Mr. Orcino's special magic there would appear four pantry girls, two cloakroom girls, a waiter to announce, and a man to summon guests' automobiles.)

"We'll get out of here probably after one," a helper said. "It won't take long to pull all this apart. We'll have a lot of help. But first there'll be dishwashing. That goes on all during the evening."

Back in the hall, I found Charles carefully passing from place to place, opening and refolding each napkin into a special shape, then standing it up on the plate.

"This shape is called a Lazy Footman," he said. "Easiest kind to make. Now a Bishop's Hat is harder." He showed me. It finished up smaller, but like a hat. "I'd leave it like that, but there's no bishop coming tonight."

Just then another waiter opened a box of demitasse cups; they were for the Italian coffee to come at the end with the liqueur. Near by was a stack of lace doilies to go under the finger bowls. But he found what he wanted, dozens of glass ash trays. White candles were already placed in the six-branched candelabra. Before Mrs. Geaney left, chandeliers and side lights were switched on in a trial run. Everything worked as it should. Twenty gold chairs for the musicians were lined up near the grand piano.

Long rectangles of late sunlight poured from the four great windows into the room, sending a golden glow into the great sweep of flags, dazzling the silver and the etched stemware. The room was empty except for me. I sat down in Secretary Dulles' place and looked about. Later, there would be beautiful women, jeweled gowns, music, yet this was probably the most enchanted moment in the whole affair.

VII

You'll See Government Girls

IF YOU FIND THIS FEDERAL CITY QUITE UNSTUFFY, even effervescing at times, there's a reason. It's that pretty girl, hatless and slim, racing for a bus. Multiply her by thousands and you have the career-girl population of Washington.

You have probably heard this well-known fact about the Government Girl: her chances of becoming a spinster are good, because there just aren't enough men here to go around. Well, this legend needs airing. Based on year-in, year-out experiences of those who help provide shelter, education, jobs, and entertainment for this segment of the population, the conservative comment is: today marriage is higher on the list of why girls leave Washington. (It still will be a long time before conditions revert to the description that one Secretary of the British Legation gave our town just after 1800—"one of the most marrying of the whole continent.")

Then there are those who marry and stay on in the Capital. A personnel director for a busy employment agency was emphatic about this. "Lots of Government Girls keep right on working after they marry. Some switch to non-Federal jobs because they think it offers more variety—or they just want to free-lance. About a fourth of those I talk to are putting their husbands through college."

And many of Uncle Sam's helpers are college-trained. That trim, shining-haired young woman coming briskly up Virginia Avenue may be a Foreign Service officer in the near-by State Department.

Often four years of college are behind her, plus difficult exams, security clearances, interviews, special schooling, and several foreign assignments. You may be looking at an expert on some small kingdom halfway across the world. Not yet thirty-five years old, she may earn a salary of seven thousand a year. (Such positions are filled by the Department of State.)

It is no longer a coincidence that an increasing number of college graduates with majors in economics, literature, and sociology (practically all but the technical fields which do their own recruiting) fill out a Form 57 even before they receive their diplomas. Or they write a masterful résumé of themselves and one day soon proceed toward Washington. For the Civil Service Commission has lately set in motion a new recruiting program, aimed directly at drawing the young graduate into training for leadership jobs. Such management training can lead to positions in general administration, communications, budget, library service, and many other branches of Government.

But many a brand-new stenographer comes right out of high school, recruited by a Government agency (or the Civil Service Commission) while still a senior. About one-third of all Federal white collar jobs were filled by women in 1954. Of this group, the stenographer, typist, clerk proportion is the largest.

Betty Lou Riggs was just seventeen when a field representative of the Federal Bureau of Investigation visited her small Pennsylvania town. She listened and came to Washington, starting work at an annual salary of about $3,000. Today, at nineteen, she is making close to $3,500 (a recent Federal pay raise helped). Now she has an apartment with a roommate (both high on a Government Girl's list of wants), sends money home, and has paid for dental work she needed done.

But after two years of working in a stenographic pool, she yearns to be a "bigger frog." Her alternatives are several. The FBI does not employ women agents, but opportunities for advancement within that agency are tremendous.

Occasionally the young Government Girl reads in the want ads of a Capitol Hill opening, paying "from $3,600 to $4,500." Clerical or stenographic, it's a start toward a rewarding potential, such as a "girl Friday" to a busy Senator. She may decide to call for an appointment, then go, wearing her best suit, to the interview during her lunch hour. In Washington, as anywhere, a pretty girl with ambition *and* brains is unbeatable.

Perhaps it *is* the Washington potential that draws and holds women—young and old.

One Government Girl, efficient, attractive, with almost twenty years in the Department of State, was quietly carrying on in her job one Friday afternoon. It was a routine sort of thing, handling inquiries, dispatching replies. Then something very unroutine happened.

A phone call from the Personnel Office came to her boss. An international conference, at that moment being held in Switzerland, was short of stenographers. This girl was picked. Passport, inoculations, clothes—all were ready for that Monday plane to New York and overseas. (Also necessary, and she had it on her record, was experience at a conference, in the United States, which had taken place months before.)

But if the Capital is glamorous, it also offers the girls real problems, as reflected by the bills in their mailboxes.

One anonymous government worker summed up her financial plight, with a low bow to John Greenleaf Whittier:

> Maud Muller on a summer's day
> Raked the meadow sweet with hay,
> She had to do this part-time work
> For she was just a U.S. clerk.

It was part of a lament appearing in Jerry Kluttz's column "The Federal Diary" in the Washington *Post and Times Herald,* before the pay-raise bill was passed.

For, from the moment she sets foot in town, her first and last problem is money. Drawn in great numbers from outside the area, she must quickly adjust to life in one of the most expensive cities in the country in terms of rent, meat and potatoes, spring suits, and bus fare.

Inadvertently, Uncle Sam himself helps start her off on the wrong foot. Her first pay check is always about three weeks late, and, according to a local credit bureau manager, some girls never recover from this setback. "But they are in the minority. Mostly, as long as they have a steady job in Government, they don't have to worry—just budget, that's all."

In its bulletin to prospective employees, the Civil Service Commission makes the suggestion that each girl plan on about $125 to safely tide her over this period.

Fifty years ago, things were at a pretty pass, too. Most women in Government departments here received from $600 to $900 a year. "Several receive over $2,500 per annum," says an old publication, "about fifty receive $1,600 per annum."

But if there is a small handful who can't keep ahead of their bills, there are others who can save enough to buy well-located real estate with income-producing units on it, who drive their own cars, take European vacations, and scan the *Wall Street Journal* while they sit under driers at their favorite beauty shops.

Old-time observers are finding a new self-sufficiency among young Government employees. This applies particularly to their manner of living. For instead of accepting the old and often dismal pattern of boarding house life, the modern youngsters are striking out on their own.

One group of Navy typists, nine in all, looked each other in the eye and decided they could get along. They rented a large furnished house in Arlington, with plenty of bedrooms and not nearly enough closets. Living separately on salaries of up to $3,000, each one could have managed well enough, but as a group they are a prosperous organization, with more than $26,000 in their total annual income. Each girl contributes $36 a month to the housekeeping kitty, which covers rent, food, and incidentals. (One hundred thirty-five quarts of milk are consumed each month!) Each one has a turn at kitchen and cleaning detail, usually in three-girl teams. First one up in the morning? The little girl born and raised on a mink ranch in Wisconsin. She opens her eyes at five-forty-five and awakens the others as she leaves for church.

An even more favored location is Georgetown. In 1955 in this charming section there was a tidy little brick house with a sign in the window calling it the "Confederate Embassy."

Inside lived seven soft-talking but wide-awake Southern girls, all employed by Southern Congressmen. They, too, decided that settling down together would be fun, and make sense economically as well. One, as house treasurer, paid the bills, and set up weekly teams to undertake the cooking, marketing, and dishwashing chores. Each contributed $75 a month toward rent and two meals each day. This was on a luxurious level, admittedly, with three bathrooms, and five cars parked outside.

An elevator operator on the Hill nicknamed the house the Confederate Embassy. Hanging on a living room wall was a Confederate hundred-dollar bill framed and with the tagline: "Save your Confederate money, boys, the South's gonna rise again!" Then one day the green hills of Virginia beckoned; the girls moved "nearer to Richmond."

But new girls coming into Washington to answer Uncle Sam's great need for stenographers and clerks don't fall into such pleasant arrangements at once. Their immediate housing need is usually handled by establishments and organizations especially fitted to provide inexpensive rooms. Perhaps the best known is the Young Women's Christian Association at Seventeenth and K streets, NW.

People shook their heads when the Y.W.C.A. bought this corner thirty years ago. Too far uptown, some said. Why, the horse-drawn street car ended its run at Eighteenth and Columbia Road. But buy it they did, and the next day even the skeptical took a second glance: the first bus went by. Today the location is ideally central, and in 1954, 960,000 girls received its many services.

Both transient and permanent quarters are available at Strong Residence, just next door to the main building. Many thousands of girls check in for a stay of one or two weeks, at $2.75 a night, while they get their bearings, arrange for interviews, or get work. Or they may have their hearts set on living on a permanent basis at Strong Residence. In that event, there is always a personal interview with the director, and an opportunity to file an application. It is a rare case when a girl can come to town and get in immediately. Permanent residence is limited to two years, and open to just seventy-seven girls. These must be employed and in the lower-income bracket of Grade 3 ($3,175) or less. They must be between the ages of eighteen and twenty-eight, although most are under twenty-four.

Each year about two thousand girls who wish to live at Strong Residence are turned away, either for lack of space or for reasons involved in the requirements. Most of these girls then find themselves at the door marked "Housing Service," just off the lobby of the main building, where another effort is made to find them suitable lodging.

The consultations in this tiny room not only cover this "overflow," but include a veritable cross section of women's housing needs and problems in Washington. Now it may be a sixteen-year-old stranded away from home, or an occasional Government Girl hoping to find "a best friend to live with." And, strange as it may seem, many who seek help at this door are not young and inexperienced. They are in retirement, on a small income, after having lived almost a lifetime in the Capital.

I listened as the able woman in charge of this office talked.

"As long as a woman is working, everything is fine. But the day comes when she retires. That means she sits home most of the day in the room where she's been living for maybe ten or fifteen years or longer. Sometimes a curious thing happens. The family in the house can't get used to it. It makes them uncomfortable to have her sitting around. It's awkward at mealtime. They like her, of course, but she's a roomer—and beginning to be a nuisance.

"So one day it turns out Uncle George is coming to live with them. It's too bad—they'll need her room. But that's the way it is. So she comes here to the Y and even while she's sitting here, the phone rings. Another room is going to be vacant—but 'don't send any retired women.' If she knew, it's her landlady."

"What do you do?" I wanted to know.

"When a woman past middle age comes in here and literally says, 'This is all the money I've got. I'll never have any more,' what can I do for her? Sometimes I want to ask *her*, 'What did you think you'd be doing at this age?' After all, she's paid out about $25,000 and lived here for thirty years. She knew she'd have to retire some day. But—of course, it's too late to ask that," she finished, then added thoughtfully, "I'd like to see more women who can afford it buy small co-operative apartments."

This idea had a sensible sound. According to this housing expert, $2,200 will buy one room and bath, plus an electric refrigerator and cooking arrangement—strictly an efficiency, with maintenance at about $12 a month.

"They could have it all paid for before they retire—through monthly payments like rent. If they get married, it's an investment. After all, everybody needs a spot they can call their own—they can fill it with their treasures."

I left with these words in my ears: "This is a big new problem, and it's growing." But out in the lobby I was brought briskly back to normal. Swarms of youngsters waited for the elevators, ballet slippers dangling on their arms. Others stopped at the long reception desk, asking for short story classes, tennis lessons, beginner's French, and Chinese cooking.

VIII

Three Girls in Georgetown

THREE GOVERNMENT GIRLS WHO ARE FAIRLY typical live in a little house with a blue door and brass knocker near Q Street. English ivy and gun-barrel fence probably can't mean much to you yet, but it's very Georgetown—and that, in Washington, means a good address. The girls rent the house for about two hundred dollars a month, which takes a pretty big bite out of their take-home pay. Unanimously they feel they are getting their money's worth.

Sheer "atmosphere," however intangible, sets Georgetown apart from other residential areas. The lure is more than gas-lighted carriage lamps glimmering in the twilight, uneven village-like streets, or walled gardens echoing with laughter on a summer evening—although all that helps. It is really a built-in charm that began gathering in long ago Federalist days.

Their neighbors are interesting, too: Foreign Service people, others with money and position who expect to round out their Government stint in one or two years, plus big names of yesterday (the "outs" who are tied to the party out of power) who just can't bear to go back home. (Just around the corner lives an ex-Secretary of State, and each of the girls has had a courtly bow from a former Attorney General, who also lives near by.)

After months in midtown boarding houses, which meant no entertaining, little home life, and no cooking, the three girls are now living their own lives and having fun doing it. It's a kind of specialized housekeeping, a trend that is springing up in the Virginia and Maryland suburbs, too.

But a certain amount of responsibility is attached to this unique pattern. Everyone who's tried it insists one girl must be responsible for seeing that the bills are paid on time, and that a routine, however casual, is worked out. Thus, Pat will keep an eye on the budget, but she must also have her menus ready when her turn comes every third Monday to set up a week of meals, with food ready on shelves and in refrigerator.

Ann has two-hour night classes in creative writing at the YWCA, and goes bowling regularly, but she still must set aside time to clean her share of the house on Friday night. In fact, there's no dating or entertaining on that clean-up night—well, hardly ever.

Mary, who spends Saturday mornings with a group of handicapped youngsters as part of her church work, and practices twice a week for choir, always gets in her turn at the ironing board on Saturday afternoon. Early in the week the girls lug a bundle of clothes to an automatic laundry and pay for it out of the housekeeping kitty.

But it's not all work. On an outdoor Saturday, Pat and friends may strike out down Wisconsin Avenue to the famous towpath of the C. & O. Canal. Here is a retreat to solitude and wilderness. In spring, Audubon Society groups (the District has one of the most active branches in the country) swarm upon the towpath with binoculars and field guides, for some of the East's finest bird-watching. For amateur artists and photographers here is the picturesque: sturdy stone lockkeeper's houses; weathered barns tumbling toward their reflections in the lazy canal; an occasional intrepid hiker, who often turns out to be an Associate Justice of the Supreme Court.

A favorite and easy hike from Georgetown is the trail to Cabin John, Maryland, about six and a half miles. Some half-dozen organized hiking clubs include this walk in their annual schedule.

The three girls with other friends, including six men living in a huge old house in the same block, have ridden the *Canal Clipper* on

Georgetown Doorway

a summer evening. It's a mule-drawn barge and its pleasant plodding trip (two hours each way) is a tourist favorite, too. The barge, complete with well-informed naturalist, mules named Donna and Dick, cold drinks, and snacks, proceeds at an all-the-time-in-the-world pace on scheduled runs Wednesday evenings and week ends. (Consult the National Capital Parks' *Outdoor Program*.)

On many another summer evening the girls go canoeing, pushing off from Dempsey's or the Washington Canoe Club (both are just under Key Bridge) in time to drift easily down the Potomac and catch the band concert at the Watergate.

Or on a middle Saturday in April, Ann and her friends will head a willing escort with a car straight for the valley country north of Baltimore where the Maryland Hunt Cup is run. Many long-time residents miss this. Yet for color, true pageantry, and excitement, this famous steeplechase has no equal. There's a parking fee, but no admission charge. (Horseback riding is expensive in Washington, but many Government Girls rise early and get in an hour or two once a week, at the nearest stables.) But Maryland and Virginia offer vicarious thrills in traditional point-to-point racing from late winter on.

It calls for a hamper of lunch to spread out when you reach lush, green Worthington Valley. After that comes the long stroll up the hill overlooking the course.

At four o'clock the cry "They're off" begins the race. It's like an old English print in motion. Watching too are the tweedy folk who live the life of landed gentry in this pleasant countryside. Scarlet coats of race officials dot the greensward; all eyes are on the beautiful horses, proud Irish hunters, carrying Social Register jockeys.

Another day-long trip out of Washington that the girls manage to take in mid-September or earlier involves a purely local recreation called "crabbing."

It may begin with the buying of bait (chunks of salted eel, chicken heads, or meat scraps) along the Maine Avenue waterfront, plus cord, sinkers, and a long-handled dip net. But this equipment is available at any place on the Chesapeake shore, the nearest one being Deale, Maryland, about thirty-five miles from the District.

Once there, the girls hire a boat, with or without motor, and pick out a likely spot inside the breakwater, perhaps near some pilings or an old wreck, to lure the tasty Chesapeake Bay blue crab. It takes a light touch and some patience, and the rewards are great. Back home about six hours later, having steamed their catch in a covered kettle with vinegar and spices, the girls sit down to the crabs, cooled and ready. (Sometimes, when the trip is not possible, they buy crabs right off the boats at the Maine Avenue wharves, pop them still scrambling into the pot with spices, and do it the easy way.) This is rather an indigenous pleasure, not one that outlanders are apt to come on, but it can be the most pleasant experience of a summer, from catching to eating.

Crab feasts happen quite often at the busy house near Q Street, because it's an easy way to keep a lot of people eating and talking at the same time. And cooking, eating, and socializing take up most at-home time in such Government Girl circles. People wander in from near and far, some bearing edible gifts, others just hungry. Almost any small event is reason for a party; a package from home, or the offer of a hoarded cache of mushrooms to a lucky possessor of a steak. A garden bursting into bloom (like the postage-stamp variety Pat faithfully manicures) is the best excuse for a garden party. In the heat of summer, after a dip in the local pool, affectionately known as the Georgetown Bath and Towel Club, the scrap of garden collects all forms of life in blue jeans, Bermuda shorts, and playsuits.

Probably the only attraction strong enough to pull the girls away from the evening get-togethers is summer ballet at the Carter Barron Amphitheater, in Rock Creek Park, or Olney Theatre, at Olney, Maryland, where the best summer theater is often to be had.

IX

Libraries of Last Resort

Hᴇʀᴇ ᴀʀᴇ ʟɪʙʀᴀʀɪᴇs ᴡɪᴛʜ ɴᴏ ʙᴏᴏᴋs, ᴀɴᴅ ᴛʜᴏsᴇ with millions of books. Here are libraries of bottles, of different kinds of hair, of collections of gunshot wounds—unique last-resort libraries, and libraries that never see a librarian.

These are Washington's knowledge collections.

These special services combine with the tremendous facilities of the Library of Congress to make this city an incomparable repository of man's accumulated learning. Safeguarding these collections, whether against small nibbling creatures or enemy bombs, is a problem that can change a smiling official into one grave with responsibility. In World War II days the problem of evacuating these tons of priceless lore was discussed concurrently with plans for evacuating people.

Here you are bound to find more than one trained librarian who has specialized in your general field, who knows where to find what you are searching for.

For an A to Z listing of Washington's special library resources, you'll find them in the thick publication called *Library and Reference Facilities in the Area of the District of Columbia* in any local public library. In 1942, when calls for special information grew frantically under stress of wartime, this compilation was born, but it had only a handful of pages then.

Consider, for example, the field of agriculture. One of the great special libraries of the world is in the Department of Agriculture's South Building, at Fourteenth and Independence Avenue, SW. It can handle any inquiry related to agricultural research and its many branches, such as botany, chemistry, dendrology, entomology, zoology, and economics. Its botanical collection includes old and rare works, herbals, and the like. Scientists come from all over the world to study here. Services include direct loan, routing of current periodicals, photostat and microfilm copying, answering reference questions, and preparation of bibliographies. This all started in 1862 with a basic book collection dating to 1839.

I talked to one remembering librarian, now retired, who could look back to the days when the "old building" stood a little north of the present main building.

"Often scientists, about to visit Washington, would send ahead long lists of references to books we would have waiting for them when they arrived. One professor would ask us to get out some of the old botanical books, then set up his camera on a reading room table, and photograph the pages or plates in which he was interested."

There were delightful incidents—such as the time a visitor said she had asked at the Smithsonian for the Aurora Borealis and was told that the Department of Agriculture had it.

The librarian remembered an exciting period when ferrets were brought in to deal with a plague of mice.

"It was in the old red-brick building. I distinctly remember one of the long, lean, cream-colored animals streaking by my desk. One day a man in one of the galleries had kicked off his shoes while he sat there reading. He felt a nibble on his toes and let out a shriek.

"'Don't be alarmed,' an attendant told him. 'It was probably a ferret.'"

The Library of Agriculture today has well over a million volumes and receives more than 23,000 current magazines and publications issued serially by countries throughout the world. The Library prepares and publishes a monthly *Bibliography of Agriculture*, which notifies the agriculturist, the scientist, the researcher, and the public what is in these thousands of new magazines, books, and pamphlets. Information on any aspect of agriculture is available for every citizen.

Perhaps you have a hobby, or a specialized profession or small business, and some problem in connection with it is giving you trouble. Your visit to Washington may serve to find the solution. The Government and non-Government libraries, chances are, contain reference material that is not available in your home town.

You don't have to be a scholar bent on dedicated digging to enter or even work in most of these highly specialized halls. Many of them are open to interested, serious users, but in most cases it is best to phone first. Staff members are few and oftentimes arrangements must be made to assemble material in advance.

You might like to know that the Washington Cathedral (Massachusetts and Wisconsin Avenues, NW) has a library devoted primarily to theology, architecture, and church music. Somewhat incongruously in these lofty Episcopal surroundings, where music usually consists of the oratorios and anthems of world-famous composers, one can find such simple but stirring songs as those in the George Stebbins Collection of Gospel Hymns. These hymns, lined out in revival tents and tabernacles, called repentant sinners to come forward as Dwight L. Moody, Billy Sunday, and others exhorted the crowds. They date from the mid-nineteenth century to the first quarter of the twentieth. George Stebbins was a compiler of songbooks, and this was his personal collection. This and the Winfred Douglas Collection of Liturgics and Hymnology are the more valuable, perhaps, because they are not duplicated in the Library of Congress.

Among the library's hundreds of Bibles and prayerbooks are about fifty which are classed as rare. One, a Confederate prayerbook, shows salt-water stains gathered when it floated in the sea off South Carolina. Southern Episcopalians planned in 1863 a prayerbook that would omit mention of the United States but carry this line: "According to the use of the Protestant Episcopal Church in the Confederate States of America."

The special printing order was sent to London; but a blockade runner carrying the finished books was intercepted by a Union ship. When the cargo was thrown overboard, the Union captain retrieved one water-soaked box. He sent the prayerbook found inside to his pastor. Today the clergyman's note on the frontispiece mentions "the box soaked by the sea."

You might like to know that the original manuscript of *Tom Sawyer,* by Mark Twain, and a manuscript copy of Richard Brinsley Sheridan's *The School for Scandal,* are in the Riggs Memorial Library of Georgetown University (Thirty-Seventh and O streets, NW). The Riggs collections also include the presentation copy of James Boswell's *Life of Samuel Johnson*—the copy he gave to the printer. Here, too, is a unique collection in which is represented just about every Catholic Bible printed in America up to 1860.

A special collection that embodies a large part of the library of a princely Italian family, the Albani of Urbino, may be found at the Catholic University of America (620 Michigan Avenue, NE). It has been called the "Clementine Library" because much of the collection belonged to the Albani Pope, Clement XI (1700–1721). Such concentration of library material once owned by a pope is exceedingly uncommon outside of Rome. The library appears to have been assembled between 1650 and 1800. The bindings are particularly notable; many are of vellum and stamped with the arms of an Albani churchman. In content, ecclesiastical matter predominates; principal languages represented are Latin, Italian, French and Greek. In 1955 more detailed cataloguing was needed to permit a full appreciation of these treasures.

Another Catholic University collection is the Lima Library, of deep interest particularly to South Americans. This, the gift of Dr. Manoel de Oliveira Lima and Mrs. Lima, contains some forty thousand volumes (many of them rare old books) on Ibero-American subjects—chiefly of Brazilian and Portuguese literature and history. A fragile tortoise-shell head comb that belonged to Simón Bolívar's mother is among the many curios in the small museum.

One of the largest collections of literature on the Negro is that in the Moorland Room of Founder's Library at Howard University

(2401 Sixth Street, NW). It runs to more than thirty thousand books and pamphlets, with many manuscripts, curios, and some pictorial material.

The collection of gunshot wounds began on a Civil War battle-field and is in the Army Medical Museum at Ninth and Independence Avenue, SW, just south of the Smithsonian Institution. On one wall hang cases with dozens of shattered limbs, remains of men who fell at places like Shiloh and Antietam. Study and treatment of battlefield wounds began from this nucleus. On two floors, history and medicine join in opening your eyes wide.

You'll find, too, a larger-than-life terra cotta frog, the "only item recovered relatively intact which was directly under the first military atom bomb." It was found in the ashes of a garden in Hiroshima, exactly at Ground Zero.

Perhaps you've always revered one William Shakespeare and want to visit the library where is housed the world's finest collection of Shakespeareana. Folger Shakespeare Library, at 201 East Capitol Street (next door to the Library of Congress Annex) welcomes you to its Elizabethan atmosphere. The exhibition hall is open to all, but only accredited scholars may retire to the reading room in pursuance of such major controversies as the Bacon authorship or minor questions as whether or not the Bard really dined on "pickled herring washed down with a lot of Ale." Inside and out, the beautiful building will charm you.

Or suppose you've heard of a tiny island somewhere on the other side of the world, or in the middle of Lake Erie, and you want to learn more about it. The library of the National Geographic Society, at Sixteenth and M streets, NW, is filled with material about world geography, plus its own files of more than fifty years of travel reporting. The library is chiefly for the Society's own staff, but generously offers help to those who seek the truth about peoples and places.

Some afternoon you may take your pencil and paper to a library in what was once an old stable. The shelves of the American Institute of Architects on the famous Octagon property at Eighteenth and New York Avenue, NW, offer extensive material on subjects ranging from fanlights to Ionic columns. You'll find, too, many of the original sketches and drawings for the base of the Statue of Liberty, by Richard Morris Hunt—for the emphasis here is on both the practical and the historic.

If you visit the library in spring, the garden, in drifts of chaste white, will be in bloom, and you may see it from the arched carriage doors that make reading room windows now.

But be careful, next door at The Octagon, not to be sidetracked into the private lives of the Madisons. Here President and Mrs. James Madison stayed after the White House had been burned and was being rebuilt. On the second floor in his circular study, the President put his name to the treaty establishing peace with Great Britain. In 1798, Dr. William Thornton, first architect of the Capitol, built the house for Colonel John Tayloe. General George Washington used to like to come here as a kind of "sidewalk superintendent" during construction. Architects, who usually know an octagon when they see it, don't seem to mind that the house has only six sides, including a circular bay in which the main entrance is placed.

If you are going to stay a while you might want to learn more about local history. The Peabody Room in the Georgetown Branch of the D.C. Public Library, at R Street and Wisconsin Avenue, NW, deals wholly with the township of Georgetown, offering plats of old streets, old directories, studies of classic Georgian houses, and memoirs of early residents. New Georgetowners often take themselves off to the Peabody Room immediately after moving in, hoping to learn something of the composite personality of their houses, and how they once looked.

The Washingtoniana Division of the Central Public Library, at K Street and Massachusetts, NW, has an outstanding collection on the District of Columbia. Old tracts, clippings, maps, files of old newspapers (including the *National Intelligencer*), plus journals and personal accounts of social life of earlier times are some of this rich store.

Also you'll find here a complete file of *Records of the Columbia Historical Society*, important chapters, indeed, in the growth of the

Capital. Since the local Society began in 1894 its periodic volumes have reported many scholarly papers read by members, and others done in the fascinating "I remember when" manner, all invaluable to historians. This organization includes many native Washingtonians, some with celebrated forebears. Major General Ulysses S. Grant, III (Ret.), was elected president in 1952.

In 1955, the Society was bequeathed the venerable Christian Heurich Memorial Home at 1307 New Hampshire, NW, as headquarters and library, in which to house its many mementos. Smallest acquisition may be the bullet that mortally wounded President Garfield; oldest may be the mantel of early proprietor Davy Burnes, saved from the homestead along the Potomac. Valuable books, prints, journals, letters, maps, and many other historic items complete the collection.

But, of course, all mention of library service in Washington must inevitably start and end with the words "Library of Congress." Surely, this is the greatest library in the world—and it awaits your visit. Here, by poring over a collection of dime novels, you may evoke memories of rainy childhood days in grandfather's attic. Or, if your tastes are more scholarly, you may explore the obscure by-paths of Orientalia.

When you report at the reception desk and ask for the regular tour, you will get a forty-minute glimpse of the library exhibits and the functions of the main reading room. But there is no reason why you cannot come back and actually use the facilities of this magnificent institution. I recommend to your particular attention the Rare Books Division and the Music Division with its Folklore Section.

If you take time to notice when you enter the reading room of the Rare Books Division on the second floor of the main building, two heavy bronze doors are thrown back. On one, carefully concealed in its rich decoration, is a vault-type lock which opens only to the right combination and secures this room against unlawful entrance after hours. The other apparent precautions are covered by a polite guard who acquaints you with simple rules, asks you to sign the visitors' book, and turns your request over to someone to assist you.

The Colonial design of this handsome room was inspired by Independence Hall in Philadelphia. Behind the walls is a honeycomb of treasures, bearing out the truth that here is the very core of the library's wealth of knowledge. Surprisingly, books falling under the heading of "rare" are not limited in subject. Of infinite range, they have in common those special aspects of age, scarcity, historic association, and distinctive characteristics in form that serve to make them unique or very nearly so. And the room attracts everyone—from curiosity seekers, who make a ten-minute visit to see the book bound in human skin, to scholars who take a familiar chair year after year, finishing one project and turning to another. Novelists and historians search through the rich mass of detail for that answer to their big question: "How did people live then?"

But there are others. A retired Midwest farmer may come in and ask to see the collection of McGuffey Readers. . . . "When I was a boy I used to read a poem in school. I'm sure it was in one of those books—I'd like to find it."

You won't see many assistants moving to and fro. A staff of five keeps the public happy. Each year some five thousand people come in, and even scholars often have to be briefed on the best way to find what they want. Over a year, a thousand inquiries are answered by mail, all taking time and research (like the origin of that phrase, "Curse you, Jack Dalton!"). Simultaneously, the staff goes quietly and steadily about the business of maintaining and adding to the more than 200,000 volumes grouped under the title "Rare Books."

Two businessmen from a large Eastern city came in recently. They, like everyone else, had the privilege of asking for special attention. They were seeking exceptional fruit or flower prints suitable for use on letterheads. It took several hours to find the right ones—in a valuable old book of richly colored engravings.

A telephone call some time ago asked for Martha Jefferson Randolph's recipe for pound cake. This request was handled quickly, for among the vast array of cookbooks known as the Katherine Golden Bitting Gastronomic Collection is a small volume entitled *The Virginia House-wife* by M. Randolph. The author was Mary Randolph, sister-in-law of Martha Jefferson Randolph, who cherished and recorded the family recipes here. Not too much later a large biscuit company's ads showed a model standing in the kitchen at Monticello mixing up "the Pound Cake inspired by Martha Jefferson's favorite recipe."

Along with expecting these experts and assistants to discuss fully the subject itself, and winnow it down to key questions, researchers often ask about the watermark, binding, author, history of a book's ownership, and a dozen other points, plus the contents itself. The range runs from early medieval manuscripts right up to books being printed today.

"The fine art of book making is not a lost art," the assistant assured me. "In France, England, Switzerland, and in the United States very limited editions of such books are being produced today. In France, fine art books are appearing, such as the series of books published by Ambroise Vollard, one of which is the well-known edition of *Cirque de l'étoile filante,* with illustrations by Georges Rouault."

Two beautifully colored illustrations from William Blake's *Songs of Innocence and of Experience* lay flat and carefully stitched between plastic on a table in the stacks. These had just been returned from the Trianon Press of Paris, where, in co-operation with Lessing J. Rosenwald, a facsimile edition was being prepared from them.

"Now the book will be put back together again," said Frederick R. Goff, Chief of the Rare Books Division. The Blake volume is one of the many outstanding books in the Rosenwald Collection, which includes some editions so rare that—strange as it may sound —few people had ever had an opportunity to see them before they were placed in the Library.

As Mr. Goff led me down one narrow, book-lined corridor of

the stacks and into the next, we passed many brown leather bindings, well worn by time and thumbed to a soft buff color.

A slim red-leather volume dated 1507 he called "the book that named America." It is *Cosmographiae introductio* by Martin Waldseemüller, and kept in excellent condition by its various owners. On one page my guide translated a paragraph which said: "Let the fourth part of the world be called America . . . because it was discovered by Amerigo Vespucci." It pointed out, too, that this seemed only fair since the names of the other continents had been taken from women.

Another, a book bound in brown cloth called *Scrap Book on Law and Politics, Men and Times,* furnishes an interesting piece of Lincolniana. In the back cover was a letter written by Abraham Lincoln thanking one George Robertson of Kentucky, the author, who gave him the book. Here, toward the letter's end, is found the first known use of the famous phrase Lincoln employed to describe a nation, "half-slave and half-free." A true Lincoln scholar would want to leaf through the original scrapbook of the Lincoln-Douglas debates, one of the many pieces in the Alfred Whital Stern Collection.

Perhaps one of the most treasured collections of all is that sold to the Library of Congress in 1815 by Thomas Jefferson. It was his private collection of books gathered from English bookshops, from two summers in Paris, "putting aside everything which related to America," and from many other sources. The collection was offered by Jefferson to replace the volumes lost when the Capitol went up in flames in 1814, and is cherished by the Library with an almost personal affection.

When the British Admiral Sir George Cockburn ordered the firing of our Capitol that fateful August day, he was not above picking up a souvenir which, in 1940, was presented to the Library. It is an undistinguished book, an official publication of the Government's budget figures for the year 1810, probably in itself as useless as many a recent GI trophy brought home from Germany or Japan. But through the passing of years it has gathered an "association" interest of much value to the Library of Congress.

Near by were sixteen large notebooks containing the revised and final version of William Somerset Maugham's novel, *Of Human Bondage*. Closely handwritten in ink on one side of the page, corrections were posted neatly on the facing page. Of much interest, too, is the accompanying book entitled *The Artistic Temperament of Stephen Carey*—the first version of the same story, which Maugham wrote years earlier. The latter volume he presented to the Library of Congress with the stipulation that it never be published but that it might be made available for study.

"A museum piece," said Mr. Goff, "is something for which there is no longer any use." So saying, he unlocked the special section where certain memorabilia are stored. Opening a wooden box, he began unfolding a packet of white tissue paper.

There lay a seed-pearl necklace, very much like the costume jewelry you see today. But these were real seed pearls set in little raised whorls on gold. There was also a broad gold bracelet decorated much like the necklace—one of a pair.

On April 28, 1862, Abraham Lincoln ordered the jewelry from Tiffany and Company in New York, and it was not cheap. He paid $180 for the necklace and $350 for two bracelets.

Mary Todd Lincoln must have prized this gift, bought for her when the Civil War had run its first sickening year, for she proudly wore the pieces at the Second Inaugural, three years later. (An old photograph in Carl Sandburg's *The War Years* shows her wearing these ornaments.) They were presented to the Library of Congress by members of the Lincoln family.

I directed my steps now toward that vast collection of musical literature in the Music Division, often called the best balanced in the world. You'll find it on the ground floor of the main building, in a rather sprawling but very crowded arm of the great Library of Congress.

Here are many musical instruments, and myriad notes dancing across the pages of 2,002,000 volumes and pieces of music. In one unique collection alone are some fifteen hundred flutes, so varied that on one shelf is a solid gold instrument, hand-wrought by the distinguished scientist and scholar, Dayton C. Miller, whose gift they were. On another is an ancient pottery whistle, curiously shaped, from a Guatemalan grave.

As I followed my guide it was plain that one could reach quickly across one century into the next. Here, in new-smelling red-leather binding was the original manuscript score of *Oklahoma!* by Richard Rodgers and Oscar Hammerstein II, its neatly penciled notes and lyrics deposited along with other works by the composer-lyricist team.

Then from a wall cabinet my guide drew the manuscript of Beethoven's Piano Sonata, Opus 109. A special acid-free, bias-cut wrapping folded smoothly around the precious paper. The separate pages were held together with green tape and blobs of red sealing wax. A large blot of black ink had long ago smeared the top sheet. The manuscript, itself, was a scramble of dots and feathery lines. (Original manuscripts are rarely made available for use, although they may be studied and frequently copied through either photostatic or photographic reproduction.)

It took the words of Edward N. Waters, Assistant Chief of the Music Division, to measure this wealth of music.

"Practically the whole field of knowledge pertaining to music in the Western world is here. People interested in music, from the most elementary aspects to the most scholarly, can satisfy their curiosity."

As an example, he proudly displayed the first printed libretto of Mozart's *Marriage of Figaro,* presumably used at the initial performance.

"Many peope seem to think they must travel to Europe to learn about opera. Yet here is the world's largest collection of opera literature—music, books, librettos."

Here, too, is a vast number of musical manuscripts and memorabilia, a great part of it the gifts of friends of the Music Division. The name of one generous donor, the late Elizabeth Sprague Coolidge, came up again and again—as we entered the acoustically perfect auditorium she presented, wherein the Library's cultivation of chamber music has achieved world-wide recognition—as we looked over the programs of concerts supported by her farsighted Foundation.

Arranged on near-by shelves, too, were more prized musical manuscripts—material of the Gertrude Clarke Whittall Foundation, but before turning to them, my guide opened an alligator case containing a rare and beautiful instrument. The lining of topaz velvet unzipped to disclose a Stradivari violin. This was one of the Stradivari group of three violins, a viola, and a cello (and Tourte bows) presented to the Library by Mrs. Whittall, with the understanding that they be actually played. (A few moments later, the Budapest String Quartet would rehearse on them for an early concert. Usually the instruments are on display in a glass case in the pavilion provided by Mrs. Whittall.)

Through these permanent foundations, it is possible for you to attend concerts held each fall and winter season. (See Chapter XI for full information.)

A great friend of the Library was Nicholas Longworth, Speaker of the House of Representatives from 1925 to 1931. An excellent amateur violinist, he belonged to a group known as the Friends of Music in the Library of Congress and was its first president. Out of this has grown the Nicholas Longworth Foundation, established for the purpose of giving occasional concerts in memory of the late Speaker.

A more recent foundation was born when the Serge Koussevitzky Music Foundation was established a few years ago. Its purpose is to assist in the development of creative music talent; each year a number of commissions are awarded.

I was pulled back into history, as I came across the favorite songs and music for pianoforte and violin of Eleanor Parke (Nelly) Custis, accomplished foster daughter of George Washington. In her day it was customary to gather together separate compositions between covers. Here, toward the front were her sacred songs, "Jubilate" and "Magnificat." At the back were lighthearted pieces, like "The

Mermaids Song" by Haydn and "The Yellow Hair'd Laddie with VARIATIONS by the late Mr. BACH."

Frequently, somewhere, someone comes across an old violin in his attic. Close inspection reveals a time-stained label inside that reads "Cremona," and then a date. The finder barely makes out the syllable "Strad-" when he sits down to write.

By airmail his inquiry speeds to the Music Division. "Is it valuable? How much is it worth?" The writer is unaware that ingenious violin makers have been copying Stradivari violins and the famous Cremona label for more than a century.

I asked my guide if he minded having to dash all these hopes. "We refer them to violin experts in their general geographical areas," he said.

Before I started toward the Folklore Section I stood at Victor Herbert's old desk in the card catalogue room. It is high, rather like an accountant's table. In another room is George Gershwin's desk, newly designed with many pigeonholes and slots, and elsewhere are the handsome desk and chair of Sergei Rachmaninov.

For an exciting, many-sided course in American beginnings go down the hall to the door marked "FOLKLORE." Here is the Archive of American Folk Song, a collection of recordings on cylinders, tape, and disks of over forty thousand different songs and ballads, fiddle tunes, harmonica and banjo pieces and other indigenous American folk music. You might call it a library of sounds. But it's much more than that. It's the largest collection of real "handed-down" folk songs in the United States.

This sweep of music is as vigorous and broad as our very folkways and history. There are "songs of track laying, driving steel spikes, cane cutting, hoe and chopping." There are work songs, union songs and blues, songs from "behind the wall" in Southern prison camps, and from Negro church congregations. There are texts and tunes from the lips of sponge fishermen and coal miners, "from an Okie balladist, a California gold miner, a Negro turpentine worker, a Bahaman ballad-maker."

The Archive of American Folk Song grew from the urgent dream of realizing for the American people a native culture and was conceived as part of the Music Division's rich resources. These ballads and tunes were fast being lost as communications improved and urban living increased. It was less than thirty years ago that the collecting of really satisfactory recordings began—not following the time-honored method of trusting just one pair of ears and one memory.

In those early years John A. Lomax and his son Alan went on field trips together. Their success was brilliant, not only in searching out the songs, but in being accepted in these hinterland areas and recording in the singers' own environment. In a two-year period of collecting for the Library of Congress in the mid-thirties, Mr. Lomax, the elder, deposited 737 completely filled records, each containing from two to twelve songs.

Some are "documentaries" in the sense that the singer does not stop with the singing of his song.

In Vermont, for example, Mr. Lomax recorded the ballad of Jim Fisk. History reports this gentleman to have been a villainous stock market speculator who made a fortune by wrecking the Erie Railroad, and caused a country-wide depression in his efforts to corner the gold market.

But when the singer had finished, Mr. Lomax asked him what kind of a man Jim Fisk really was.

"Why, he was one of the kindest men who ever lived," the singer replied. "He'd pat a dog on the head." Speaking out of the everyday pattern of his own experience, the singer went on to breathe life into his description of Jim Fisk. "When the record was cut," Mr. Lomax pointed out, "the Archive had a full-sized portrait of an American folk-hero, illuminated by the individual qualities of the teller of the tale."

But not so many songs are brought in from the country's by-ways today. Funds for such collecting have shrunk, and it is largely through colleges and universities that this field work continues. Some sixty-five educational institutions are giving courses in folk music, and are alert to the needs of the Archive. If a professor finds a folk singer in his area, he makes recordings and sends them along to the Library.

Some songs literally "walk in." One day a tall man with a shock of blond hair walked in with a bag on his shoulder. It was Percy Grainger, the renowned pianist, bringing to the Folklore Section his prized personal recordings of Danish, English, and Australian folk music—too precious to trust to shipment.

Another time a retired sea captain, salty and in good voice, arrived. He offered to sing some of his sea chanteys—songs he learned in a long life on windjammers. He was Captain Leighton Robinson, eighty-four years old. His songs are work songs, chanteys used in the heavy hauling up of the anchor, halyard chanteys for hoisting the yards, and short haul chanteys when a short hard pull was necessary. They were recorded and are now for sale as examples of American sea songs.

Another interesting recording was made recently when a Pakistani student brought in his "sitar," a guitar-like instrument, and sang the folk songs of his country. (The Recording Laboratory, another section of the Music Division, established by gift, makes it possible to enlarge the collection without ever leaving the Library.)

This tremendous miscellany of songs, and bits of songs, goes into a great file, arranged primarily by geographical location. When a record is to be cut which will draw on many separate items, such qualifications must be taken into account as source of origin, type of song, date, or its place in history. The completed record is then a veritable cross section of authentic American folklore or music.

Twenty-two albums and thirty-three long-playing records are on sale here to the public. A catalogue of folk music records will be sent on request; cost ten cents. (Ten albums and twelve records of poetry reading also are available—the most popular probably those of T. S. Eliot and Robert Frost. Catalogue sent on request for five cents.) In the listening room set apart from the Laboratory and main offices, you can hear any one of these; the records are sold on a non-profit basis, at prices that cover only the cost of producing them.

Many come here. The day you visit, you may well be among scholars intent on Indian cultures or a Hollywood director or two in search of authentic frontier songs. In 1955 a café singer borrowed from the Library's Mississippi River songs the recorded calls of a steamboat leadsman, "Mark four, mark twain," for his act.

Perhaps your favorite record will be "Songs and Ballads of American History" which includes a song sung by Judge Learned Hand, or "Songs and Ballads of the Assassination of Presidents." One ballad is a first-person account called "Mr. Garfield." The verses discovered in North Carolina by the Library include these lines about Mrs. Garfield:

"Well, after Mrs. Garfield got through washing the dishes, she come on in, sit down on the bedside where her husband was. She says, 'Mr. Garfield, if the worst should come to the worst, and you shouldn't get well, would you be willing for me to marry again?'"

Some of the most recent recordings are in Gullah dialect. The late Albert H. Stoddard, the narrator, grew up on an island plantation in South Carolina where he learned this colorful speech. When he recorded the tales for the Library—he was nearly eighty—it was to set down permanently an American dialect that is no longer heard. The "Br'er Rabbit" stories fascinated him and he relates these tales of Uncle Remus fame the way he heard them.

As I left, somewhere a square dance call went its rollicking way:

> Meet your pardner, pat her on the head,
> If she don't like biscuit, feed her corn bread.

X

Could It All Be a Real Estate Dream?

SOMEDAY SOON, WHEN YOU HAVE LISTENED LONG enough to your favorite solon in the Senate chamber, take a short walk out the east entrance of the Capitol, down East Capitol Street.

This, of course, is where it all started. And don't mind if it happens to be a foggy day in late March. That is altogether fitting and proper. L'Enfant, you recall, scouted for hours in chill and fog up here on Jenkins Hill, riding among the trees, just to be able to report to General George Washington that this site was the right one. His own words were that here was "a pedestal waiting for a monument." And he knew that on his plan that monument would be the Capitol.

Look past Folger Shakespeare Library, down East Capitol Street with its small stores and dreary late-nineteenth-century houses, some shabby, some trim. No "grand avenue" here, yet this was also on his plan: a street 160 feet wide, from the Capitol to a bridge across the Anacostia River; the street passing under "an arched way . . . whose . . . shops will be most conveniently and agreeably situated." But no impatience, please. The bridge L'Enfant foresaw has just been finished, and opened with suitable ribbon-cutting. A bare 160 years have passed, not very long in a city's history.

A sharp right turn at the Capitol's east front leads into the broad, tree-lined New Jersey Avenue. This was one of the Frenchman's

favorite thoroughfares, even on paper. Walking down the slope
about three blocks, you'll see the approximate spot of the mansion
that Daniel Carroll started to build. If Carroll was shocked to find
it tumbling down, instead of going up, this note to L'Enfant from
the Commissioners shows their amazed and hurt feelings:

SIR

On our meeting this day, we were equally surprised, and concerned to
find that you had proceeded to demolish Mr. Carroll's house. We were
impelled by many considerations to give immediate directions to those
acting in your absence to desist. We must observe to you, that allowing
the measure to have been absolutely necessary, and such an one as Mr.
Carroll might be compelled to acquiesce in from the terms he has entered
into; still our opinions ought to have been previously taken on a subject
so delicate and so interesting.

We are Sir,
Your Ob't Serv'ts.

You are, of course, off usual sandstone-and-marble tourist ter-
ritory, in slipping away from the crowds to explore old Capitol
Hill. But here, on the one hand, you are immersed in history;
while on the other, you are looking in on an exciting restoration, a
face-lifting that may, one day, bring realization of a long-time dream.
Many believe that this is the section L'Enfant meant to be the
Capital's choicest neighborhood, beautiful, functional, alive. Those
who base such opinion on the Capitol's east front prominence prefer
to ignore the fact that it was Latrobe and not L'Enfant who planned
the great sweep of steps for what was to have had a simple arched
basement entrance.

You might like to sit down, as I did the first time I visited old
Capitol Hill, on decaying steps only a block or two from the Capitol.
Behind me that day a green door, its intricate carving chipped and
marred, bore the sign "CONDEMNED." Weeds grew high in the small
front yard. I counted five "CONDEMNED" signs down the street. This
was spreading, like an outcropping of measles. But next door,
against the street's wreckage, a restored brick shimmered, pink,
composed, and ageless behind trim ironwork and a miniature ivy-

deep yard. A colored maid went humming down the steps with a clothes basket on her arm.

Here was no quiet street that could relate itself to broad farm country of early proprietor Daniel Carroll of Duddington, from whom land was acquired to build the Capitol. Cars were parked bumper to bumper, dusty pickup truck and impeccable Cadillac. A corner grocer's untidy window shouted "Bologna—½ lb. 25c." I heard hammering, and ripping plaster. Two men walked past toward their car. Obviously one was a seller, one was a buyer.

First big Capitol Hill real estate dealer was probably George Thompson, attorney, who in 1663 acquired title to a vast area stretching from Anacostia into Capitol Hill and the Northwest area.

These lands were then part of Maryland, where only a bare thirty years before Cecilius Calvert had sent a company to settle the province.

Provincial court proceedings for the year 1670 in Maryland covering first grants of Capitol Hill lands show that Thompson leased three tracts—Duddington Manor, Duddington Pasture, and New Troy—to Thomas Notley for one thousand years. For Duddington Manor alone, Thompson charged Notley forty thousand pounds of tobacco. (That was when the "long green" was ready currency.) Notley was a merchant and lawyer and was later to be deputy governor of the province. The next year, the title was corrected and he petitioned the court to unite the three tracts under the name "Cerne Abbey Manor."

Through marriage lines Duddington and Duddington Pasture fell to Charles Carroll when the Manor was divided. Since then, the distinguished Carroll family, with its profusion of branches and its devotion to the Christian names Charles and Daniel, has been the despair of historians and genealogists.

The Charles Carroll who acquired Duddington and Duddington Pasture added "of Carrollsburgh" after his name to distinguish himself from his famous cousin, Charles Carroll of Carrollton, last surviving signer of the Declaration of Independence. A son, Daniel Carroll of Duddington, became the man who sold acreage for use in the Federal City, and whose mansion was razed at L'Enfant's command. Another Daniel (of Rock Creek) was a commissioner of the new Capital.

Although there were about nineteen original landowners, three men owned most of the land on which this city was founded. They were Daniel Carroll, Notley Young, and David Burnes. Under President Washington's arrangements with landowners, they were to receive $66.67 per acre for all land to be used for public buildings and improvements. (This price was favorable to the owners, more than they could command at farmland prices.)

Well before the public sales of lots started, it was assumed quite naturally that a land boom was ahead. (Perhaps it was because L'Enfant was so worried by the threat of speculation that he refused to give up his large plan to the engraver.) From the first, new settlers seemed disinclined to buy, although some did buy, but more considered prices too high, and chose to buy and build in the section north of the Capitol site. (By 1808 a little village had grown up between the Capitol and the White House.) Every means of promoting private building in the area was tried, for on this hinged funds for the Government building program. Lotteries were held. Daniel Carroll placed advertisements in the press of other cities, offering to donate whole sides of squares to persons who would undertake to build.

James Greenleaf, a transplanted Bostonian, who would probably be called a "shrewd operator" today, formed a syndicate with John Nicholson and wealthy Philadelphian Robert Morris. Into this land speculation went thousands of dollars as men of wealth invested and lost. Captain William Mayne Duncanson (whose home has grown into what is now Friendship House, which you will want to see), for one, lost over seventy thousand dollars.

During the speculation, Greenleaf contracted with Daniel Carroll of Duddington for the first houses to go up on Capitol Hill. The project was described thirty-one years later by an anonymous journalist:

On a knowl south of Capitol Hill stands an object of peculiar dreari-

Antique Shop, Georgetown

ness [wrote the journalist, an eccentric speller]. It is a row of twenty brick buildings; without ever having been inhabited, have fallen into delapidation and ruin. They were put up when speculation was at its height—the ground on which they stood became the subject of a suit; they were locked up, broken into, and at length suffered to be pulled down peacemeal, and the doors and floors used for fuel. There they stand with roofs sunk in, the grass growing in the windows . . .

Nor did the original landowners make the fortunes attributed to them. David Burnes, who was admittedly a cantankerous one, spent his remaining years writing letters to the Commissioners, complaining that his crops had suffered, that bill collectors were after him since his farmlands had gone into the Federal City. (But his lovely daughter Marcia gained substantially from the transaction.)

Summing it up, Daniel Carroll, who prospered and outlived most of his contemporaries, wrote in a letter about the fate of the first proprietors: "After nearly a half century the result is now fully known; the unfortunate proprietors are generally brought to ruin, and some with scarcely enough to buy daily food for their families. . . ."

The city grew the other way: from forests, bogs, commons, steep hills, and plunging ravines the Northwest area has been cultivated to parks, heights, and terraces. (Remembering natives sigh and echo the words of an old real-estate folder, ". . . where was I when Dupont Circle and Washington Heights property sold at 10¢ a foot?")

Strangely enough, Washington still has not lost touch with its early proprietors. The present direct lineal descendant of Notley Young well remembers many a family conclave before the turn of the century.

For according to family records, the land at Pennsylvania Avenue near Seventh Street, NW, on which the old Center Market was located, formed a part of Notley Young's early holdings. The deed stipulated that when the land had served its original purpose—that of providing ground for the Center Market—the land would revert to the Young heirs. But the deed has been missing many years, and some think it was burned in the British invasion. Over the years the location in the heart of downtown Washington has grown very valuable. But the Young descendants decided not to press for the land.

Aloof and serene, the fortress-like National Archives building stands on the site where old market stalls once held cackling hens and fresh-caught shad. Just the same, as one member of the family says, "every descendant of the Youngs (and they are legion) has been raised on the story of Center Market!"

During that anguished early period around 1800 visitors began to come to town, and slipped about in the mud of Pennsylvania Avenue (much time passed before the city could afford to pave its wide streets). For years a number achieved some fame by calling the Federal City slightingly "the city of magnificent distances," or "a thick wood pierced by avenues." One visitor looked around him in the year 1801 and wrote his wife:

Our local situation is far from being pleasant, or even convenient. Around the Capitol are seven or eight boarding-houses, one tailor, one shoemaker, one printer, a washing-woman, a grocery shop, a pamphlets and stationery shop, a small dry-goods shop, and an oyster house. This makes the whole of the Federal City as connected with the Capitol.

But the future looked bright for a knowing advertiser in the *National Intelligencer* later that year. He advised the public that he had

To Let, During the Session of Congress or Longer A Handsome two story brickhouse, with the liberty of a large garden, an excellent kitchen, with a pump of good water in the same, a good eight stall stable and coach house, with every conveniency; situate in the New Jersey Avenue; Enquire on the premises of

John Fownes

who has lately laid in a general assortment of Dry Goods, such as superfine broad cloths, cassmeres, coatings, woollens of all kinds, linens, muslins, stockings, Hats &c, Likewise all kinds of groceries. He returns his sincere thanks to his friends and the public for the encouragement he has already met with since his residence here and hopes for a continuance of their favor which will be gratefully acknowledged.

As the decades rolled by, humble cottages and fine mansions took root on the Hill, but again and again in early annals there are signs that this section was allowed to lose step with the growing city. In city records showing new houses built, "low places filled in," and streets graded, ward by ward, Capitol Hill wards too often carried the brief notation, "No improvements made."

Then in 1834 a spurt of building began with expansion of the Washington Navy Yard and additions to both the Capitol Building, and Congressional Cemetery at Eighteenth and E streets, SE. Records for 1855 note that the Gas Company has "commenced laying pipes" from the Capitol to Eighth Street east on Pennsylvania Avenue. (The local expression "laying pipes," meaning to make plans, must have derived from this period. Even now you can hear a native say, "I'm laying pipes to buy a new car.")

"Philadelphia Row," patterned on Rittenhouse Square in Philadelphia, was built on Eleventh Street, SE, after the Civil War. Today this flat-front row of sixteen arched doorways set in red brick still stands, as distinguished as ever, the white stone steps hardly worn.

Many historic buildings on the Hill were gradually abandoned. Some, such as the National Bank of Washington (Daniel Carroll was its first president), moved to a more central location in Northwest. Old Carroll's Row, with the Bank's first offices at one end, was later torn down to make way for the Library of Congress, just as another landmark, the Brick Capitol, was pulled down to make way for the Supreme Court Building. The small Brick Capitol was built to house legislators while the Capitol was being rebuilt following the War of 1812. (Later it became a prison, with notorious residents, and toward the last was rebuilt as living quarters.) Big homes became shabby-genteel rooming houses and squalid tenements after owners moved away, until finally slums settled almost undisturbed next door to Government buildings.

There is a legend that during President Grover Cleveland's administration a country seat on Capitol Hill was considered for the Chief Executive, away from summer miasmas of the low-placed

White House. But that old ghost, speculation, is said to have walked again and real estate prices went up. At any rate, a country house was finally chosen in Northwest, afterward called Cleveland Park. But even before this, Presidents Van Buren, Tyler, and Buchanan had summered at Woodley on the edge of Rock Creek Park.

During this decline only a small core of die-hard Washingtonians stood fast.

And now, so unobtrusively that many have been unaware of it, a benevolent whirlwind has aroused Capitol Hill. Crumbling slums are being scoured clean. Old houses, abandoned in neglect, live again in beauty they knew when occupied by our earliest law-makers. Windows that looked out on the smoldering Capital now gleam in dwellings whose honest timbers and sound foundations have warranted restoration. Since the early 1940's close to five hundred dwellings have undergone an inspired face-lifting.

Today some of the old streets are like a catalogue of American architecture. A few early Federal houses rub shoulders with more numerous Civil War bricks. Prim Victorian relics, wearing their "bustles" in front and high arched "eyebrows" over the windows, nudge ponderous monuments to late nineteenth-century taste. But the red-brick row house, put up after 1850, predominates.

Some architects, however, deem it best to replan along modern lines. "Amputate those bay windows," they order. Then they throw the small dark rooms together, and create added living space with a paved garden area in place of the old-fashioned back yard.

There is the air of a country town about these streets, even today. Old residents tell about the colored preacher who used to come to the door, selling oysters from a tin pail, and others recall old tales like "The cows used to roam and get locked up at night on the Capitol grounds." Closely set sycamores line some streets, and roots of giant elms and oaks buckle the brick sidewalks in places. Of all the thoroughfares shaded by Washington trees (all 180,000 of them), these ample, untrafficked streets seem to offer the most breathing space.

The restoration story is one of bits and pieces, gathered from

new and old residents, builders, churchmen, teachers and those
who work on Capitol Hill.

"The street was shabby," one Navy wife recalled, as we talked
in her charming remodeled living room. She and her family, back
together again after World War II, had looked at this Victorian
house, a stone's throw from the Capitol. That was when Washington was literally popping its seams. After weeks of vain searching,
an advertisement brought the family here.

"They were singing the 'Jubilate' at the old church across the
street—we hoped it was a good omen. We needed the house—but
the house needed so much done." The neighbors, she then discovered, were dreaming of moving Northwest.

For here were sociological problems, some almost unanswerable,
involving a growing Negro population of substandard economic
level, plus shortsighted landlords who sought to exploit this group.
There were too few building inspectors then, to examine and con-
demn the spreading slums. (A new District housing code remedied
this in 1955.)

The problem called for hard work plus imagination, courage, and
money. Many people have figured in it.

One, an attractive Englishwoman, fell in love with the historic
section and envisioned sagging wrecks giving way to town houses
for statesmen. Her interest began one Sunday afternoon when she
strolled about Capitol Hill.

"From that first look I felt this was the area that in a sense should
recommend Washington to visitors. I was enchanted with the old
doorways, the brick sidewalks. It reminded me of the mews of London. But conditions were appalling, simply awful. People slept in
relays; twenty-four occupied one dwelling. They were without heat
or water—just a faucet in the yard, and sickening outbuildings."

As momentum gathered, more newcomers bought houses. Some
began the remodeling themselves, as time and money permitted;
others discovered it was not a "calcimine and thumbtacks job" but
one for experts. Old residents saw the changes taking place about
them, and the effect was electric.

In April, 1950, "Operation Paintbrush" set off a four-month clean-up contest sponsored by a businessmen's group. Near-by Eastern High School youngsters took the lead and organized SCROOCH (Students Committee for the Restoration of Old Capitol Hill). In one hundred energy-packed minutes SCROOCH transformed six dingy, peeling, row-type brick homes to clean, fresh-painted exteriors.

Builders, investors, and householders both obscure and famous quickly gave evidence of their confidence in the Hill's future. A new hotel went up and immediately became a social rendezvous for legislators and their friends. A new apartment house drew a large delegation of lawmakers.

A three-story brick house was converted into the plush Capitol Hill Club, where Republican legislators relax between quorum calls. (One Congressman who lost in his bid for re-election leased his Capitol Hill house to his opposite number, the man who beat him.)

The restoration is not finished yet. In fact, it is only beginning. Now and again there are rumors. Some say prices have gone too high, that it threatens to be the old story all over again of speculation by a few. But others insist that restoration is expensive, and point to mellow, ivy-decked town houses that consumed twice the original budgets set for the work.

One thing is certain, Major Pierre Charles L'Enfant has not given up.

Before you leave the Hill you'll want to stop over on G Street, near Sixth, SE, where old Christ Church, Washington Parish, stands firm, unmindful of real estate or political fortunes.

"Few tours stop at our church," the Rector says with a smile. "It's not fashionable, but it's been here for 148 years, and will survive."

First services were held in a tobacco barn on New Jersey Avenue for want of a better place, but in 1794 the Maryland Assembly established Washington Parish so that planners and artisans engaged in building the Capitol City might have a place to worship. (Thomas Jefferson used to tie his horse to a certain tree when he attended services, carrying his big red prayerbook.)

Benjamin H. Latrobe, your old friend from Decatur House and St. John's Church, and probably America's first professional architect, designed Christ Church while working on the south wing of the Capitol. The little Gothic building of hand-pressed brick was completed in 1807. Only recently, however, was uncovered the extent of the deviation from Latrobe's original design—for on the Hill, architect can turn archaeologist faster than you can say restoration.

An astute contemporary architect, Horace W. Peaslee, who also restored Latrobe's St. John's Church on Lafayette Square, was sure that no designer of Latrobe's stature would have fathered such a hit-or-miss combination of conflicting elements.

"Those were times of scant funds, few people, and great need for a place to worship," he said. "Latrobe's church was a simple rectangular room, clearly indicated by the old foundations, but it had been extended with a chancel added four years after Latrobe's death." The extent of the additions and alterations made their integration problems of "reconciliation" rather than restoration. Perhaps the most interesting of these early additions was the little balcony for the United States Marines who marched over from the Marine Barracks only a block or two away.

Sharing Capitol Hill's early history is this famous institution, with the Commandant's House claiming title to being the oldest official residence continuously "lived in" in Washington. The soft-toned salmon-colored bricks and three-foot-thick walls of the original building are much the same today as when first planned, but who created those plans is still a mystery. Marine Corps historians continue to search for the answer among papers of early architects—Thornton, Latrobe, Bulfinch, and others.

Residence in the Commandant's House is one of the privileges of the general commanding the Marine Corps. In near-by buildings surrounding the velvety green Quadrangle live other Corps "brass," and the Barracks house the famous Marine Band and a detachment which provides personnel for parade, funeral, and special guard details. Here also is headquarters of the Marine Corps Institute, which conducts correspondence courses for Leathernecks stationed all over the world.

That native Washingtonian, John Philip Sousa, Marine band-master, is memorialized countless times, as his "Stars and Stripes Forever" and "Washington Post March" fill the air, particularly at Sunset Parade time, held on Friday afternoon at five o'clock during Daylight Saving Time. The famous composer lived in several locations on Capitol Hill.

You can't spend much time on the Hill without hearing about Friendship House at 619 D Street, SE. It was once called The Maples, but today no maple remains; there are many fine old trees, but only an ancient horse chestnut is left of early trees, for this is one of Washington's oldest houses.

In its infancy, George Washington described the then frame dwelling as a "fine house in the woods between Capitol Hill and the Navy Yard." In its maturity, today, it ranks as one of the most beautiful community houses in the country.

During the time between, great men—Lafayette, Webster, Clay, Lincoln—were entertained here. A gentle ghost tarried in the winding corridors for many years. It is said the wife of Captain Augustus A. Nicholson, USN, committed suicide shortly after the Nicholsons bought the dwelling in 1838, and tales of strange music and spectral visitations by night kept the house vacant.

The Maples began as a pioneer's cabin in a forest clearing. The nearest neighbor was in Georgetown. Then in 1796 a British soldier, Captain William Mayne Duncanson, remodeled the cabin into a comfortable frame dwelling. In 1815, Francis Scott Key, author of the *Star Spangled Banner*, bought the house and lived there for many years. Many changes were made until in 1871 the house was bought by Emily Edson Briggs, known as "Olivia," Civil War correspondent for Ferney's *Philadelphia Press*, and probably the first woman admitted to the White House press room. Mrs. Briggs' daughter sold The Maples to Friendship House in 1937.

Today its white painted brick walls enclose an ever widening circle of young and old who seek its many services, ranging from day care for children of working mothers to classes in ceramics, sewing, carpentry, individual tutoring, clubs for mothers, teen-agers, oldsters, neighbors, and a host of other activities.

Walk with me along famous Virginia Avenue, SE. On one corner, opposite houses soon to be razed to make way for public housing, a carpet-cleaning firm occupies an old church building that a hundred years ago was new. I asked a colored man working inside the door about it.

"I knew a lady who went to church here," he said. "It was Methodist. Sometimes it was called Frog-eye Methodist Church." He came outside and pointed to a single window high above. Shutters covered it.

"When that's open, it looks like a frog-eye," he said. "The steeple fell in, right through the church, one day."

In back, a brick stable remained; the workman reminisced on: "After the church was closed, the city kept big broom straws here for the street cleaners. In those days they were horse-drawn, with big rolling brushes."

Farther south on Virginia Avenue at Eighth and M, SE, is the United States Naval Gun Factory, formerly known as the Navy Yard. For security reasons, this facility is no longer open to the public; but it deserves mention because only the Capitol itself and the U.S. Marine Corps are so closely identified with the area during the past 150 years.

Of the thousands of immigrants flocking to the city in 1800 many found work at the Yard, established homes near by, and spent their entire lives in this section of Washington. Indeed, this section and another in the area of Southwest Washington, called "the Island," formed a well-remembered stronghold of native Washingtonians.

In L'Enfant's plan there was space for a Navy yard but those twelve acres were hardly enough and more land was added, until today the plant covers 125 acres and is Washington's only heavy industry.

To Captain Thomas Tingey, the first superintendent, came the painful order to burn the Yard at that critical moment before its stores fell into British hands in 1814. Legend says the captain watched the flames consume the buildings as he left in his gig, and the awful sight condemned him to years of "haunting." Until the Yard was renamed the United States Naval Gun Factory in 1945, the nautical specter returned to his rebuilt quarters often, striding along in a white nightshirt, gold-braided hat, brass spyglass in hand.

During the Civil War, the Potomac Flotilla operated out of the Yard. More and more, the nature of its work changed from shipyard to armorer, until today the services are unique in this, the world's largest naval ordnance plant. Through six wars the factory has helped the Navy progress from frigates to fast carriers, from round shot and smooth-bore carronades to rockets and guided missiles.

Leafing through yellowing city records, I found the name of one Marmaduke Dove, sailing master at the Navy Yard in those first years. But it was over another paper that I lingered. It was headed "Inventory of Books, Plans, Instruments, Etc., Belonging to the Public in the Surveyor's Office, May 31, 1802, by R. King." (This was Robert King, who arrived from England in 1797 to follow his son Nicholas as Public Surveyor.) Just two years had elapsed since Congress moved to Washington, and every architect, surveyor, builder, planner, and craftsman could only be occupied with building the new Capital.

"In the drawer under the case of files," he listed dozens of plans, large and small, not only for all parts of the city, but for circles, squares, small parks, walks, and so on. Item No. 8 was "Major L'Enfant's old plan by Hallet." Item No. 15 was "plan shewing areas, footways, trees, carriage roads, etc., in the streets." In the "south middle drawer" were more; items 5 and 6 were plans for the President's Square.

From his list, it was easy to imagine the surveyor's office—a room with many tables. On one, a large plan of the city rested "very much wore and torn." There were five chairs, three of them red, and an iron stove stood there, also a footstool. Andirons suggested a fireplace. A pine chest held a miscellany of T squares, bevel, fifty-foot chain, measuring rods, spirit level with two ten-foot staves, and theodolite.

XI

Restaurants, Theaters, and Relaxation

MOST WASHINGTON VISITORS SOONER OR LATER express an eagerness to sample the famous seafood of Chesapeake Bay, a body of water described by the late H. L. Mencken as an "immense protein factory." Oysters are usually what the visitors have in mind.

Our seafood is good, all right, and easily obtainable. But you may be surprised to learn that the tastiest oysters—the salty ones that are eaten raw, on the half-shell—do not come from Chesapeake Bay at all, but from Chincoteague, which is a smaller neighboring bay. Other choice oysters eaten locally come from such distant places as New Jersey and Long Island Sound. Most bivalves from the Chesapeake and its tributaries, less flavorsome but no less nutritious than the majestic Chincoteagues, wind up as canned oysters, to be stewed or fried. Vast quantities of them are shipped to all parts of the United States.

Chincoteague Bay and the lower Chesapeake also yield excellent clams, the hard-shell variety known to New Englanders as quahogs, and these, too, are available locally. In fact, the name "cherrystone," which refers to the small clam served freshly opened on the half-shell, originated in the vicinity of Cherrystone Inlet in Chesapeake Bay. Soft-shell clams, the kind that are featured in New England clambakes, come from Chesapeake Bay and its tidal estuaries. These succulent mollusks have always been present in these waters, but not

112

until recently was anyone able to devise an economical way of extracting them from their sandy hiding places. Now, thanks to an ingenious hydraulic dredge invented by a Marylander, soft-shell clams, or "steamers," are harvested in huge quantities. Many are shipped to New York and New England. A kettle of steamers, with drawn butter to dip them in and cold beer or chilled white wine to wash them down, makes a fine light luncheon or late evening snack.

If any foods can be said to be indigenous to the Washington-Baltimore area, they are diamondback terrapin and the Chesapeake blue crab. Terrapin stew is so costly and difficult to prepare that it is seldom seen these days. Should you encounter it in a restaurant, a smallish bowl would set you back about $3.50.

The crab is a different and happier story. This noble crustacean, caught throughout Tidewater Maryland and Virginia, finds its way to table in many forms: crab imperial, deviled crab, crab Norfolk, crab cakes, crab soup, crab salad, etc. Connoisseurs prefer their crabs steamed alive in a subtle mixture of vinegar and spices. They come out of the pot bright red, like boiled lobsters; then they are cracked with wooden hammers and torn apart and the meat extracted from claws and body interstices. Cooking and eating them in this style is such an untidy and space-consuming business that only a few places serve them. Most of the seafood shops along the Maine Avenue waterfront sell steamed crabs to be consumed off the premises. Or you may buy them alive, from the shops or from crabbers aboard their boats docked near by, and steam them yourself.

Soft-shell crabs, of course, are simply the same blue crabs caught during their growth periods—that is, when they have shed their old shells and are in the process of growing new and larger ones. If you order soft-shell crabs in a restaurant, be sure to specify that they be floured but lightly and then sautéed in butter. Otherwise, as far as taste is concerned, you might as well have ordered breaded veal cutlet, for the crabs will come to you encased in a thick armor plating of batter that destroys the creature's true delightful character.

Here, as elsewhere, the seasons govern the availability of seafood. During the R months there are oysters; in springtime, shad and shad roe; in summer, crabs. Clams, both hard-shell and soft-shell, are here the year round, as are many kinds of fin fish other than the aforementioned shad.

Aside from seafood, what do Washington's restaurants offer? The answer is that dining out here is pretty much like dining out in any other large American city—conceding, of course, the long-established superiority of such gourmet centers as New York, New Orleans, Baltimore, or San Francisco. Where and what you eat will be determined largely by two factors: (a) your personal taste and (b) the state of your pocketbook. But whether your taste runs to pheasant or pizza, you can eat well here, and within the price range of your choosing.

Suppose, for example, that you are staying at either the Shoreham or the Sheraton-Park (both of which, incidentally, have excellent dining rooms and coffee shops). A short stroll from either hotel will take you to Connecticut Avenue, and there, in the single block between Calvert Street and Woodley Road, are eating places covering a remarkable range. On the moderately expensive side are Ted Lewis's, a handsomely decorated New York-type restaurant, and Napoleon's, where dining is in the more intimate French manner. A few doors away are Rocco's, a sumptuous Italian basement, and the New Smörgåsbord, which features serve-yourself Swedish food. All these are on the east side of the street, and so are Garvin's, a standard American establishment, and El Mexico, which—unsurprisingly —serves Mexican dishes. Across the street are Arbaugh's, a long-time Washington favorite, and the Chinese-American Chin's. Around the corner, on Calvert Street, is Fogan's, a good steak house.

So it goes in most Washington neighborhoods. Whether you are uptown, downtown, or in the suburbs, you are not far from a good restaurant, or at least a satisfactory one.

If you are feeling particularly festive and have a well-stocked wallet, you should head for either the Colony or La Salle du Bois. These restaurants, both under the same ownership, are Washington's counterparts of the Chambord in New York (though not that expensive) and Antoine's in New Orleans. It is wise to make reservations at both. Another in the plush category is Espionage, housed in a former undertaking parlor in Georgetown. Reservations here, too.

Also in or near the topflight bracket, but not particularly expensive, are the famous old Washington stand-bys: Harvey's, the Occidental, and Olmsted. Billy Martin's Carriage House and the Town House, both in Georgetown, have established excellent reputations in the few years they have been in business. Pierre, on Q Street at Connecticut Avenue, draws a distinguished clientele. On the tearoomy side, but not excessively cute, is Water Gate Inn on the Potomac; it specializes in Pennsylvania Dutch dishes. Michel's, a pleasant place on Vermont Avenue, is highly regarded for both its food and its gypsy music. The Eight Twenty Three, Fifteenth Street near I Street, has Viennese music and German food. Old New Orleans, Eighteenth Street off Connecticut Avenue, and the Madrillon, New York Avenue at Fifteenth Street, are favorites with those who like dancing and entertainment with dinner.

All the leading hotels, of course, are prepared to do well by the inner man. The Sheraton-Carlton is outstanding among these, but the Mayflower, Statler, Sheraton-Park, Shoreham, Willard, Hay-Adams, and other hostelries also make stout claims for their cookery and service. The Hotel Washington's rooftop dining room offers, along with good food, a superb view of the city.

Most of the restaurants listed below are known to me through personal experience. As for the others, I rely upon their general reputations, or, in many cases, upon the reports of discerning friends. They are classified according to nationality, but this does not mean that their menus are necessarily limited. Most places described as French, Italian, Oriental, or the like will serve you a charcoal-broiled steak just as readily as they will their special dishes. The list is by no means all-inclusive and it is subject to change, since restaurants have a way of suddenly changing hands, moving, or going out of business. Here goes:

AMERICAN

Alfonso's, 1403 L Street, NW*
Allies' Inn, 1703 New York Avenue, NW
Arbaugh's, 2606 Connecticut Avenue, NW
Billy Martin's Carriage House, 1238 Wisconsin Avenue, NW
Cannon's, 1270 Fifth Street, NE*
Caruso's, 1035 Connecticut Avenue, NW
Costin Sirloin Room, National Press Building*
Duke Zeibert's, 1730 L Street, NW
Fan & Bill's, 1132 Connecticut Avenue, NW*
Flame, 1629 Connecticut Avenue, NW
Fogan's, 2317 Calvert Street, NW*
Garden Gate, 1530 Wisconsin Avenue, NW
Garden T Shoppe, 1835 Columbia Road, NW
Golden Parrot, 1701 Twentieth Street, NW
Goldie Ahearn's, Connecticut Avenue at M Street, NW*
Hall's, 1000 Seventh Street, SW†
Hamilton Arms Coffee House, 1232 Thirty-first Street, NW
Hammel's, 416 Tenth Street, NW*
Harvey's, 1107 Connecticut Avenue, NW*†
Hendrix's, 1252 Fourth Street, NE*
Herzog's, Eleventh Street and Maine Avenue, SW†
Hogate's, Ninth Street and Maine Avenue, SW†
Hunt's Raw Bar, 1743½ Pennsylvania Avenue, NW†
Iron Gate Inn, 1734 N Street, NW
Lee Lounge, Fifteenth and L Streets, NW
Longchamps, Fourteenth Street and New York Avenue, NW
Madrillon, New York Avenue at Fifteenth Street, NW
Mozart Room, 2300 Connecticut Avenue, NW
Naylor's, 20 Municipal Fish Wharf, SW†
New England Raw Bar, 23 Municipal Fish Wharf, SW†
Occidental, 1411 Pennsylvania Avenue, NW*†
O'Donnell's, 1221 E Street, NW†

* Steaks a specialty.
† Seafood a specialty.

Old Ebbitt Grill, 1427 F Street, NW
Olmsted, 1356 G Street, NW*†
Parchey's, 1900 K Street, NW*
Potomac, 1113 Maine Avenue, SW†
Silver Fox, 5324 Wisconsin Avenue, NW*†
Tally-Ho, 812 Seventeenth Street, NW
Ted Lewis's, 2655 Connecticut Avenue, NW*
Water Gate Inn, 2700 F Street, NW
Wearley's, 516 North Capitol Street†

FRENCH

Aux Trois Mousquetaires, 820 Connecticut Avenue, NW
Avignone Frères, 1777 Columbia Road, NW
Bonat, 1022 Vermont Avenue, NW
Burgundy, 5031 Connecticut Avenue, NW
Colony, 1737 DeSales Street, NW
Espionage, 2900 M Street, NW
La Salle du Bois, 1800 M Street, NW
Maxime, 1731 Connecticut Avenue, NW
Michel's, 1020 Vermont Avenue, NW
Napoleon's, 2649 Connecticut Avenue, NW
Old New Orleans, Eighteenth Street at Connecticut Avenue, NW
Pierre, 1929 Q Street, NW
Place Vendôme, 722 Seventeenth Street, NW
Pouget's, 3309 Connecticut Avenue, NW
Town House, 1365 Wisconsin Avenue, NW

GERMAN

Eight Twenty Three, 823 Fifteenth Street, NW
Old Europe, 2434 Wisconsin Avenue, NW
Old Heidelburg, 515 Eleventh Street, NW

ITALIAN

Aldo Café, 1143 New Hampshire Avenue, NW

* Steaks a specialty.
† Seafood a specialty.

A. V. Ristorante Italiano, 607 New York Avenue, NW
Ciro's, 1707 DeSales Street, NW
Gusti's, 1837 M Street, NW
Livera's, 1314 L Street, NW
Mickey Grasso's, 732 Fourteenth Street, NW
Rocco's, 2637 Connecticut Avenue, NW
Roma, 3419 Connecticut Avenue, NW
Torino, 909 H Street, NW

MEXICAN

El Mexico, 2603 Connecticut Avenue, NW
Ernesto's, 1735 F Street, NW

NEAR AND MIDDLE EAST

Athens, 804 Ninth Street, NW
Bagdad, 1733 I Street, NW
Desert Inn, 1202 St. Matthews Court, NW
New Athens, 1741 K Street, NW
Sheherazade, 709 Eighteenth Street, NW

ORIENTAL

China Boy, 809 H Street, NW
China Doll, 627 H Street, NW
China Inn, 631 H Street, NW
Chin's, 2614 Connecticut Avenue, NW
Dragon, 1329 G Street, NW
Good Earth, 1117 Seventeenth Street, NW
Jade Bowl, 1018 Vermont Avenue, NW
Kwang Chow, 600 G Street, NW
Nanking, 901 New York Avenue, NW
Orient, 1715 Wisconsin Avenue, NW
Peking, 5522 Connecticut Avenue, NW
Ruby Foo's, 728 Thirteenth Street, NW
Wing's, 622 H Street, NW
Yenching Palace, 3524 Connecticut Avenue, NW

SCANDINAVIAN

New Smörgåsbord, 2641 Connecticut Avenue, NW

SPANISH

La Fonda, 1637 R Street, NW

If you want to combine dining with a pleasant drive in the country, several outstanding places wait to serve you. One is Normandy Farm at Potomac, Maryland, about twenty miles from downtown Washington via Massachusetts Avenue and River Road. Others are Olney Inn at Olney, Maryland, twelve miles north of Silver Spring on Routh 97 (Georgia Avenue extended), and Mrs. K's Toll House in Silver Spring. In Virginia there are Collingwood on the Potomac, five miles south of Alexandria on the Mount Vernon Memorial Highway; Evans Coffee Shop, at 4770 Lee Highway (Route 29–211), and Allison's Little Tea House, 1301 South Arlington Ridge Road.

Virtually all restaurants on the list serve mixed drinks, wines, or beer, and in most cases all three. The main exceptions are tearooms and cafeterias. In the District of Columbia no alcoholic beverages may be sold after 2:00 A.M. during the week or after midnight Saturday. District liquor stores are open from 10:00 A.M. to 9 P.M. during the week; a few stay open until midnight Saturday. On Sunday in the District, only beer and light wines may be sold legally from 1:00 P.M. to midnight, and then only for consumption on the premises of eating places.

In Montgomery County, Maryland (northwest of Washington), the law permits sale of beer and light wines in public places and hard liquor through county dispensaries. Normandy Farm, Olney Inn, and certain private clubs, however, are licensed to sell mixed drinks on Sunday as well as weekdays. In Washington's Virginia suburbs, only beer and light wines may be served in public places at any time; on Sunday, these bottled wares may be bought in grocery stores and other such licensed places as happen to be open. Sale of hard liquor in Virginia is confined to State-operated dispensaries, open from 10:00 A.M. to 6:00 P.M. daily except Sunday.

In both Washington Sunday newspapers, itemized lists of recreational events for each week are given much space. Musicals, with times and cost, if any, are scheduled for a variety of organizations ranging from the Ancient Instruments Society of Washington to the United States Navy Band concerts.

The same is true of art exhibits which are to be found not only in the formal galleries, but in movie theater lobbies, bookshops, in the Smithsonian's National Museum, and in countless small galleries in the Northwest area.

Below are some of the places where you can spend a pleasant afternoon or evening.

PHILLIPS GALLERY at 1600 Twenty-first Street, NW. (No admission charge.) This is located in the comfortable red-brick, four-storied former home of Mr. and Mrs. Duncan Phillips. The gallery is built around Renoir's *The Luncheon of the Boating Party* and is considered one of America's finest collections of modern paintings. The Phillips Collection is open from 11:00 A.M. to 10:00 P.M. Mondays; from 11:00 A.M. to 6:00 P.M. Tuesdays through Saturdays; and from 2:00 to 7:00 P.M. Sundays. Free musical recitals are usually at 5:00 P.M. on Sundays; at 8:30 P.M. on Mondays.

CORCORAN GALLERY OF ART, Seventeenth and New York Avenue, NW. Important exhibitions, concerts, film programs and lectures are scheduled at this Gallery over the year for members of the Association of the Gallery. For information write Corcoran Gallery of Art. The Gallery and its collections are open to the public.

NATIONAL SYMPHONY ORCHESTRA. Washington's twenty-five-year-old symphony orchestra has a full season of concerts October to April, in Constitution Hall. These include performances by other orchestras, such as the Philadelphia and Boston. Beginning in 1956 the orchestra inaugurated a series of concerts for visiting high school students, scheduled from late April through the month of May. For details call or write the National Symphony Orchestra, Washington.

PATRICK HAYES CONCERT BUREAU each season brings entertainers representing ballet, choral groups, and including nationally known artists. Tickets may be purchased at Campbell's Music Company, 1108 G Street, NW. Watch the newspapers for announcements.

WATERGATE CONCERTS. From 8:30 P.M. to 10:00 on four summer evenings each week (June through August) service bands hold free concerts in the Watergate near the Lincoln Memorial. On Tuesdays, the United States Army Band performs; Thursdays, the United States Navy Band; on Fridays, the United States Air Force Symphony Orchestra; and on Sundays, the United States Marine Band.

COOLIDGE AUDITORIUM. The Library of Congress regularly offers a series of literary readings and lectures in this Auditorium in the Library, bringing outstanding literary figures to participate. The series is sponsored by the Gertrude Clarke Whittall Poetry and Literature Fund. Programs usually fall on a dozen or so Monday evenings, beginning in October and closing in late spring. Tickets, always in great demand, become available on the Wednesday preceding the lecture, and cost only the amount of the handling charge, twenty-five cents. These may be obtained, two to a person, from a downtown box office. Announcements of lectures appear in local newspapers.

Through the Gertrude Clarke Whittall Foundation and the Elizabeth Sprague Coolidge Foundation, and other gifts, the Library of Congress also presents distinguished performers in a large number of concerts, beginning in October and ending in April. These feature string quartets, or other chamber music ensembles. Some concerts make use of the rare Stradivari instruments presented to the Library by Mrs. Whittall. Tickets for these concerts, two to a person, may be obtained from a downtown box office. Watch local newspapers for details.

NATIONAL THEATRE, E Street between Thirteenth and Fourteenth, NW. The Theatre Guild—American Theatre Wing Society's eight thousand subscribers, plus others, form a solid backbone of playgoers. The Guild offers nine plays a season—divided between the National and the Shubert. (Students get a special low subscription rate.) Other plays come from Broadway; or are frequently those being groomed for Broadway openings. Legitimate theater; see box office for tickets.

SHUBERT THEATER, on Ninth Street near E Street, NW. This was renovated in early 1950's from a darkened burlesque house (the rosy little cupids are holdovers). Legitimate theater; see box-office for tickets.

MOVIE HOUSES. More than a dozen movie theaters are scattered through the F Street and uptown areas. Some, like the Dupont, feature only foreign films; others, like the MacArthur, present only British movies; while the Capitol, Columbia, Palace, Keith's, and Playhouse have first-run Hollywood productions.

AMATEUR THEATER. The Speech and Drama Department of Catholic University is headquarters of amateur theater in Washington. The schedule calls for five shows a year, presented in the University Theater at Fourth Street and Michigan Avenue, NE. In summer the University's graduate players perform in the air-conditioned theater at Olney, in the Maryland countryside north of Washington.

CARTER BARRON AMPHITHEATER, near Sixteenth Street and Colorado Avenue, NW. A selection that may draw on Broadway musicals, opera, ballet, symphony, Spanish dancers, is presented each summer under the stars in Rock Creek Park. Tickets on sale at Amphitheater box office or write or call at Super Music City box-office, 1350 F Street, NW.

GLEN ECHO PARK, about six miles from Key Bridge along the Maryland shore. Complete with picnic tables, speed rides, and swimming pool, plus a vast dance floor. No admission charge to enter the park.

U.S. NAVAL OBSERVATORY, at Thirty-fourth and Massachusetts, NW (no admission charge). Children under 12 are not admitted. Open Monday through Friday (except holidays) for conducted tours of about forty minutes, at 10:00 A.M. and 2:00 P.M. Evening tours are held once a month, usually on a Wednesday between first quarter and full moon. The two-hour evening tour includes viewing the sky through three telescopes. Reservations are open six weeks in advance of tour; inquire by mail or phone.

For exploring in and around outdoor Washington you can make excellent use of three publications:

Outdoor Program, booklet scheduling activities provided by the National Capital Parks, published about April 1 annually; free. To get a copy call United States Department of Interior's National Capital Parks office, asking for either Park Naturalist or Park Historian.

Summer Fun, pamphlet of the Volunteer Information Services, a *Digest of Summer Activities in the Washington Area for Men and Women of the Armed Forces;* price 35 cents. This lists recreation from archery to zoo, prices, and how to get there. Available from Armed Services Hospitality Committee, Room 27-A, Old Post Office Building, Twelfth and Pennsylvania, NW.

Atlantic Naturalist, magazine published five times a year by the Audubon Society of the District of Columbia, Inc., price about 50 cents each. Available from William Ballantyne and Sons, 1421 F Street, NW, Francis Scott Key Book Shop, Twenty-eighth and O, NW (Georgetown); Whyte Book Shop & Gallery, 1518 Connecticut Avenue, NW.

Probably the most popular title is the National Capital Parks' free *Outdoor Program,* giving a concentrated bill of things to do from April 1 to November 30. To follow it completely would keep you breathless, but to take part in even a small selection will bring you many insights into the city's rich background, from the standpoints of history, nature, and science.

XII

This Is Washington

THIS MAY BE THE TIME FOR YOU TO MULL OVER and sort out the feelings you have had so far, experiences bringing small or great surprises. Perhaps you already have discovered currents drifting around you that blend into the special charm of this city.

This is the town where a local minister on a rare "day off" visits the Senate for four hours; where a young couple leave their small farm and children twenty miles away in Virginia in the care of an all-night baby-sitter and check in to a downtown hotel, have breakfast in bed and papers sent up, just to get away from it all.

But it's cosmopolitan, as shown by those three French officers striding along Sixteenth Street, and the tribal chieftain from Africa entering the Shoreham Hotel to attend an international conference, or that young woman in the gold-banded sari, stepping into a cab. Interesting, too, is the uncurious attitude toward this native dress. Rarely does a head turn for a second glance. (In the yardgoods department of local stores you can find women asking in foreign accents for the tissue-like fabric, to wrap into this graceful costume.)

A city of cold monuments? Each year around February 12, dozens of letters arrive addressed to Mr. Abraham Lincoln, Washington, D.C., or in care of the Lincoln Memorial. They are written mostly by children and lend the Capital's most beautiful memorial a strange, elusive warmth. They usually are delivered to the offices of the National Capital Parks.

You may want to skip George Washington's birthday in this Capital which was named in his honor. It is celebrated as a shopper's carnival called Washington Birthday Sales. All night on the

Islamic Center

twenty-first of February lines form at midtown shops, awaiting opening time. Next day a hundred or more extra police are assigned to control traffic as crowds, now on their mark, feverishly get set and go—for a ninety-nine-cent typewriter, an eighty-eight-cent washing machine or nineteen-cent outboard motor.

But there's unexpected kindness, too. If you were here during the fifty-odd-day transit strike in 1955, unhappily coinciding with a heat wave, you would have seen many a car pull up to a sweating, overworked policeman in the center of a traffic maelstrom. Someone would reach out and hand him an ice-cold bottled drink.

A completely different kind of warmhearted enthusiasm is demonstrated each Friday in the winter audience of the National Geographic Society lectures in Constitution Hall. These three thousand people are there because they can't stay away. Films show a tender blossom opening in brilliant Kodachrome close-ups, or baby birds crowding a nest, or romantic trips to distant lands. Lecturers soon learn to expect the very audible, breathless "Oh-hhhh" followed by repeated, scattered handclapping—a response they say they receive only in Washington.

But the individual exists here, too. On the edge of Georgetown each fall when the purple grapes on a certain fence have ripened, a conservative gentleman gathers them into his basement. Suitably garbed and with bare feet he stomps them to a pulp, and in due time bottles what he likes to call an "adequate little red."

This is a town where a rash of Presidential aspirations breaks out every four years, and where fiery John C. Calhoun always greeted John Randolph of Roanoke when they met with the words, "Who, please God, will never be President."

It's a town publicly affected by spring fever. And when the herring and shad runs in the Potomac reach Chain Bridge, it's more finny than beautiful. Cab drivers and clerks desert their callings, and if you drive over that way yourself, you'll see thousands of local fishermen clinging to rocks intent only on snaring the fish flashing in the river's muddy freshet.

It's a city everyone wants to define. "Washington is a big motel—somebody is always coming or going." Someone else compares it to "a White House in a green city." In spite of this, it goes right on being quiet and serene. Its gracious air of hospitality makes itself felt right along with an impressive dignity.

Oh, yes, it's historic. And if, standing off looking at the glowing Capitol dome lifted almost like a crown into a fading twilight, you suddenly realize that you are "posterity"—the one that Washington and Jefferson and all the others knew would come along some day to receive all this—you'll never be quite the same again.

Now, as you turn to the pleasant business of sight-seeing, let me borrow a few words from a follower of L'Enfant: "Make no little plans—"

PART II

Ten Tours for Easy Sight-seeing

Tour I

Washington Monument, Pan American Union, American Red Cross, Continental Hall (DAR Building), Corcoran Gallery of Art, Bureau of Engraving and Printing, Aquarium

WASHINGTON MONUMENT, on The Mall. (Elevator charge: 10 cents; free to children and educational groups; open 9:00 A.M. to 5:00 P.M. daily.)

Plan to visit this most famous of Capital sights in midmorning or early afternoon. Visibility from the 555-foot summit is best then, and you may be able to board the elevator before you are number 1,380 in line. Riding up and walking down is a favorite way of seeing everything, for even walking down 898 steps calls for stamina.

The interior walls bear 189 carved memorial stones from the States and from foreign governments, benevolent societies and the like. Landings off the iron stairway are frequent and so arranged that six memorial stones can usually be studied from each one. Some stones are touched with gold leaf, some are phrased in Greek, Arabic, and other languages; all record great respect for George Washington.

If L'Enfant were here today, this monument, in one sense, would be no surprise. It was Item A on his famous plan, calling for an "equestrian figure of George Washington, a Monument voted in 1783 by the late Continental Congress," in this approximate location on The Mall. Architect Robert Mills designed such a monument—which looked rather like an immense wedding cake—to have a colossal statue of Washington inside and a shaft thrusting out of its center. Before actual building began in 1848, however, these plans were sharply revised to produce plans for the classic memorial you are climbing today. (L'Enfant would have to go to Washington Circle to see "Mounted Washington," created by Clark Mills and dedicated in 1860). Viewed from almost any distant approach, the obelisk's grace and simplicity of outline somehow belie its great size. Only when you are walking at the base, or riding up-up-up for one minute and ten seconds, do the gigantic dimensions become real.

As you watch fireworks at any Fourth of July celebration on the Monument grounds, you are honoring the Father of his Country in the best tradition. The laying of the cornerstone of this memorial took place on that day in 1848. Dolley Madison, who was ill, sent her regrets the day before, but Mrs. Alexander Hamilton and George Washington Parke Custis, both very old, were among the notables attending, plus a great live black eagle. It was the same eagle that welcomed Lafayette on his visit to Alexandria years earlier. (The gallant bird was old too, probably creaking a bit, but on its perch it made a spirited and dramatic symbol.)

A postscript to this historic scene is this: today the cornerstone can't be located, although it's believed to be in the northeast corner, remote and hidden by foundation additions. Buried inside among the seventy-odd mementos are copies of the Constitution and Declaration of Independence, Washington's portrait and coat-of-arms, a city map, a *Godey's Lady's Book;* and newspapers including the *Western Citizen* of Paris, Kentucky, and the Baltimore *Daily Sun.*

Either before or after your ascent, take a moment to study the framed prints and documents on the walls inside the base. These are telling highlights in the uneven rise of the Monument. For a time, the entire city was in an uproar, due to the machinations of the Know-Nothing Party, a pre-Civil War political group which did much damage to the Monument. (One particularly violent Know-Nothing orator in the mayoralty campaign threatened to crop the opposing candidate's ears.) Before they were put down they defaced and threw into the Potomac a marble block sent by Pope Pius IX and seized the papers and plans for the Monument from the Washington National Monument Society, then virtually captured the unfinished marble shaft. In spite of these delays, the monument was dedicated February 21, 1885.

The view from the top, no matter how many times you see it, is breath-taking and will revitalize your mental geography of the city. As you look through the windows you may want to give a thankful little nod to the west where on a Virginia hill L'Enfant sleeps. As you peer out of the north windows, there is the White House in miniature, looking serenely beautiful, secure, and well cared for.

By all means, look eastward and salute the Capitol, Washington's other skyline landmark, standing head and shoulders above the city. No unsightly canal splits the green Mall as it did one hundred years ago.

Look east across to the red turrets of the Smithsonian Institution, called "Uncle Sam's Attic." A back yard full of wild animals that was once fenced in just south of the building is gone now. It aided taxidermists in their work of mounting the various specimens in the National Museum and preceded the National Zoological Park, located uptown.

Around to the southeast you'll see the Department of Agriculture's vast buildings, with not so much as a hint of the old stockyards located on that site during the Civil War. The land was used as a holding ground for cattle; here the animals milled around in seas of dust until time to be slaughtered to feed the troops.

Across from Agriculture, you'll look down on the Bureau of Engraving and Printing's sprawling operation. Once a historic residence stood near this site, commanding a splendid view of the Potomac. It was of brick, with porches and porticoes hung with purple wisteria and yellow roses, and the home of a descendant of Notley Young, an original landowner in the Federal City.

Before you turn away, let your eyes move west of the White

House, past the old State Department Building to Seventeenth Street, NW. Follow the street south as it crosses Constitution Avenue—that's the broad, tree-lined thoroughfare which separates the Monument from the parklike Ellipse. The Zero Milestone, from which all distances on the continent are supposed to be computed, is located here, nine hundred feet south of the White House. L'Enfant's plan called for an "itinerary column" on Capitol Hill. Each Christmas season the Ellipse becomes a fairyland of lights, music, and dancing when the Pageant of Peace is given under the sponsorship of the Washington Board of Trade. Dedicated to international peace and good will, the pageant features dozens of local organizations; embassy groups also take part. A giant tree, lighted and trimmed, surrounded by life-size Nativity scenes, adds beauty after dark. By day Santa Claus and live reindeer provide realism as the fourteen-day pageant runs its course. The traditional Christmas tree lighting ceremony by the President marks the official opening of the pageant.

Back on Constitution Avenue, walk west to Seventeenth Street. You are, of course, crossing David Burnes's farm. This first proprietor made his crusty reputation by "talking back" to General George Washington, and was put down as "obstinant" in Washington's diary.

(On the southwest corner is the lock keeper's house, remnant of the famous Washington Canal.) Davy's dwelling (a story and a half with dormers and solid-looking structure in the old photograph belonging to the Columbia Historical Society) remained standing many years. Parts were still there when, in the same area, the fine house of Davy's daughter began crumbling in neglect shortly after the owners died. Said to be the most lavish house of its time, it was built for Marcia by her prominent Congressman husband, John P. Van Ness. Benjamin H. Latrobe was the architect. Like many another in its day, the Van Ness mansion was famous as a gathering place for political leaders. Who can say what history was made or policies adopted that first began as ideas exchanged at such social functions? The Van Ness place was razed after Congress in 1906 gave the land to the International Union of American Republics as the site for the Pan American Union. Each of the Latin American Republics contributed a share, which, together with a gift from Andrew Carnegie, paid for the Union's building.

Davy himself would beam today at the exotic beauty created on his acres (only a plaque on one of the trees reminds you of the early history).

On this northwest corner of Seventeenth and Constitution, NW, stands the PAN AMERICAN UNION. (No admission charge.) Open 9:30 A.M. to 5:30 P.M., Monday through Friday; Saturday, 9:00 A.M. to 12:00 noon; closed Sundays and holidays. This marble structure in graceful Hispanic style is often described as Washington's most beautiful building.

Each year many visitors are drawn here to what is often called the "home of the Americas," as peoples of the world dream of living together in peace and understanding. For the Pan American Union is a symbol. Sixty-six years ago, leading statesmen of the American Republics met in Washington and revitalized Simón Bolívar's plan (which he visualized in 1826) for a union of American nations.

The Organization of American States, conceived then, was born at the Bogotá Conference in 1948. It has its General Secretariat in the Pan American Union, devoted to maintaining peace and promoting human welfare in this hemisphere. Three hundred and thirty-two million people of different nationalities, creeds, and cultures are thus uniquely bound together in friendship.

Step inside where a tropical patio with bubbling fountain, lush vegetation, and an eighty-year-old parrot invite you to rest for a moment on white stone benches. (That parrot, by the way, is a comparatively recent arrival. Panchito, his predecessor, died a few years ago, but is still remembered for his gay choruses of "Rock-a-By-Baby," and "Where O Where Has My Little Dog Gone?")

Beyond the patio, an art gallery exhibits the works of artists from all the Americas; to the left is a gift shop. The Columbus Memorial Library, with 150,000 books in English, Spanish, and Portuguese inviting research in Latin-American activities, is found at the rear.

Upstairs is the Hall of the Americas, busy with international conferences, concerts, and diplomatic dinners. (The hundred-foot room is for the exclusive use of each one of the twenty-one member nations.) Some night you may see lights burning late. I have heard the strains of "Tico Tico" and a rich guitar accompaniment from upstairs windows.

Separated from the main building by the colorful Aztec Garden is the Secretary General's residence. The only part open to the public is the arched terrace with its blue tiles inset with Mayan figures of carved wood. On an adjacent triangular plot facing on Constitution Avenue is the Administration Building with offices and cafeteria. A tunnel connects it with the main building, enabling staff members to go back and forth without going outside.

THE AMERICAN RED CROSS headquarters building, on Seventeenth between D and E streets, NW (no admission charge), is dedicated to the memory of the women who cared for the ill and wounded of both the North and the South during the Civil War.

In the spacious lobby and the floor below are historical exhibits, statuary, and displays of current projects. A broad marble stairway leads to an assembly hall on the second floor where the famous stained-glass windows designed by Louis Tiffany will capture your attention. Special exhibits are arranged from time to time. Nineteen fifty-six marked the celebration of seventy-five years of service to humanity by the organization.

Continuing north on Seventeenth Street between C and D, you are at MEMORIAL CONTINENTAL HALL, where are housed the twenty-eight period State Rooms (open to the public) and the excellent genealogical library of the National Society of the Daughters of the American Revolution. (The museum at 1776 D Street, NW, in the Administration Building, is open to the public. No admission charge; free guide service 9:00 A.M. to 3:00 P.M. Monday through Friday. Closed Saturday, Sunday, and holidays.)

As you enter the museum room, a larger-than-life oil portrait of

Martha Washington standing in a cherry-red gown beckons to you. The portrait is the work of E. F. Andrews; a similar one by Andrews hangs in the East Room of the White House. You'll discover an air of intimacy lingers about the cherished belongings on display from all parts of the country.

No story of "how it all began" is more interesting. In 1890 a Washington member named Mary E. Letts had in her possession a rose-patterned beaded bag. The DAR itself had been founded that same year. Mary Letts could think of no better, safer place than the DAR for her prize—the bag which had been carried by her great-grandmother, a descendant of a *Mayflower* passenger and wife of a Revolutionary soldier.

Thus it began. Relics have been showering down ever since to build a collection now numbering some ten thousand pieces.

The State Rooms are located on all four floors in Continental Hall. Marble columns usher you into the impressive foyer furnished by the State Society of Pennsylvania.

Louisiana's contribution is a brick-paved courtyard; New Jersey's room is Jacobean, furnished with wood from a British frigate sunk in 1777. New Hampshire has created a nostalgic "children's attic." You'll want to rock the hand-fashioned cradles as little faces smile above the covers. There are china-headed dolls, a little pine desk from a New England schoolhouse of 1825, and a collection of toy banks that move when pennies are dropped in.

As you leave this building, remember stately Constitution Hall, the famous DAR auditorium, is at the other end of the block. There concerts, lectures, and musicals are held except during the week of April 19, Battle of Lexington Day, when the Daughters reserve the Hall for their annual Continental Congress.

CORCORAN GALLERY OF ART, located at Seventeenth and New York Avenue, NW. (No admission charge.) Open: Tuesday through Friday, 10:00 A.M. to 4:30 P.M.; Saturday: 9:00 A.M. to 4:30 P.M.; Sunday and holidays: 2:00 to 5:00 P.M. Closed: Mondays, Christmas, New Year's Day, and July 4.

Before you step inside the Corcoran Gallery of Art you might want to look north for a glimpse of the handsome brick building occupying the northeast corner of Pennsylvania Avenue and Seventeenth. Now the United States Court of Claims, this was the first home of the Gallery, started by wealthy William Wilson Corcoran in 1859. The art collection of this philanthropist was housed here in 1869 as a gift to the public, while he commissioned men of judgment to buy treasures around the world to fill it. Before long, it was apparent that the quarters were too small; in 1897 the present gallery on the east side of Seventeenth Street was opened.

But the history of the first brick building has its own highlights. A great ball attended by the leaders of the day was held there in 1871, and in magnificence it surpassed anything Washington had ever seen. (The occasion itself was memorable; it marked not only the paving of Pennsylvania Avenue, but the passage by the Congress of a bill providing for a new District Government and regarded generally as a panacea for all the city's ills.)

The present Gallery offers, among many things, complete contrasts. In the west portion of the building is the Clark wing, bequeathed by William Andrews Clark. In the wing's twenty rooms are assembled a Louis XVI salon, purchased intact by the late Senator from Montana from the Paris townhouse of the Duc de la Tremoille, a wealth of Gothic, Gobelin and Beauvais tapestries, rare laces and faïence, plus a rich representation of European art. Included among the paintings are Rembrandts, Van Dycks, Rubenses, Corots, and others. (A private apartment for the W. A. Clark Collection's curator is also provided.)

On the Seventeenth Street side of the Gallery is the growing American collection. It is particularly strong in portraiture; Copley, the Peales, Sully, and Stuart are there. Of special interest are the two Athenaeum portraits of George Washington by Gilbert Stuart; the artist referred to them as his "hundred-dollar bills." He made more than seventy variations of this one type. This is the head you see reproduced today in the design for the one-dollar bill and the one-cent stamp; it is probably the best-known portrait ever painted.

As you go from room to room, the wider range of pictorial subject matter which began in the nineteenth century is strongly evident—still lifes, marines, landscapes, and genre paintings. You find yourself swept from Colonial drawing-room manners to the pioneer West. Truly magnificent is the painting by Albert Bierstadt, *The Last of the Buffalo*. John Singer Sargent's *Mrs. Henry White* is a striking full-length portrait, and there are mystery and grace in Thomas Eakins' *The Pathetic Song*, painted in 1881.

But the Corcoran's most important canvas, the one you must not miss, is *The Old House of Representatives*, by Samuel F. B. Morse. Aside from the fifty or so individual portraits you see in the painting, it is remarkable in being among the first to handle the difficulties of artificial light. Against the red hangings there is a glow that makes you believe you are looking through a window into the famous chamber. It was painted in 1822 by the versatile artist-inventor.

Of special interest, too, is a little-known portrait of Abraham Lincoln, executed from life by George P. A. Healy in 1860. It shows the beardless Lincoln, and the portrait's great distinction is the warmth and inspiration of the portrayal.

In sculpture, the Corcoran has such pioneers of American realism as Clark Mills (of Jackson statue fame). One work is a marble bust of John C. Calhoun presented to the Gallery by the sculptor.

On permanent display in the atrium is a replica of Hiram Powers' *Greek Slave*, probably the most widely publicized statue of its day. The undraped female figure, though gentle of mien, was considered in shocking bad taste in the 1850's.

Don't overlook the fine collection of animals in bronze by Antoine Louis Barye, one of the acquisitions Mr. Corcoran commissioned personally.

The Corcoran Gallery of Art holds an unusual place in Washington, quite apart from its permanent collections. It is a kind of community art center, offering many cultural programs and events in the allied arts, and bringing pleasure to thousands each year.

The Corcoran's Annual Area Exhibition offers the local artist opportunity to show his work; the Biennial Show, in turn, brings in original art works from all over the United States. Through the purchase of significant works from these exhibitions, the Collection of Contemporary American Artists is increased.

The Gallery operates a flourishing Art School, with day and evening classes, for both adults and children. Painting, sculpture, and commercial art are taught. (Any Saturday you may meet a ten-year-old coming proudly down the steps holding a still life or a clay beast on a cardboard, just past the moist state of creation.)

BUREAU OF ENGRAVING AND PRINTING, Fourteenth and C streets, SW. (No admission charge.) Open with conducted tours 8:00 A.M. to 11:00 A.M. and 12:30 P.M. to 2:00 P.M. Monday through Friday. Closed Saturday, Sunday, and holidays.

Watching Uncle Sam literally making money in this, the world's largest plant of its kind, is a favorite pastime for visitors. The intensely interesting thirty-five-minute tour takes you along high galleries stretching well over the heads of the busy employees, mostly women, who go about stacking, counting, and examining freshly printed currency. (There's always a wit or two on the tour, delighting to ask the guide for samples, or remarking that it is just like any other factory—"just a better product, that's all!")

Along the way you'll see one-dollar bills in uncut sheets of eighteen printed first on the backs in green, then on the fronts in black. What workers call the "octopus," a contrivance with small suction cups, lifts one sheet at a time, as each is printed, into a neat pile.

More than thirty-one million dollars in paper money is printed here each day, at a cost of slightly less than one cent per note. It's awe-inspiring to see the stacks of money spread on long tables. Denominations run from $1 to $100,000—that big one is for banking purposes only.

The special paper, part cotton, part linen, is made under strict Government supervision, and before the large blank sheets are ready for the presses the paper must be "aged"—a wetting and drying process that brings each sheet to the desired stage of absorption.

Every day money which in the judgment of banking institutions is damaged beyond use is taken out of circulation and destroyed by burning. This incinerating process is carried out in Washington and at Federal Reserve Banks throughout the country. The average life of a dollar bill is about twelve months, but even then it varies according to the business and habits of those handling it. Money circulated in coal-mining areas or oil fields suffers much more in handling than, say, bills exchanged by New York business firms. That is why 68 per cent of the currency printed here is in dollar bills, the most circulated bill in American money.

In one section you'll discover the reason for a tiny star on an occasional note in your wallet. In the examination of currency after the sheets have been cut five hundred at a time, the inspector expertly and instantly spots mutilated notes, discards them, and inserts a note carrying the small star. You might say the star stands for a flaw that kept the original bill from passing muster. Here, too, the money gets a final counting, and it is understandable why this is one of the top sections in terms of skill and rewards.

It's fascinating to watch the flying fingers of these experts handle the huge packages of money. Learning to count the bills is one of the first duties the new worker must master. You'll watch their speed with real admiration. In the guide's words, "You don't think you'll ever get it—fanning out four bills at a time. You practice on the telephone book or any book every chance you get—and then suddenly you've got it."

The first time I saw the Bureau's operation, some years ago, the inking of the plate and removal of excess ink was followed by a light hand polishing. Then the guide had said that nothing had ever been found to replace this polishing by hand. Now a fat roll of paper does the job.

The Bureau began in a small way in 1862, finding space in the attic of the new Treasury to turn out greenbacks in two- and five-dollar denominations. These helped not only to finance the Civil War, but they inspired the Greenback Party, which in 1876 nominated eighty-five-year-old Peter Cooper of New York for President.

Today the mammoth operation produces United States notes, silver certificates, Federal Reserve notes, Treasury bonds, and many more valuable pieces of paper. Across the street in the Annex, stamps by the millions are printed. Every once in a while a small printing error will slip by to gladden the hearts of philatelists. Bureau people still talk about the flurry caused in philatelic circles when, somehow, a new stamp carried the picture of an airplane flying upside down.

In a display case in the Bureau's Fifteenth Street lobby, an exhibition of currency and stamps includes a $100,000 bill, with Woodrow Wilson's picture on it. "Just think," said a young bride to her husband, "one little bill could represent the earnings of a lifetime."

AQUARIUM, located in the basement of the Department of Commerce Building, Fourteenth and Fifteenth Streets at E Street, NW. (No admission charge.) Open daily 9:00 A.M. to 5:00 P.M.

Arranged along the walls of this large room, forty attractively lighted tanks display to great advantage a variety of fishes, alligators, frogs, turtles, and many more species that are common to the waters of the United States.

For lunch try Allies' Inn, at Seventeenth and New York Avenue, NW, for good food at reasonable cost. (Closed Saturdays; open Sundays.) This cafeteria is frequented weekdays at noon by Government people—some you may recognize.

This is very near the American Automobile Association's offices at 1712 G Street, NW, where you can find out about tours and new tourist entertainment.

For dinner, just over on Pennsylvania Avenue, NW, at 1743½, is Jack Hunt's. Good food, not exorbitantly priced.

Tour II

Lafayette Square, Decatur House, Truxtun-Decatur Naval Museum, St. John's Church and Parish House, White House, Treasury Building

LAFAYETTE SQUARE, DECATUR HOUSE (not open to the public), Truxtun-Decatur Naval Museum (no admission charge; open 12:00 noon to 5:00 P.M. weekdays and Sunday; 10:30 A.M. to 5:00 P.M. Saturday; closed Monday), St. John's Church and Parish House (no admission charge); The White House (no admission charge; open Tuesday through Saturday, 10:00 A.M. to 12:00 noon); Treasury Building: Exhibition Room open Monday through Friday, 9:30 A.M. to 3:45 P.M.

The White House won't open until ten o'clock, so there's time to look back.

A little Washington lady now in her eighties belonged to an old bicycle club whose members used to spin swiftly by here. She recalled, "Why, I could go down Pennsylvania Avenue from the State Department to the Capitol without ever touching the handle bars." (The pre-1900 version of "Look, Ma—no hands"?) She went on: "A man asked Papa if he could put me on the stage—imagine!"

But on just such a bench as yours one July 1, a man sat watching the White House. He was short, spare, with a grudge in his unhappy mind and a revolver in his pocket. He was waiting for President James A. Garfield to come out, cross the Avenue alone, as he did, and stroll into Secretary of State James G. Blaine's house on Madison Place. From an adjacent alley, later, the little man followed as Garfield and Blaine returned arm in arm to the White House. He followed but did not shoot. "It was a very hot, sultry night, and I felt tired and wearied by the heat," he said later.

But the next morning Charles J. Guiteau was back on his La-fayette Square bench until he boarded a horsecar for the railway station at the foot of Capitol Hill. There he shot the President, who was about to leave on a brief trip. And the Square never saw either man again as he had been before that day.

The area got its first fling at historic holidays in 1801, when hundreds of Americans, fresh-minted and free, gathered from dawn to dusk to celebrate the Fourth of July. Frigates on the Potomac fired salutes. United States Marines passed in review before President Thomas Jefferson, probably on the South Lawn; it was the first time a party of regular troops was reviewed by a President at his official Washington residence. The Marine Band played, and refreshments were served to staff officials, Cherokee chiefs, and solid citizens.

Some say the people of Washington named the Square after La-fayette when he returned as a beloved guest of the city in 1824 and was entertained at the most brilliant social season the Capital had yet seen. But others insist that General Washington himself, years before, had bestowed the name. (If you have a taste for unraveling historical mysteries, such questions, great and small, about the Capital's first 150 years are in good supply.) The breath of scandal has blown across the Square. All Washington was shocked when, outside the old National Club in February, 1859, Congressman Daniel E. Sickles fatally wounded Philip Barton Key; Sickles believed Key was enamored of his young wife. In the sensational trial which followed, the defense set a precedent by pleading temporary derangement; Sickles was acquitted. (A physical reminder of the eccentric Sickles is on view today in a case in the Army Medical Museum. It is his right leg, amputated because of wounds suffered at Gettysburg. The limb, in a crude wooden box, arrived at the

Museum with a card saying, "With the compliments of Maj. Gen. Daniel E. Sickles, U.S. Vols." For some years after the war, Sickles called regularly at the Museum to see his leg.)

Prairie dogs and deer caused only a slight stir when they turned up in the Square as late as 1878, probably because it was only a few years since pigs, goats, and other animals ceased to have the run of the little patch of land. That statue of General Andrew Jackson—today as much a piece of Americana as a Currier and Ives print —made the difference. Cast from melted-down cannon captured by Jackson during his campaigns, it marked a new respectability, with iron fence to follow. Erected in 1853, this was the first of many equestrian statues to rear, canter, or plunge in the city's circles, squares, triangles, and vistas. (You'll probably detect a Cinderella quality in some Washington statuary. Clark Mills, who designed, modeled, and cast the Jackson statue, was a gifted plasterer from New York State who made up with great devotion to authentic detail for what he lacked in training.) There's a helter-skelter touch, too. Here is Old Hickory triumphing over the central spot, facing not the Capitol, nor even the White House lawn with the magnolias he planted, but just west. And the Frenchman whose name the park bears is often overlooked; his statue stands on the tree-shaded southeast corner.

Formal invitations were sent out in 1910 for the unveiling of the statue of General Thaddeus Kosciusko by Anton Popiel at the northeast corner; but formal receptions were held for all: for the statue of Baron von Steuben by Albert Jaegers in the northwest corner that same year; and for the statue of Rochambeau in the southwest corner. The latter was a gift from France and is a copy by Ferdinand Hamar of the memorial to honor Rochambeau at Vendôme, France.

Sitting here some seventy years ago, you might have seen a waffle vendor over on the White House lawn. An old photograph shows hungry lads gathered around as he carried on a lively business, while off to one side a bearded fellow in a high hat, with an early camera in his hands, looked about for a picture. On the snow-covered Avenue a horsecar made its careful plodding way.

Look around now at the houses that face on the Square. The National Science Foundation now occupies the old wrought-iron-trimmed mansion at the northeast corner of Madison Place. A plaque marks the site where Dolley Madison, great and beloved lady, held court for many years after the death of her husband, James Madison, the fourth President. In April, great swags of wisteria drift fragrantly over the building and onto the adjacent Tayloe-Cameron House, known during the McKinley administration as the "Little White House." President William McKinley frequently breakfasted with Senator Marcus A. Hanna, who lived there; the winning campaign of 1900, when Republicans wooed labor with promises of the "full dinner pail," was mapped in this house. The Cosmos Club for years had its home here. When this social club for men distinguished in science and letters moved recently to new headquarters in the sumptuous Sumner Welles mansion at Florida Avenue and Twentieth Street, NW, it took along colorful murals depicting houses facing the Square.

The Belasco Theater, now a USO service club, is another old landmark. Lillian Russell played here in 1895, when it was the newly built Lafayette Square Opera House. As the Belasco Theater a decade later, it drew such performers as Julia Marlowe and Blanche Bates. But there's a plaque telling that Commodore John Rodgers built a house here long years before, and it in turn became a fashionable boarding house for such great as Henry Clay and John C. Calhoun. Soon after, it became the exclusive National Club whose membership included political and social leaders. During the Civil War the red brick house again turned private residence for Lincoln's Secretary of State William H. Seward. The night Lincoln was shot, Seward, ill in his third-floor bedroom, was stabbed by Lewis Paine (born Lewis Powell), John Wilkes Booth's fellow conspirator. Later when James G. Blaine moved in, he was warned that it was an unlucky house.

On the northwest, Decatur House is the Square's most famous

St. John's Church

private dwelling, and the first to go up, back in 1819. That year, the Decaturs could stand in their doorway greeting guests—the Monroes, the Calhouns, the Madisons—and see the newly painted White House (restored after the burning by the British in 1814), or look at the other structure also still making history on the Square: St. John's Church on H Street. (A much needed bell was placed in the steeple in 1822, but Decatur did not live to hear it.) Decatur's words "Our country! In her intercourse with foreign nations may she always be right, but our country right or wrong!" echoed down the years in American schoolhouses. Take another look at Decatur House, note its satisfying scale and simplicity, and remember the name Benjamin H. Latrobe, for he designed other buildings, notably St. John's Church and the south wing of the Capitol.

Stop by the old carriage house of the Decatur residence just next door for a fascinating collection of naval documents, uniforms, weapons and ship models at the TRUXTUN-DECATUR NAVAL MUSEUM, 1610 H Street, NW. Open noon to 5:00 P.M. weekdays and Sunday; 10:30 A.M. to 5:00 P.M. Saturday; closed Monday. No admission charge.

This Naval Museum houses many exhibits of the Naval Historical Foundation, and is dedicated to the preservation of the Nation's rich heritage of maritime history and tradition. Exhibits are devoted to seapower not alone in the Navy, but in the Marine Corps, Coast Guard, Merchant Marine, and all other components.

In little ST. JOHN'S, the Church of Presidents, ten of the nation's Chief Executives have held pews and worshiped; almost all have occasionally sought its quiet for meditation. Brick pavings inside were replaced long ago; box pews were used for a time. The portico and tower were added in 1820. About thirty-five years ago the church received a needed refurbishing, with much new richness in gold and other colors. The story goes that on the Sunday it was reopened to service there was audible distressed whispering—"So much gold, my dear." As an old parishioner tells it, "Whereat it was difficult to keep sober when just then the choir burst into 'Take all my guilt away'!"

But the burnished dome today makes it especially appealing to photographers who take color pictures from the Hay-Adams House corner across Sixteenth Street, "just to get it in." The church owns a prized 1818 water color by Latrobe, with a view of the partially burned White House in the background and St. John's as it looked then. Sit down in a quiet pew as the morning sun falls through stained-glass windows and traffic is muffled. After James Madison had Pew 54 it was set aside for Presidents; Dolley, although a Quaker, was baptized and confirmed an Episcopalian here.

Famous old Ashburton House, as the result of a well-considered swap, is now the Parish House of St. John's Church. The new AFL-CIO headquarters building rises on the site of the back lawn and stable of Ashburton House, around the corner on Sixteenth Street. The four-story brown stucco house on H Street is well over a hundred years old. After being purchased by Joseph Gales, wealthy editor of the *National Intelligencer*, it attracted many of social prominence to its rooms. Daniel Webster, then Secretary of State, became a frequent caller when Lord Ashburton took up residence, having been sent here to handle the United States–Canadian boundary question. Webster lived just down the street in a mansion on the present site of the United States Chamber of Commerce Building. But it proved too expensive, and he sold the home to the wealthy William W. Corcoran. It was while he lived here that Webster now and then sent his servant across the street to Dolley Madison's house, with a basketful of good things. During these later years, the extravagances of Dolley's only son reduced her to near-poverty.

Fine foods and good wines were known to inhabit this side of H Street, despite the tempering presence of the good church. Ashburton fancied such delicacies as rare French desserts described as "seductive," and fine wines, while Webster himself went to market to select oysters, terrapin, crabs, and ducks. The Arlington Hotel graced the Square for nearly fifty years, offering in that time hospitality to many Presidents-elect as they awaited inauguration. Now the Veterans Administration Building marks the spot.

If you find yourself at Lafayette Square around lunchtime, try the quiet air-conditioned grill of the Hay-Adams House. This hotel, opposite St. John's Church on Sixteenth Street, takes its name from the living quarters once occupied by historian Henry Adams and statesman John Hay. Here, as in other dwellings on the Square, foregathered the great men of their times—leaders in statecraft, art, and literature.

Now for the WHITE HOUSE. First of all, I hope before you have gotten this far that you have written to National Capital Parks, U.S. Department of Interior, Washington 25, D.C., for a copy of the eight-page White House booklet giving facts and figures about the First Family's dwelling. In limited edition, it is not distributed locally, but it is sent out on request. You'll learn, among many facts, that there are 132 rooms and 20 baths in the newly renovated White House; that the residence has seen many weddings but only one of a President, that of Grover Cleveland and Frances Folsom in the Blue Room.

The Capital's first days were busy ones for architects. Even Thomas Jefferson secretly submitted plans (after writing the advertisement for the competition which appeared in principal newspapers) for a suitable President's House. But James Hoban won the $500 first prize with a plan that has been compared with Dublin's Leinster House, although it resembles more closely a "Design for a Gentleman's House" from *A Book of Architecture* by one James Gibbs, follower of Christopher Wren. The exact site was General Washington's choice, a sufficient distance from the Capitol and in harmony with L'Enfant's plan.

Aside from its historic meaning, here is a rare chance for you to stroll through a house costing $16,000,000. That doesn't include the estimated cost of the original structure at the time the cornerstone was laid in 1792, but starts with the bill for rebuilding in 1815, after the burning, and comes right down to 1952. The intervening years saw many piecemeal alterations and improvements. What a change the new gas lighting must have made in 1848, and later, during the Pierce administration, the first hot water furnace!

An efficient staff of seventy-two maids, butlers, cooks, gardeners, maintenance men, and others toil, mostly behind the scenes, to make this beautiful mansion a spotless miracle of good house-keeping. In 1954 a House appropriation amounting to $367,200 paid for these services. But it wasn't always so. In early times a President was forced to find much of the money and even the furnishings to keep his ménage going. Abigail Adams was only a week in the White House when she sagely observed, "But this House is built for ages to come. The establishment necessary is a tax which cannot be borne by the present salary."

She arrived in the wilderness city on a cold Sunday in November, to become the initial First Lady to occupy the famous house. In a lively letter, she wrote: "The house is upon a grand and superb scale, requiring about thirty servants to attend and keep the apartments in proper order." But the damp, Potomac-laden wind was blowing through these drafty rooms and she was cold. "Shiver, shiver, shiver. . . . No wood-cutters nor carters to be had at any rate. We are now indebted to a Pennsylvania wagon to bring us, through the first clerk in the Treasury Office, one cord and a half of wood, which is all we have for this house, where 12 fires are constantly required."

How Mrs. Adams would have welcomed the "elegant stove" advertised in the *National Intelligencer* the following winter! It was pyramidal, "standing 6 feet, 6 inches high, with lion's feet, the bust of Gen. Washington on the top, and the arms of the United States on each side . . . for coal or wood . . . for churches, Public office, Halls, or large stores."

Your official free tour of the White House, on any day except Sundays, Mondays, and holidays, starts at the ground floor from the East Wing. You continue down the long corridor, past the portraits of several Presidents to the foot of what is known as the public stairs, and up to the main hall. You are then on the first floor of the White House. Next in order is the State Dining Room, then on to the Red, Blue, and Green Rooms, and finally through the East Room.

If it's April, May, or June you'll likely get to walk *through* these rooms and find yourself standing outside at the north portico when it's quickly over. (All those heel marks sometimes make it necessary to close the White House to visitors for a few weeks to restore the worn spots.) But at other seasons, velvet ropes at the doorways keep observers looking on from the hall. That's when there's time for loitering.

As I went through the east entrance recently, carried along with half a hundred teen-agers, we came to the first large portrait, that of President Millard Fillmore. "What a hair-do!" laughed a small voice behind me.

Perhaps today's slim five-minute tour has resulted from the public's past wanton disregard for their First Family's home and feelings. Long ago it was the practice of the White House to throw open its doors once in every fortnight and let the public meet the President and his Lady. A leading newspaper mentioned such an evening when the Monroes lived here, reporting that Senators, consuls, farmers, merchants, auctioneers, judges, "and nothingarians, all with their wives and some with their gawky offspring, crowd to the President's house, some in shoes, most in boots, and many in spurs; some snuffing, others chewing, and many longing for their cigars and whiskey-punch left at home. Some with powdered heads, others frizzled and oiled, with some whose heads a comb has never touched, half-hid by dirty collars, far above their ears, as stiff as pasteboard."

Ransacking as well as rudeness is not new to White House occupants. In Lincoln's time, determined visitors thought nothing of tearing great souvenir patches from the draperies, and apparently there's no sure cure, in spite of velvet ropes and alert guarding. Only recently, a socially prominent out-of-towner on a privately conducted tour had to be separated from a heavy crystal ashtray bearing the President's seal which she was observed trying to filch.

Up to fifty years ago, the Chief Executive's offices were on the second floor. The President, to cross the corridor, was forced to step over office-seekers and cranks who could literally bar his path. This unhappy situation ended with President Theodore Roosevelt's sweeping changes; an executive west wing provided office space.

Today, officially invited guests must assemble in the palatial East Room or one of the other first-floor rooms to wait upon the President and his Lady, who make their appearance from private apartments upstairs. Uninvited guests never get past the White House police except during public tours. As an *invited* guest yourself (holding your invitation in your warm little hand) you could be arriving for a special function, say on a February evening, at this east entrance. Cabinet members roll up to the north or south portico, and special intimates (those of whom the First Lady says, "It's been ages since we played bridge—let's invite the Smiths on Friday night, dear") come in at a specified entrance.

The White House has long been Washington's first interest to strangers. Travelers who are in town for a few hours will often hail a cab and ask just to drive around the mansion. "They never take their eyes off it—and I go slow," one driver said.

The delightful story of "two plain ladies from the West," in the city just overnight and determined to see Mrs. Dolley Madison, is told in *The Ladies of the White House*, by L. C. Holloway, written in 1882:

Meeting in the street an old gentleman they timidly approached and asked him to show them the way to the President's House. Being an old acquaintance of Mrs. Madison, he took pleasure in conducting the strangers to the White House. The President's family were at breakfast when the party arrived, but Mrs. Madison good-naturedly went in to be seen by the curious old ladies. . . . Her friendly welcome soon put them at ease, and rising to leave . . . one of them said "P'haps you wouldn't mind if I jest kissed you, to tell my gals about." Mrs. Madison, not to be outdone by her guest's politeness, gracefully saluted each of the delighted old ladies, who adjusted their spectacles, and, with evident admiration, departed.

It was the same Dolley Madison who sat at a small desk in the White House on that dark day, August 22, 1814, when all Washington was caught in a paralyzing fear of unpreparedness. She wrote to her sister that afternoon, words like lines in a play making a kind of poetry of anxiety:

Three o'clock. Will you believe it, my sister? We have had a battle, or skirmish, near Bladensburg, and I am still here within sound of the cannon. Mr. Madison comes not—may God protect him! Two messengers, covered with dust, come to bid me fly; but I wait for him. . . .

In the same letter she describes how her good friend, Mr. Charles Carroll, has come to aid in her departure and is

in very bad humor with me because I insist on waiting until the large picture of General Washington is secured, and it requires that it be unscrewed from the wall. This process was found too tedious for these perilous moments; I have ordered the frame to be broken and the canvas taken out; it is done—and the precious portrait placed in the hands of two gentlemen of New York for safe keeping.

The full-length portrait of Washington which hangs today in the East Room carries a label saying it is the original painting that Dolley Madison removed during the British invasion.

But this single portrait proves what a merry business inquiring into history can be. A receipt (still in the Treasury Department in 1881), dated July 5, 1800, signed by the Secretary of the Navy, Benjamin Stoddert, who misspelled his own name on it, records that eight hundred dollars was paid to "Thomas Lang" for a full-length "Stewart" portrait. History shows that a William Laing did sell a Gilbert Stuart painting to the Committee in charge of furnishing the White House. But when Laing directed Winstanley, the English landscape painter, to forward the portrait to the White House, Winstanley is said to have made off to England with it, and "packed up one of his copies instead," which was hung in the mansion. When Stuart saw the painting three years later, he forthwith disclaimed it. (Mr. Laing, in despair, is believed to have finally refunded the eight hundred dollars to the Government.) Present-day opinion, in the face of too frequent cleaning, a partial repainting in 1862 and more restoring in 1932, is still undecided as to whether this portrait is by Stuart, or a copy.

Add to this a bitter controversy which boiled up after a Carroll descendant insisted it was his father who had saved the portrait. Dolley Madison finally was moved to send a clarifying note to the public press. But even now there are opinions on both sides.

Many today seeing the portrait and knowing the story wonder why the canvas bears no sign of cutting. Records show that only the heavy gilt frame was broken. The canvas itself is stretched on an inner frame of wood and was undamaged through it all.

Another fascinating footnote to that day's confusion concerns the Declaration of Independence. Some believe that when President Madison urged his wife in his absence to save White House valuables, Dolley personally rescued the Declaration of Independence.

But records in the National Archives tell a different story. Before the enemy could set fire to the building "west of the President's house" which the Departments of State, War, and Navy all shared, papers of first importance were removed. A State Department clerk wrote fully about it (thirty-four years later) telling of fellow clerks placing the records (including the Declaration) in coarse linen bags, loading them on carts and setting out for a grist mill above Chain Bridge on the Virginia shore. A second security move took the records on to Leesburg, on the very day of the battle. They remained there in complete safety for several weeks.

At the west end of the first-floor corridor is the

State Dining Room. Gone is the heavy atmosphere of dark oak paneling and American big game trophies beloved of Theodore Roosevelt. Paint of a soft blue-green hue now covers the dark wood; gold damask draperies add rich contrast. Parting with this "heavy" atmosphere was almost sacrilegious for some, but history shows that light tones antedated the clubroom-like interior. This ample room, the largest except for the East Room, can seat about one hundred in horseshoe and E-shape arrangement. Then the carved and gilded centerpiece that President Monroe had sent from France may be used. The centerpiece or "mirror plateau," often mentioned in local social columns when a White House dinner is taking place, is made up of sixteen small figures bearing crowns to hold candles, or cups for fresh flowers. A mirror base reflects the flickering light or graceful orchids sometimes used, and the whole stretches an eye-filling thirteen and a half feet down the table. These Monroe pieces are among the few "heirlooms" of those early days.

But at Christmas the mirror often catches red holly berries spilling from the small cups, and miniature yew trees bright with red and gold balls against a background of gilded magnolia leaves. Those decorative touches have been used for the White House dinner traditionally honoring the members of the Supreme Court, the first of the official dinners usually given here between mid-December and Ash Wednesday. (In December, 1954, banks of white poinsettias turned up in the Red Room; great sprays of greens with pine cones and pots of yellow chrysanthemums in the Blue Room; red poinsettias in the Green and East Rooms marked the holiday spirit. A week or two before Christmas great trees usually are set up and decorated in a corner of the East Room and the Blue Room. Lucky, indeed, is the visitor at the holiday season.)

In an old letter a visitor to Mr. Monroe's table writes:

The dining room was in better taste than is common here, being quite simply and but little furnished. The table was large and quite handsome. The service was in china. . . . There was, however, a rich plateau, and a great abundance of the smaller articles of table-plate. The cloth, napkins, etc., etc., were fine and beautiful. The dinner was served in the French style, a little Americanized. The dishes were handed around, though some of the guests, appearing to prefer their own customs, coolly helped themselves to what they found at hand.

The "overmantel" on the north wall is a painting of flowers framed in gilt over a mirror; this and the candelabra just below were presented for the late King George VI of England by the present Queen Elizabeth II when she was a princess.

The Red Room. This is the First Lady's reception room. On formal occasions it has become one of a series of state apartments. President Rutherford B. Hayes took the oath of office here on a Saturday to prevent the country from being without a Chief Executive over Sunday, March 4, 1877. The conversational groupings of furniture are almost cozy, and against the striking white wainscoting, woodwork, and marble, make a pleasant welcome. Take a second look at the Carrara marble mantel. It and one in the Green Room were both imported from Italy for the newly rebuilt White House after the War of 1812. The eighteenth-century candelabra and the musical clock centered there were gifts of the President of France in April, 1952.

Wall coverings and draperies are red silk damask and the rug on the oak floor is chenille, replacing a red Aubusson rug. A new crystal chandelier, more lacy-looking than the last, hangs from the ceiling.

The Blue Room. When Abigail Adams looked around the unfinished mansion and wrote: "There is an oval room, which is designed for the drawing room, and has the crimson furniture in it. It is a very handsome room now, but when completed will be beautiful," she was describing the second-floor oval room, now the President's Study. (With plenty of candlelight and roaring fires, the Adamses had the first reception, on New Year's Day in 1801, in that upstairs "Oval Room." The Marine Band made its official White House debut on the same occasion.)

Today, in the oval Blue Room on the first floor, blue silk damask with classic gold motif covers walls and is repeated in the draperies and upholstery. This room is considered the most beautiful in the White House, and is where the President often receives official guests.

Furniture was so scarce when the Monroes planned to reopen the rebuilt White House on New Year's Day in 1818 that they sold the Government some of their choice possessions. (Monroe bought the pieces back at the end of his second term.) Also, they sent to France, where James Monroe had twice served as Minister, for public room pieces, including some for what is today the Blue Room. The furniture arrived the fall of 1817, described on the bill of lading as "a set of drawing room furniture of gilded wood carved with branched olive leaves and covered with a heavy satin material of delicate crimson color, with a pattern of laurel leaves in two tones of gold." But the expensive satin didn't wear well and needed to be replaced during the John Quincy Adams administration. Gilt candle-sticks now on the mantel and the French Minerva clock were part of the Monroe purchases.

The white marble mantel dates from 1902; bundles of arrows tipped with bronze form the supports.

The Green Room. Here, green silk damask covers walls, forms draperies, and makes striking contrast with the spanking white wainscoting and woodwork. The white marble mantel is a duplicate of one in the Red Room. The gilt bronze clock representing Hanni-bal after the Battle of Cannae and gilt vases on the mantel were pur-chased in France during Monroe's administration. The Great Seal of the President is woven dramatically into the Savonnerie rug covering the oak floor.

The room is used for formal and informal receptions; or on such occasions as the White House Diplomatic Reception, the Green Room might be reserved for members of the Senate Foreign Rela-tions Committee, the House Foreign Affairs Committee, and the Little Cabinet, and wives.

The East Room. In 1954 a social note in the *Post and Times Herald* began: "The President and Mrs. Eisenhower received the guests at the entrance to the East Room (where yellow gladiolas added a festive note to the décor), and then proceeded down the red-carpeted hall to the State Dining Room."

State receptions and balls, weddings and funerals have taken place in this great hall, the largest room in the house. In the recent renovation walls were redecorated in white and gold, with lemon-yellow and white silk damask draperies. The old white enamel wood paneling was replaced; but retained were six bas-relief panels done by the Piccirilli Brothers in 1902. New mantels were installed, also, gift of one State which especially desired to contribute these pieces. (Some of the discarded paneling, pilasters, and marble mantels you'll find gracing the reconstructed East Room background in the First Ladies Hall in the Smithsonian Institution.)

At the north end of the room is a mahogany concert piano de-signed in the grand manner for the White House. It was a gift to the nation by the Steinway family in 1938. Carved and gilded eagles form the legs, and decorations along the sides represent American folk dancing and musical forms. (Guests often return here after state dinners to hear artists perform.)

On the broad east wall is the famous portrait of General Washington, often attributed to Gilbert Stuart and rescued by Dolley Madison. A portrait of Martha Washington, by E. F. Andrews and presented by the Daughters of the American Revolution, hangs near by. It was copied from the unfinished head of Mrs. Washington by Gilbert Stuart, which portrait now hangs in the Boston Museum of Fine Arts.

Three crystal chandeliers were purchased in 1902 to replace gas and candlelight. These can be dimmed to the soft glow of candlelight.

When you hear that Abigail Adams used the East Room to dry her wash, try not to put her down for an uncouth pioneer. This was a big unfinished barn of a room then; the only heat was thrown off by fires in the fireplaces to help dry the wet, rankly smelling plaster. Out of doors was a morass of mud. Abigail had had her fifty-sixth birthday that same chill November, was a grandmother, and had just recovered from a serious illness, yet could look about and say, "I am determined to be satisfied and content." Although this resourceful and witty First Lady lived here just three months, her brief experiences taken from her warm, spirited letters have made sparkling reading for many years.

Many affairs of the White House social season take place within the East Room. The scarlet of the Marine Band adds brilliance as the President and the First Lady receive members of Congress, and others.

Today the "Blue Danube" is not played so often as it once was for parties. As for the light step and the quick repartee—perhaps it was in the East Room where a Foreign Minister once said to his dancing partner, "Madam, you dance with the grace of a Parisienne. I can hardly realize you were educated in Tennessee."

"Count, you forget," was the spirited reply, "that grace is a cos-

mopolite, and like a wild flower, is much oftener found in the woods
than in the streets of a city."

On the second and third floors are family living quarters and
guest rooms. On the top is the new sun parlor or solarium above
the south portico.

The 18½ acres of lawn rolling up to this famous house are landscaped with great care to create a scene of natural beauty and
simple dignity. That solid green velvet look comes from fescue, rye,
and blue grasses. Three hundred or so trees, many of them American elms, plus two acres of flowers, keep the chief gardener and his
staff busy. While some flowers are cut in season from these gardens,
fresh flowers are bought daily in local markets, and often held for
special state affairs for days at 40 degrees in a special cooling
chamber. Eventually these bouquets find their way to local hos-
pitals.

English boxwood as old as the White House marks borders.
Andrew Jackson's thriving magnolia trees, near the President's rose
gardens on the south portico, were planted in memory of his Rachel,
who never saw the White House but died before he took office. The
magnolias were brought from the Hermitage, his estate in Tennessee.

Birds have been contented visitors here too. When Theodore
Roosevelt was Chief Executive he made a list of ninety-three species
of birds he saw on the White House grounds and in his pursuit of
the "strenuous life" elsewhere about Washington. He recorded a
pair of redheaded woodpeckers nesting on the grounds, and spotted
other nests there—redstart, flicker, wood thrush, catbird, screech
owl, and sparrow hawk.

Squirrels flourish today, saved in 1955 in a flurry of publicity after
it seemed they might be banished for ignoring the "off limits" sign
on the President's putting green. (In President Garfield's last days,
two children offered to give up their pet squirrel when they learned
the very ill Chief Executive had expressed a wish for such a dish.)

When twelve noon comes and the last tourist quits the north
portico, an air of new activity fills the rooms. Down come the velvet

barriers. Soon floor polishers and cleaners remove footprints down to the last heel mark. A long red rug is unrolled from the East Room to the State Dining Room. Vases of flowers complete the arrangements, and the White House once again becomes the private home of the President of the United States.

In the TREASURY BUILDING, at the southwest corner of Fifteenth Street and Pennsylvania Avenue, visitors are invited to examine displays in the Exhibition Room on the second floor. One case displays samples of Armed Services decorations, ranging from the Good Conduct Medal to the Congressional Medal of Honor. The Secret Service exhibit presents the revolver used by Giuseppe Zangara when he fired at President-elect Franklin D. Roosevelt and mortally wounded Mayor Anton Cermak of Chicago, at Miami on February 15, 1933. The Secret Service also displays a case of counterfeiters' equipment and some remarkable examples of bogus money, including a fifty-dollar bill thoughtlessly decorated with the head of George Washington. An illegal whisky still seized by the Alcohol Tax Unit fills a whole corner of the room. Other Treasury agencies represented by exhibits are the Bureau of Customs, the Bureau of Engraving and Printing, and the Bureau of Narcotics.

Tour III

Smithsonian Institution Group: Smithsonian Building; Arts and Industries Building: First Ladies Hall; Aircraft Building; Freer Gallery of Art; Natural History Building: Hall of North American Mammals, Hall of Birds, and Hall of Indians

SMITHSONIAN INSTITUTION GROUP: (No admission charge.) Smithsonian Building; Arts and Industries Building: First Ladies Hall; Aircraft Building; Freer Gallery of Art. This group is located between The Mall and Independence Avenue, SW. Natural History Building: Hall of North American Mammals, Hall of Birds, and Hall of Indians. This building is located between The Mall and Constitution Avenue, NW. (*Note:* Two other departments of the Smithsonian—the National Gallery of Art and the National Zoological Park—are included in separate tours.) All buildings open every day from 9:00 A.M. to 4:30 P.M.

Nowhere else in Washington or in the world, for that matter, will you get so close to so many items that have figured in the year-by-year growth of American customs and traditions as in the Smithsonian Institution. The list of what you can find in any given building is so staggering that one must be selective, indeed. The portable mahogany desk on which Thomas Jefferson wrote the Declaration of Independence—George Washington's field kit from his

Revolutionary campaigns—the American flag that waved over Fort McHenry and inspired the writing of the "Star Spangled Banner"— dresses of First Ladies of the White House from Martha Washington to Mamie Eisenhower—early steam engines, first automobiles including a "merrie Oldsmobile" and a 1903 Winton, the Wright

Smithsonian Institution

brothers' plane and Lindbergh's *Spirit of St. Louis* are only a few of the historic milestones to be found in the Arts and Industries Building.

But if from that brief list you may think the Smithsonian is largely history, then consider that archaeology, geology (the largest mineral collection in the world, including beautiful gem stones), the study of cultures of American Indians and other primitive peoples make up a large part of the Natural History Building. Too, there are new halls of mounted animals in lifelike and natural surroundings, and of birds from all over the world. If you are in quest of restorations of strange prehistoric monsters, you'll find them here, including one plant-eating dinosaur which looks rather forbidding for a vegetarian because it's seventy feet long. In the National Collection of Fine Arts are rare paintings, sculptures, ceramics, and many other choice items valued in 1955 at more than $10,000,000.

In all the buildings there are some 35,000,000 catalogued items which, for the most part, make up a priceless collection of Americana. But as you go from one exhibit to the next, you'll discover that just a portion of this vast store is in sight. Behind the scenes these old halls are jammed, literally to the rafters, waiting for new buildings into which to expand. The oldest building is now more than a hundred years old.

In 1829 the English scientist James Smithson died and bequeathed half a million dollars "to found at Washington under the name of the Smithsonian Institution, an establishment for the increase and diffusion of knowledge among men." The bequest came as a surprise, for Smithson had never visited this country. So it's not too astonishing that it took Congress eight years to decide just how to interpret the wording of the will after accepting the money. A host of schemes were suggested, further confusing and delaying the decision.

Finally Congress acted and the Smithsonian was established. The charming red-turreted central building, known as the SMITHSONIAN BUILDING, was the first of the group to go up. That was in 1852. For a time all the scientists and their families lived in apartments in the building. Joseph Henry, the first Secretary, lived in the building with his family all through the years of the Civil War. Samuel P. Langley, the third Secretary of the Smithsonian, became an aviation pioneer and had his shop outside; his planes are now on exhibit at the Institution. At the entrance to this building is a small chapel where the remains of James Smithson are entombed.

As established by Congress, a board of regents is the governing body, and a secretary directs the affairs of the Institution. The board is composed of the Vice President of the United States and the Chief Justice of the United States—one, usually the Chief Justice, acting as Chancellor—three United States Senators and three members of the House of Representatives plus six eminent private citizens.

Many Presidents have served on the board of regents: Fillmore, Johnson, Garfield, Arthur, Theodore Roosevelt, Taft, Coolidge, and Truman, as well as others illustrious in their fields, such as Louis Agassiz, Stephen A. Douglas, and Alexander Graham Bell.

The first thirty years brought in a wealth of specimens—from exploring expeditions, Government surveys of the Western frontier land, the newly established Fish Commission, and the 1876 Philadelphia Centennial Exposition where a number of exhibits had been prepared. To meet the urgent need for space, the ARTS AND INDUSTRIES BUILDING was completed in 1881. Even before it was quite finished, the lavish inaugural ball of President Garfield was held in the great hall.

By the turn of the century it was time for another building, and so in 1909 the Natural History Building was ready. A one-story aircraft building was built during World War I when the Museum's collection of historic aircraft suddenly grew. As you explore this little shedlike building today, it's well to remember that many of the Museum's famous exhibits—like the B-29 superfortress which dropped the first atomic bomb on Japan—are stored elsewhere, awaiting a larger housing arrangement in or near Washington.

If you wonder what's going on behind the walls where hammers are tapping, and corridors are temporarily closed it's pretty sure to be the birth of a new exhibit. Also, you may know the curator is not far away.

For these exhibits are ideally created first in a curator's script. It is composed as fully and dramatically as a script for a play, complete with "plot," stage directions, and lighting. (The curator is actually the playright, director, stage manager, and property man.) For the manuscript carries detailed reference not only to what specimens shall be used but stresses the underlying theme, detailing how much and how little will carry the thread of the story. (In the "Story of Power" in Arts and Industries, which was a-building for many months, the script ran to many pages, and countless specimens were examined before the right ones were selected—right in size, application, date, and a dozen other qualifications.

You may always have wondered just what a curator does. You rarely see him as you go from exhibit to exhibit. He's a very busy man. In a museum concerned with history he must know his history thoroughly, and know exactly what he wants to express in every exhibit. That's true of the curator of geology, birds, or mammals. One of his everlasting problems is: Where in creating an exhibit can the line be drawn in number and kinds of items, in order to reach the greatest number of people? If you put in too few specimens, you may bore people; if you put in too many, it's confusing. (Ideally, the specimens should be so displayed that the exhibit device is secondary.)

Aside from writing the script for the displays and supervising it to the last detail, the curator must also conduct original research on the study collection—the great portion you never see. It is through this scientific investigation that new knowledge is discovered. New life forms are made known, past geologic eras get a new chapter, as scientists behind the scenes count fish scales, bones, or grains of sand.

Perhaps the most glamorous research you'll see is in the new First Ladies Hall in the Arts and Industries Building, which took two years to complete. The display of dresses of First Ladies has always been popular. But when Mamie Eisenhower officially pressed the master switch to light up the new First Ladies Hall in May, 1955, she illuminated actual rooms in history where for the first time authentic old and new costumes belonging to First Ladies were enhanced by period settings. You may find it hard to believe that these are the same gowns you saw on an earlier visit, lined up as they were then in dimly lighted cases.

Now in a nineteenth-century music room, an old-time Blue Room, and the Red Room of the twenties—to mention only three of the eight—furnishings such as portraits, musical instruments, and wall hangings help recreate the background typical of the period. There are fascinating small details about the figures themselves: a fine pocket handkerchief tucked there, a jeweled sorority pin, a small hand-made satin bag. In the alcove cases between the rooms are many more, such as pewter-rimmed eyeglasses, or a pair of pale green silk stockings.

The idea of creating such graphic backgrounds for the dresses was not a new one. Museum officials had long recognized that the display as it stood for some forty years left much to be desired. But the needed spark that gave the new conception its start was the gift of several marble mantelpieces at the time of the White House renovation. For in the Truman administration the Executive Mansion was getting its first thorough reconstruction since the rebuilding by James Hoban in 1815 (modern architects found charred beams still in place). Before the tremendous job was completed, drastic renovation had taken place. From the East Room came wood paneling, pilasters, and molding. The Smithsonian's staff on civil history received each precious offering gratefully. It was already visualizing from these discards a partial East Room setting which, as you see it, closely approximates in many of its authentic appointments the present East Room of the White House.

Among the millions of items which the Smithsonian has accumulated over the years—intimate articles such as an old tin box of General U. S. Grant's favorite cigars as he received them during his military career—was a store of period furnishings. Many were from earlier White House redecoration. Now each piece was carefully studied for possible use.

There was the gold furniture which had been purchased in the Buchanan administration and used until the Franklin D. Roosevelts came to the White House in 1933. Mrs. Roosevelt, considering it too shabby and fragile for continued use, presented it to the Museum. Some of the pieces were badly chipped; all were losing their gilt. Rebuilding and refinishing the furniture brought up new problems.

Some staff members took a short course in restoring gold leaf. The job was not to renew the furniture, but to effect that exact condition that would denote long years of careful use. (You'll find the gold furniture in four of the First Ladies' period settings.)

In the old days, each new President was largely responsible for the redecoration of his official home, as well as the cost attached thereto. Often he brought family pieces with him. Thus, when his term of office ended, it was not unlikely that he took those new furnishings with him into private life.

While that may account for the disappearance of some White House furniture since 1800, another practice also abetted this loss. Periodically auctions were held to rid the White House of undesirable furnishings, very often the "old-fashioned" things used by previous Presidents. Indeed, an auction might well result from some casual remark as "Why don't you get some of the *new* furniture?" to a new First Lady. At one time public feeling was opposed to the use of the French furnishings introduced into the White House by the Monroes, and the Monroe descendants were able gradually to gather them up.

With high hopes of recalling some of these cherished White House pieces, which they felt might be languishing in a Pennsylvania parlor or a Midwest sitting room, Museum officials sent out a news release frankly asking for such originals to put into the new Hall. The request has not yet produced the desired reaction. Some of the possessions that were received had to be returned regretfully with the word that they did not appear on any authentic lists. But the Museum still dreams that among those who visit the First Ladies Hall and see the tremendous interest it is attracting will be some who own such treasures, who may return home and send back a valued relic to be enjoyed by a broad and appreciative segment of the public.

The figures as well as the dresses presented problems as the Hall moved toward completion.

The entire figure on which each dress is worn is made in the Smithsonian. The head is a cast of a sculptured head, the classic

Cordelia from *King Lear,* executed by Pierce Connelly during the Civil War, and all faces are meant to look alike. True enough, each has been "fatted up or leaned down" as the true size of the lady required. But discerning staff members insist that the faces have other subtle differences. Over the last four decades several different sculptors have modeled the heads, copying Cordelia's regular features faithfully, but they have mysteriously added something of themselves. (By careful study it is even possible to tell where one sculptor's work ends and another's begins.) But the power of suggestion is mostly responsible for the chance remark about a First Lady (the varying hair styles help, too): "I don't think this one is as good a likeness as that."

The dresses themselves were in excellent condition except for a few minor defects that could be repaired by the staff. But not since the display began in 1912 had the gowns been examined carefully. Now it was discovered that some had small changes that carefully disguised the original line. For example, net inserts were decorously added to a neckline that must have seemed to dip too low for the conservative first years of this century. Those little touches have been removed and First Ladies, vivacious or otherwise, are wearing their gowns as they were designed.

Understandably, hundreds of relatives of First Ladies have mingled with the crowds and studied the work done on their own particular kinfolk. Imagine what could happen if true facial likenesses had been attempted. "The mouth is much too big . . . the nose too pointed. . . . I know because my grandmother told me. . . ." It was a sure stroke of diplomacy to present the great ladies to their own families as well as to the public with those calm and gracious countenances.

To create rooms of the first fifty years, researchers in the absence of documentary photographs had to rely heavily on letters, diaries, and paintings. From 1860 on, however, photographic evidence was of great value, and some of the rooms, such as the Blue Room, drew with great fidelity on detailed old photographs. But, perhaps aside from the need for funds, which is perennial with museums, the biggest problem arose in fitting the pieces into the space allotted to each setting. The ceiling of the Hall is a full three feet lower than White House ceilings, and scale in furniture and paneling presented difficulties which were finally met.

For example, the pilasters from the East Room not only had to be cut down to fit, but one "flute" had to be removed from each to keep them in proportion. Luckily, however, the flutes thus assembled were put together to form an extra column which was needed to complete the setting.

If you follow your personal tour of the White House almost at once with a visit to the First Ladies Hall, it will add immensely to your feeling for these authentic dresses with their intimate associations and sympathetic backgrounds. Each case contains dresses representing a time span of about twenty-five years. If it surprises you to discover that some cases are crowded with First Ladies, while others less so, this springs from the sad circumstances that many wives of Presidents were physically unable to carry out their hostess duties. Thus, they and the relatives who shared such duties must be represented.

Look first to the right as you enter First Ladies Hall. You will find Abigail Adams, Martha Jefferson Randolph, and Dolley Madison joining Martha Washington as she sits beside her tea table. But the stage belongs to Mrs. Washington, for the room is completely furnished (except for the rug) with Washington possessions. The tables were once in the parlor at Mount Vernon, and the handsome red wing chair was in General Washington's bedroom. The Sheraton chairs were purchased by Washington in Philadelphia in 1797; the green patterned horsehair covers are originals. Flanking the mirror are silver Argand lamps which were said to give out such a brilliant light that dark blue chimneys were used; the oil flowed from the adjoining raised mount.

Martha Washington's dress is one of the most interesting in the entire Hall. Close scrutiny reveals that it is hand-painted. The motifs include more than fifty different tiny insects, each daintily set in a wreath or garland. So unusual was the fabric considered at one point in its early history that the seams of the gown were opened and it was used as a piano throw. Since then, however, loving hands turned fine stitches to put it back together again. Martha's little brown satin bag on her wrist, with "M. Washington" faintly visible in front, is one she made.

The figure of Dolley Madison, her hair style reflecting her love of the turban, and in a rich-looking gold ball gown, takes a favorite position. The book at her side is a copy of *Paradise Lost*. Dolley's social posture usually included a book in her hand or near by.

The Abigail Adams dress, a rather plain one, is not one she wore while in the White House (she was there barely three months), but it did belong to her.

Martha Jefferson Randolph, hostess for her father, Thomas Jefferson, is wearing her black shawl over a simple white dress. When descendants were asked if they could supply a White House gown of Mrs. Randolph's, it was disclosed that all such clothes had been cut up and remade into other garments.

Much of the porcelain, silver, and glassware, along with the painting of Great Falls by Winstanley, the English landscape artist, is from the valuable collection of Washington relics purchased by the Government from heirs of Eleanor Parke (Nelly) Custis in 1878.

This setting covers the period 1789–1817.

At the immediate right as you enter First Ladies Hall is a White House music room as it might have looked during the John Quincy Adams administration. The setting is of the period 1817–1829. The portrait of Mrs. Adams by Charles Bird King is an original and the more interesting in that the harp in the picture is the same one standing beside the mantel. The music stand and music books also belonged to the First Lady. The handsome brocatel curtains and much of the Adams memorabilia are on loan from the Adams-Clement Collection. The twin pictures on the left wall are in needlepoint worked by Mrs. Adams' mother, Mrs. Joshua Johnson.

The dress of Louisa Catherine Adams is a late example of the Empire style which was worn in this country at that period. President Monroe's daughter, Mrs. Maria Monroe Gouverneur, has on a gown that is particularly unusual. The embroidered detail is made of softened strands of wheat carefully worked into the skirt. This was the first dress received from the Monroe family. Mrs. James Monroe, wearing her own topaz necklace, has an elaborate costume. Not only is it decorated in self-fabric, but the petticoat is made of the same material, and the shoulder-high sweep of the full back is rather regal.

The adjoining alcove discloses much about Mrs. John Quincy Adams. She was well educated and much traveled, and one of the very few First Ladies who entered the White House familiar with the social demands of official life. Her open visiting book is carefully kept, showing on the left visits received and the date; on the right, visits returned. Times have changed; First Ladies do not return calls.

On to the next room on the left, which presents a reception room during the Van Buren administration. The star-spangled wallpaper was especially designed for use in this room, from a description of a White House interior of this period—"white paper sprinkled with gold stars and a gilt border." The curly maple divan is of the type popular in the early nineteenth century. The rug in this setting is especially important, for it was a gift to President Van Buren from the Imam of Muscat.

The beautiful blue velvet gown worn by Angelica Van Buren (the President's daughter-in-law, a distant relative of Dolley Madison) is probably the most popular dress among all those presented. With little change it could easily be worn as an evening dress today. Titian-haired Emily Donelson, in the earliest inaugural gown in the collection, must have been most attractive; she made a charming official hostess for her uncle, President Andrew Jackson.

This setting spans the years 1829 to 1849.

Next on the left is one of the most interesting rooms in the group.

It shows the way a Victorian parlor in the White House might have looked during the period 1849–1869.

The room is built around a white marble mantel that came out of the White House and dates back to the Franklin Pierce administration. It was removed in an effort to restore the mansion to the Federal period. The wallpaper here was actually copied from a small scrap found under layers of plaster when the wood paneling was recently removed from the State Dining Room.

In the mid-nineteenth century laminated rosewood furniture from J. H. Belter, New York cabinetmaker, was very popular. (The word "laminated" seems to be new, but the technique is an old one.) The cloverleaf sofa, the inlaid marble table, and the carpet with floral pattern were all "good" at this time.

Center of interest among the First Ladies is Harriet Lane, who acted as hostess for her bachelor uncle, President James Buchanan. Her oyster-white satin gown is exceptionally lovely. The plaid dress to the extreme left worn by Betty Taylor Bliss, daughter of President Zachary Taylor, is made of grenadine and is the earliest First Ladies' dress to have machine stitching on it.

Mary Todd Lincoln in her purple velvet wears her favorite head-dress—a wreath of flowers. The Lincoln gown has innovations more modern than you would guess. There are two bodices (like our "separates" today), the one Mrs. Lincoln is wearing for formal use, and another tailored one (not shown) for other occasions.

Martha Johnson Patterson, President Andrew Johnson's daughter, wears a white wool cloak like an Arab's burnoose. It was one of the outer garments suitable to cover the hoop skirts of the period. Abigail Powers Fillmore and Jane Appleton Pierce also appear in the setting.

Cross over to the room second on the right for the old-time Blue Room of the White House as it looked during the Grant administration. Here the dresses and background reflect the "fuss and feathers" period, 1869–1893. All the dresses have bustles, or overdrapery, and much beaded decoration. The walls, too, bear a similar influence.

The black and gold borders were taken from an early photograph of the Blue Room. This is the gold furniture that was refurbished after its long service from James Buchanan to Franklin D. Roosevelt.

If you look closely you will see that Lucy Webb Hayes wears a sorority pin—a Kappa Kappa Gamma key. Mrs. Hayes was the first college graduate to become First Lady, and the key was presented to her almost at the inception of the organization.

The setting also includes the dresses of Julia Dent Grant; Lucretia Rudolph Garfield; Mary Arthur McElroy, sister of President Chester Arthur; and Caroline Scott Harrison and Mary Harrison McKee, who represent the administration of President Benjamin Harrison.

This oval rug was woven especially for the room, to represent one shown in the photograph on which the setting was based. The black marble mantel dates from the Grant administration, but was not the one used in the Blue Room.

On to the third room on the right, where a new version of the Blue Room, as it existed during the McKinley administration, is presented.

At once the over-all elegance in the First Lady gowns finds a similar richness in the fabric-paneled walls and tasteful ornamentation. There is a feeling of wealth here, and rightly so, for this (1893–1921) is the era of the grand tour abroad, of the millionaire at home—and the White House, too, felt the trend.

The gold furniture is now upholstered to emphasize the delicate blue of the walls, and these First Ladies seem well aware that they are regally dressed.

The material in the gown worn by Mrs. Helen Herron Taft was especially sent to Japan for this handwork. The dress on Mrs. Ida Saxton McKinley, satin covered with pearls, was the dress that President Eisenhower marked as his favorite at the opening ceremony for the rooms.

The dresses of Frances Folsom Cleveland (who was married in

the Blue Room), Edith Kermit Roosevelt, Ellen Axson Wilson, and Edith Bolling Wilson complete the display.

Up to the right to the Red Room of the White House.

Velvet in a deep maroon tone covers the walls, complementing the dresses of the flapper twenties. You'll notice that Florence Kling Harding and Grace Goodhue Coolidge are the first to show their feet, as fashion lifted skirts. (Almost all the figures are on pedestal bases for better balance.) Mrs. Coolidge's velvet dress has pinned to it a Pi Beta Phi sorority pin; that First Lady put it there herself.

This is very much like the present-day Red Room with its red fabric-covered walls. The gold furniture is upholstered in oyster white. The blue porcelain vase was given especially from Mrs. Herbert Hoover's collection for use in the room.

In the alcove to the right of the Red Room are a variety of objects, including knitted bed slippers made by Mrs. McKinley, pale green silk stockings and white gloves that belonged to Mrs. Harding, and valuable gifts presented to Mrs. Woodrow Wilson by the people of Europe and brought back from the Peace Conference which she attended with the President.

The East Room across the end of the Hall is a grand finale, larger and, in its contemporary feeling, more meaningful than any other. The wall paneling, with bas-relief and pilasters, came from the East Room and was cut down to fit these dimensions.

The beautiful Siena marble mantel also came out of the East Room's recent renovation. The mirror is from the White House, and the Steinway gold piano decorated by Tiffany you may remember if you visited the White House before December, 1938. It was made for the White House in 1902.

The crystal chandelier is similar to the type found throughout the White House before the turn of the century, when gaslight fixtures were used.

Anna Eleanor Roosevelt and Bess Wallace Truman were not present at the ceremonies inaugurating the new First Ladies Hall.

But Mamie Doud Eisenhower was there and could study her figure with its bangs, the pink taffeta gown, even recognize the pearl choker, earrings, and bracelet as exactly like a set she has at the White House. (The designers made duplicate pieces which she could retain.)

As you can see, room has been left here for First Ladies yet to come.

AIRCRAFT BUILDING, west of the Arts and Industries Building. In this small building are comparatively few of the historic airplanes acquired by the Smithsonian, yet what you see is the best aeronautical collection in the world.

The fascinating development of aeronautics is recorded in extensive exhibits; historic planes such as General Billy Mitchell's *Spad XVI*; the NC4, first aircraft to fly the Atlantic, although not nonstop, and the *Excalibur III*, in which Captain Charles Blair made the first solo flight over the North Pole.

Here is the gondola of a balloon that reached the highest altitude ever attained by man. You'll find also relics from the achievements of Admiral Byrd, Wiley Post, Amelia Earhart, and many others. Old Chinese kites, acquired almost eighty years ago, mark early efforts to solve the mysteries of flight.

FREER GALLERY OF ART, corner of Independence Avenue at Twelfth, SW, just west of the Smithsonian Building. (No admission charge.)

When Charles Lang Freer of Detroit presented his unusual collection of American and Oriental art objects to the Smithsonian Institution, he also provided funds for a gallery. This is the building you see today, a Florentine Renaissance type building with three arches, and surmounted with a stone balustrade. The building was opened to the public in 1923, presenting in the American material the largest collection extant of James McNeill Whistler, plus paintings by other American artists.

Even before you reach the Oriental bronzes, paintings, sculpture, pottery, and metalwork from the Far and Near East, you'll recognize the Oriental influences in Whistler's work.

The Peacock Room is a dining room decorated by Whistler for a London shipbuilder. Whistler is said to have meant the decorations as a prank. However, the room is in the Freer Gallery, complete with the golden peacocks with crystal eyes.

Other artists among the American collection are Homer, Sargent, Tryon, Dewing, and Thayer.

In the Asiatic collection are examples of Chinese art over many centuries—paintings on album, scroll, and screen, sculptures in wood and stone, ceramics, and bronzes. One portrait on silk of the philosopher Lao-tzu is attributed to a court painter of A.D. 786–805. Exquisite landscapes in ink and soft colors on silk depict mountain retreats; others quails and grasses.

A collection of Japanese screens is most interesting, showing the decorated folding screen which, as a wall, was highly functional. One, *Pines on a Wintery Mountain*, by Yeitoku (1543–90) is particularly lovely.

NATURAL HISTORY BUILDING, Tenth and Constitution Avenue, NW.

One of these days you're bound to find yourself standing before a case in the new Hall of North American Mammals, perhaps looking on an Alpine meadow where a mother grizzly digs out a ground squirrel while her three cubs stand around in inquiring, expectant attitudes. You may even wonder how that glint was put in the mother grizzly's eye.

The morning I walked in to see William Brown, exhibit specialist and taxidermist, the big mammal exhibit was just out of the planning stage. On his desk were "blueprints," he called them—models of the cases. A few bison modeled in clay mingled with some pheasants on the file case. (On his desk was a "blue-bearded bee eater" which he himself marveled at—"probably came out of a white egg shell, at that!") When he saw me admiring a puma and some elephants, he said with a twinkle that he was expecting an elephant in the mail— just the hide.

Mr. Brown had just returned from his annual trip to gather authentic background material. This time he had been to Glacier

National Park, Montana, to get the setting for the grizzly bear group. That was in September; now outside his door in huge tanks were soil, rocks, plants, and trees which he had brought back from the site—hundreds of pounds of scenery. "It's a part of Glacier," he explained, "from the exact location on Logan Pass."

The particular spot he selected was about thirty miles out from West Glacier by automobile and trailer, and at an altitude of 6,664 feet. The site is just about at timberline and famous as old grizzly country. "The meadow was beginning to change from green to shades of brown," he went on. "Two weeks earlier there had been flowers; four weeks later, three feet of snow." In four trips to the Pass, he gathered growing specimens of Alpine fire and clumps of grass, and made numerous color photographs to capture the setting permanently for the artist's later guidance.

"The bearskins will come from Yellowstone Park," Mr. Brown explained. "The scene will show a mother grizzly digging out a ground squirrel hole—these occur about every two feet in the meadow. The little animals are like prairie dogs, popping up and standing on their hind legs and diving back into their holes. The cubs will be around the mother bear, one peering, another sitting down, and the third watching every movement."

Guided by the projected color slides, an artist first makes a preliminary sketch of the setting and the specimens of plants and trees. Then he makes a diorama (a large curved view) on a scale of two inches to the foot, very accurate in detail, which will be followed in the final painting.

That glint in the eye of the grizzly is done literally with mirrors. They are carefully embedded in rock or ground cover at strategic places, so that reflected light is beamed directly into the animal's glass eye.

These groups in the Hall of Mammals are designed primarily to show those animals which existed in pioneer times. The bison, or American buffalo, is one of the most important. Mr. Brown admits this is his favorite beast. "It was so useful to the Indians, then later to the pioneers. The Indians made tents of the skins, implements from the bones, and ate the meat.

"I was up in Bismarck, North Dakota, working on a coyote and bobcat group, and I began to think of bison," he recounted. "I knew this was once great bison country. I decided to look over some dozens of color slides made by a local professional photographer, and finally selected one of a beautiful spot in the Badlands. The next thing was to find it. I had a trapper friend up there, and I knew if anyone could find it, he could. It was quite a while before we did find it—in Slope County, North Dakota, near the Montana border. When buffalo herds were plentiful they were found in this location."

I looked at the color slide. A columnar cedar was the only object in the picture; the ground cover was typical Badlands—brown, with distant buttes low on the horizon. That was all I saw, but Mr. Brown could see bison herds thundering in the background and three magnificent specimens in the foreground (if you care to look at the thirty-foot case today).

The bison skins, tanned and soft as a kid glove, came from Montana's National Bison Range. I walked past Mr. Brown's desk back into the studio, where a big-as-life female bison was receiving a coat of shellac over a foundation of cloth and plaster. The clay model that had preceded this step had been destroyed after the quarter-inch cast was made. Now, with the cast in place, it was almost ready for the skin to be stretched over it and affixed and sewed together. Standing next to the cow was a great bull bison with its interior of wire and wood showing, waiting for the clay covering.

It was while Mr. Brown was at Yellowstone, seeing about the grizzly bears, that he made plans to modernize the elk group for the big exhibit. It had been collected out there in 1914. In the park naturalist's files he discovered a number of pictures that would provide a new and authentic setting. The scene as you see it is familiar: Gardiner area in the background; mountain peaks rise beyond a snow-covered foreground, with Mount Electric, the second highest peak, prominent.

Before the age of color slides all such documentary photographs were black and white. It took an exceptional artist, Mr. Brown said, to work from a black and white picture and turn out a colored replica authentic in atmosphere and detail. One such artist, Arthur Jansson, could do just that in those early days, and even today his backgrounds are considered excellent conceptions of locale.

Photography also has contributed a new method of making leaves in naturalistic backgrounds. By photographing one leaf—maple, beech, or quaking aspen—full scale, then coloring it, much time and expense is saved. The older method required the molding and casting of each one separately. "Now," Mr. Brown said, "five hundred or fifty can be turned out in the dark room on any mat paper for texture—and then there's the added advantage of showing the natural veining in the leaf."

He went over the plans he had for each of the cases. "The Virginia deer will be a summer group—South Carolina swamp with cypress trees and knees. . . . There will be five deer sloshing through the swamp. The caribou will be shown against an Alaskan mountain range, with a glacier stream and an outcropping stony bar in the foreground. . . . I used to drink that water . . . good and cold. I got the moose and caribou up in Alaska. The Alaskan wolf group will be on snow—three mounted wolves converging on a moose painted on the background."

There are other groups, too: a black bear scene in Pennsylvania, with very young cubs just out of hibernation, Rocky Mountain goats, Rocky Mountain sheep, pronghorn antelope, puma.

As I got up reluctantly to leave this pleasant place, Mr. Brown with a chuckle told me he liked to stump visiting ornithologists by slipping a plastic penguin bill over the slender beak of a mounted plover on his desk. "That makes 'em mighty quiet . . . they recognize the markings, the feet, the head, but that bill . . ."

I took a last look around. Among the fascinating miscellany a small plastic fish eye, hand-painted and disembodied, stared back at me. Miniature animals were grouped around the picture of a sailfish caught by President Franklin D. Roosevelt. Beyond in the workroom, a tiger with its skin carefully folded around it was getting some finishing touches to its beautifully mounted head. Smells of shellac and mothballs mingled. Birds with outstretched wings hung from the ceiling; a life-size American eagle stood on the floor. On a table lay a cast of a silver-blue fish, and just above it the magnificent tail of a peacock was pinned in full spread, until such time as its place in the new Hall of Birds should be ready.

The day I came on this new bird exhibit it had just reached the background painting stage. I cautiously rounded a corridor only to meet two huge ostriches covered with brown paper standing between two lines of unfinished cases. Artists were busy. One was putting the last strokes on a tropic scene where a hornbill of Malaya would flash its crimson beak in a lush tropic setting of thick vines. Past cans of paint, ladders, and hundreds of specimens I found Dr. Herbert Friedmann, curator, carefully working out labels to go on the many alcoves that would reveal the story.

As you see it today, the new Hall of Birds displays and groups birds of the world in many fascinating ways. For example, ten habitat groups feature birds of special interest portrayed against naturalistic backgrounds, each contrasting spectacularly with the next.

But on my visit, Dr. Friedmann pointed to the large case where penguins in sedate two-by-two's walked over the ice. "Penguins are highly adapted to life in the Antarctic—they do all their flying in the water," he said. The painted background was deceptively real, as pairs of black and white birds receded into the cold, snowy landscape.

"Ostriches are the biggest of living birds." Dr. Friedmann indicated the big unfinished case where they would go. "Theodore Roosevelt brought these specimens back from a hunting expedition in 1909." (It was on this expedition to British East Africa that the former President brought back an excellent live collection, including five lions, which added materially to the original nucleus in the National Zoological Park.)

Next came a bird whose special point of interest rose from enormous feathers patterned in shades of brown. It was the Argus pheasant, and was one of several displays in habitat groups probably unique in American museums.

Another was the exhibit demonstrating the amazing teamwork between a bird and a mammal. There the bird known as the greater honey-guide leads the honey badger to a wild bees' nest—the bird watching from a safe branch as the badger breaks into the comb, gets its fill of honey, the bees making no inroads into the thick fur. The honey-guide later sups on honeycomb and bee grubs.

Another unique habitat group is that of the palm chat of Haiti and Santo Domingo. Flocks of these small striped birds build their own communal nest; inside, each pair has its own small cubbyhole.

Facing these habitat groups you find alcoves treating different phases in the life of a bird—such as courtship; nest, eggs, and young; plumage and variation; evolution; birds in relation to man—economically, in sports and in art and legend.

In the latter group are two unexpectedly familiar ones—the Plymouth Rock and the tame duck (mallard). Economically, these two are most important as the basis of the poultry industry. In this same case a little goldfinch is dramatized beside its portrait in the reproduction of *Madonna and the Goldfinch,* by Tiepolo, the original of which hangs in the National Gallery of Art.

Don't miss the dodo, the great auk, and the Carolina parakeet (the only parrot ever native to the Eastern United States) which along with the passenger pigeon, shown in a group coming over a hilltop to alight in a tree, are among twenty or so birds which are extinct. In the same alcove are several birds just on the verge of extinction. The whooping crane is one here which is threatened with extinction, as the known number of this species dwindles.

Two large alcoves in the center of the Hall are filled with representatives of the 160 families of birds. If you have always wanted to see an oriole or some other favorite bird close enough to identify it, here is your opportunity.

Be sure to look above and see the familiar silhouettes of birds in flight painted on the ceiling of the Hall. Toward the rotunda are marine birds as you might see them from an ocean liner in the southern oceans; in the center are nine different species of hawks of the Eastern United States (particularly interesting if you plan to visit Hawk Mountain, Pennsylvania, with the fall pilgrimage of the Audubon Society), and at the other end is a large V-shaped flock of Canada geese in flight.

The new Hall of Indians of North America will fascinate you with its full-scale figures in carefully authentic groupings. Their beautiful sculptured faces, natural poses and sparkling presentation show up remarkably as they go about their daily chores or dance the snake dance.

Remembering your Western trip, you'll enjoy studying the small-scale reproduction of an Indian village in Yosemite Valley, with Half-Dome in the background. Near by is an elaborate ceremonial costume made of a deerksin decorated with woodpecker scalps (very recognizable, too). Still another display shows shell money. One yard of clamshell beads was worth $2.50 in Central California before 1880.

Another striking display, called "Lucayan Indians Discover Columbus," shows the alarm of the Indians as they looked up to find the explorer's ship coming toward them like a great white bird in the late afternoon of October 17, 1492. Ethnologist H. W. Krieger of the Smithsonian unearthed the remains of the Lucayan village on Long Island in the Bahamas, the third island Columbus visited. On San Salvador and Rum Cay, according to his journal, Columbus saw no villages.

Also in the Natural History Building is the new Colonial Hall—with something so big you can't possibly overlook it: a seventeenth-century Colonial American house. Timbers, chipped bricks, and kegs of rusty hand-forged nails of the 1678 New England structure were received; for weeks the job was one of sorting out the different pieces. Suddenly several million disturbed carpenter ants swarmed out of the cracks and crevices of the old lumber, and down the elevators. As fumigators put an end to the hordes, one veteran employee is said to have remarked, "I knew this old Museum would come to life someday."

The 8″ x 8″ crossbeams in the ceilings hang barely 5½ feet above the floor. Such ceilings doubtless conserved heat in those days. Hand-forged strap hinges are used on the front door. Authentic materials went into the Museum's reconstruction work wherever possible; plaster for one wall, true to the seventeenth-century method, had goat hair applied as a binder.

Simple, functional furnishings, with pewter, woodenware, and primitive paintings, mark the exhibit. Here are authentic living conditions of an American family of moderate means in the seventeenth and eighteenth centuries—in sharp contrast to the rich brocades and expensive appointments of Mount Vernon or Gunston Hall.

These short tours are only a brief sampling of what awaits you at the Smithsonian.

Tour IV

A Day with Lincoln

AN OLD description of Abraham Lincoln revealed him in the White House "dressed in a rather dusty suit of black," resembling "some rural tourist who had blundered into the place."

You will make your own important discoveries as you go about this Capital City, particularly as you visit a few of the places marked with happy as well as tragic associations of Lincoln's Washington years.

It might well start on a Sunday morning attending regular services at what was known as "Lincoln's Church"—the New York Avenue Presbyterian Church, at Fourteenth Street and New York Avenue, NW. (The ideal Sunday would be that closest to February 12, when special services honor this famous one-time member of the congregation.) The church was organized in 1803 at an F Street location. The present structure has been much rebuilt and enlarged over the years. Only recently the church gained wide distinction through the preaching of the late Rev. Peter Marshall. In your tour of the church, conducted after services, be sure to see the original of Lincoln's first proposal leading to the Emancipation Proclamation.

Near the church's center aisle a small plate marks the pew which the Lincolns occupied. According to old records, Mrs. Lincoln personally selected the pew from a seating chart a deacon took to her at the White House. She saw that these seats were vacant and chose them unaware that her husband's White House predecessor, James Buchanan, had only just released them.

While the pew was no different from any other during Lincoln's time, today it is distinctive. New pews since Lincoln's day have been so cut that the Lincoln pew could be joined and installed in exactly the same numbered position it occupied in the 1860's.

After the family first arrived in the city, the children went regularly with two young friends, Bud and Holly Taft, and their older sister, Julia, to the "Old Fourth Church" which stood at the corner of Ninth Street and Grant Place (opposite the present Tenth Congregational Church). The boys found the Fourth Presbyterian Church "much livelier," particularly when secessionists, after the pastor asked the Lord's blessing on the President of the United States, rose and left noisily, banging the pew doors behind them.

A detailed Sunday school treasurer's report for March, 1862, records that among the contributions was five dollars given to the Sunday school by Mrs. Lincoln—"being the amount of money found in Willie's possession at his death." Willie died in the White House at the age of twelve.

Lincoln frequently attended midweek prayer meeting in the lecture room beneath the sanctuary. But when politicians pursued the President here, too, the pastor, Rev. Phineas D. Gurley, invited him to listen from the study, leaving the door ajar. One evening two boys (one grew up to become a deacon and delighted to recall the story) saw a tall figure, silhouetted between a flickering candle and the door glass, remove his stovepipe hat and put it on the table. When the familiar figure came out the boys followed him to the White House. After that they often watched for the President on prayer-meeting night.

Not far away, at what is now 1207 New York Avenue, the little toyshop of Joseph Stuntz once stood. Here Mr. Lincoln brought energetic young Tad and they looked about, selecting brightly colored tin and wooden soldiers and captains with swords from the shelves. Just before Christmas Mr. Lincoln would come alone and pick other playthings from Stuntz's stock. (One Washingtonian remembered the "pretty little china dolls made all in one piece" that she bought there for five cents in the 1880's. She lived on L Street, but was allowed to walk alone to the shop because it was not far and the few carriages made little traffic hazard. At that time, however, Stuntz's daughter, a "middle-aged German woman," kept the shop.)

Continuing south on Fourteenth Street brings you to the Willard Hotel, which occupies the west side of the street between Pennsylvania Avenue and F Street. In Lincoln's day the hostelry was called Willard's Hotel and was run most successfully by two brothers, Henry and Joseph Willard. Since that time, the famous hotel has been much rebuilt and passed from the Willard family.

When Mr. Lincoln was elected President, Willard's was selected to put up the Presidential party for a brief time until March 4, when they would move on to the White House. A letter dated February 21, 1861, to the hotel from Ward H. Lamon, Lincoln's friend, began, "We have decided after consultation with Mr. Lincoln, that he, his family and party will stop at your house."

Mr. Lincoln's arrival occurred before daylight, as part of a plan to keep the President-elect's whereabouts secret. North and South differences had risen to such bitterness in the area, especially Baltimore, that fear was expressed for Mr. Lincoln's safety. He entered the hotel by the side entrance on Fourteenth Street, wearing "a soft crowned hat, a muffler around his neck and a short, bobtailed coat," as described by Elihu B. Washburne, the only man who met the train when it came in at the depot (then at the foot of the Capitol). Henry Willard welcomed Lincoln. The family arrived later that day, as crowds, hearing rumors, gathered around Willard's.

Staying up early and late was part of successful hotelkeeping then. Almost every day Henry Willard arose at 3 A.M. and went to old Center Market, where he personally selected provisions for the hotel. Invariably he presided over the carving table in the anteroom, especially at the dinner hour, making sure there was no waste.

Almost immediately the hotel came to Mr. Lincoln's aid in a very personal way. He soon discovered his comfortable slippers had been overlooked in packing, and he needed something to change into. Henry Willard could think of none in the hotel large enough, but his wife's grandfather was visiting across the street and was delighted to send his extra-large slippers to the President-elect. The slippers, with a handwritten note of the incident on the back of one, have been handed down as treasured heirlooms in the Willard family.

That Henry Willard had a special gift for meeting emergencies was apparent on another day when a slight fire broke out on one of the hotel's five floors. A panicky guest rushed to the office shouting, "Mr. Willard, the hotel is on fire! Where is it? Where is it?" Calmly, Mr. Willard summoned a bellboy. "John," he said, "will you take the gentleman upstairs and show him the fire?"

Today as you stroll through "Peacock Alley" you can read the large plaque near the lobby commemorating the writing of "The Battle Hymn of the Republic" by Julia Ward Howe.

On down to the Smithsonian's Arts and Industries Building, you'll find in the Lincoln case a model for "A Device for Buoying Vessels over Shoals," on which a patent was granted to Lincoln in 1849. The model is one he whittled for his invention prompted when two boats he was on ran aground.

A next stop might take you to the United States Capitol where Gutzon Borglum's colossal marble head of Lincoln stands in the Rotunda. It was presented in 1908 by Eugene Meyer, Jr.

As you examine this powerful study of Lincoln, you discover a remarkable fact: the sculptor has chosen to emphasize the right side of Lincoln's face, seeming to slight the left. In a letter to a Congressional committee, Borglum wrote: "Lincoln's face was so much more developed on the right side that I have carved this head in the same way—that is, developing that side. . . ."

Robert Lincoln, in a note to Borglum, called the head "the most extraordinarily good portrait of my father that I have ever seen."

Also in the Rotunda is the marble statue of Lincoln by Vinnie Ream acquired by purchase in 1871.

On the gallery floor in the Senate wing of the Capitol, is a marble bust of Lincoln purchased in 1868—the work of Sarah Fisher Ames. In the old Supreme Court chamber is the celebrated painting, *The First Reading of the Emancipation Proclamation,* by Francis Bicknell Carpenter. It shows Lincoln's Cabinet in the White House.

The first public monument erected in Washington to Lincoln's memory is in the court of the old City Hall, on Indiana Avenue between Fourth and Fifth streets, NW. It was executed by Lot Flannery, who had known Lincoln personally, and was dedicated in the rain on April 15, 1868.

Another statue, the Emancipation Monument, you will find over on East Capitol Street in a small square called Lincoln Park. The monument is the work of Thomas Ball and was paid for through voluntary subscription by emancipated Negroes. It was unveiled in 1876.

The next important stop might be at the Lincoln Museum in old Ford's Theater, on Tenth Street between E and F Streets, NW. The Museum is open 9:00 A.M. to 9:00 P.M. Monday through Saturday, 12:30 P.M. to 9:00 P.M. Sunday and holidays; admission charge: 10 cents.

The old theater, where the Lincolns attended a performance of *Our American Cousin* the night of the assassination, contains thousands of relics gathered from many sources and exhibited in cases and along the walls. There is a miniature reproduction of Ford's Theater as it was on that Good Friday night of 1865. By pushing a button you may hear a recording of details of the tragedy. On the floor of the museum are a man's footprints, leading from the outlined edge of the theater box to the diagramed door, following the path of John Wilkes Booth, assassin, as he jumped, fell, and made his escape.

A part of the collection was assembled by Osborn H. Oldroyd over a lifetime and later purchased by the United States Government. Political overtones are many. The Republican "Wide-Awakes," in the campaign that elected Lincoln, ironed out some problems before leaving for Washington. One member wrote: "What arrangements have you made for our meals? Will it be necessary for us to bring coal oil and our torches?" There's a political prop that was used in the campaign—a fence rail made by Lincoln in 1830.

But tragedy is the dominant note here. There is much documentary evidence of Booth's association with Dr. Samuel A. Mudd, and of his mad ride southward from Washington—such as the slit boot, and the red pocket compass upon which Booth spilled candle grease as he tried to read it while crossing the Potomac at night. The Museum will sell you a booklet with map of Booth's escape route, if you should care to follow it yourself. Also for sale are photostatic copies of the New York *Herald's* Saturday edition, with long columns about the assassination.

There is always a special ceremony in the Museum on February 12, to honor the memory of Lincoln on his birth date, and the meeting is open to the public. Year after year, some of the same oldsters attend. Many are members of a local organization known as the Lincoln Group of the District of Columbia, and some have hiked the trail that Booth followed before he crossed over into Virginia.

Directly across Tenth Street is the Petersen House, called the House Where Lincoln Died, where the mortally wounded President was taken from the theater (open 9:00 A.M. to 5:30 P.M. weekdays, 12:30 P.M. to 5:30 P.M. Sunday and holidays; admission charge: 10 cents). Even today it is a sad little house, seemingly bowed down under the weight of its history. The bed similar to the one on which Lincoln died almost fills the room, and yet it was too small for his long, gaunt form. (Rocking chairs, old-time pictures, pitcher in basin, and Victorian furnishings will take you back to old rooms you have known.)

Final grim and relentless reminders of the death of Lincoln are in the Army Medical Museum at Ninth Street and Independence Avenue, SW, just south of the Smithsonian Building. (Open daily and Sunday 9:00 A.M. to 5:00 P.M.; no admission charge.)

Out of the Medical Museum's records have come the results of the autopsy, and a sketch of the deathbed scene made by Hermann Faber, then medical artist of the museum. Faber's sketch captures the group of more than two dozen men in attitudes of hopeless waiting. There are the blood-stained cuffs of Dr. E. Curtis, who with Dr. J. J. Woodward performed the autopsy; a splinter of bone from Dr. Curtis's surgical probe, and a bit of Lincoln's dark hair.

Another and happier stop is at the Corcoran Gallery of Art, at Seventeenth Street and New York Avenue, NW. On your way glance at the buff-colored Blair House on Pennsylvania Avenue opposite the old State Department Building; the Civil War President occasionally stopped in here to see Montgomery Blair, his Postmaster General. The baroque old State Department Building is now occupied largely by White House executive offices (since the location of the new State Department Building on Virginia Avenue in Foggy Bottom). On this site in Lincoln's day, however, was also located the War Department, and both day and night the President could be seen anxiously visiting the Army telegraph office that had been set up inside.

Once at the Corcoran, ask to see the Healy portrait of Lincoln, recently restored and relatively unknown. This painting was executed from life by George Peter Alexander Healy, one of the foremost artists of his time, about ten days after Lincoln's election to the Presidency. It presents a beardless Lincoln, young-looking for his fifty-one years, and the eyes are alight with a special feeling—a sense of the man "standing on the threshold." Lincoln sat for the portrait probably no more than three times in mid-November, 1860, in a large chamber in the Statehouse in Springfield, Illinois. (Discover the interesting "ghost image" where the artist painted over the left cheekbone. As the paint grows translucent with age, the two contours show.)

Years later, Healy recalled that his sitter—with whom he was immediately congenial—mentioned a young correspondent who would have him grow whiskers to hide his lantern jaws. "Will you paint me with whiskers? No? I thought not." (It was only a few days later that Lincoln told his barber to give his whiskers a "chance to grow.")

A visitor who looked in on this scene later wrote: ". . . he [Lincoln] chatted, told stories, laughed at his own wit—and the humor of others—and in one way and another made a couple of hours pass merrily and never once lost his dignity or committed himself to an opinion. . . ."

Healy's work was quick and sure; Mrs. Lincoln approved of it, and Thomas B. Bryan, wealthy Chicago land promoter and art collector, liked it. It was Bryan who had commissioned the portrait to add to his growing collection of Presidents, all by the same artist. Then in 1879 the Washington philanthropist, W. W. Corcoran, wrote Healy: "I have just purchased from Bryan your collection of portraits of the Presidents."

Like a case history, the details unfold in the Gallery's records. William MacLeod, curator, next noted that the Lincoln portrait arrived April 26, 1879. It followed by a day the arrival of sixteen other Presidential portraits. After a time the feeling for Healy paintings began to wane, and the collection was taken down to make room for more current favorites. The Gallery adopted a policy which sent the pictures on loan to those city schools bearing Presidents' names, and March, 1926, found the Lincoln hanging in the Abraham Lincoln School for colored children at Second and C streets, in Southeast Washington.

Not until 1943 were the portraits recalled to the Corcoran. The beardless Lincoln was fresh from the hands of the Gallery's expert restorer when a Washington art historian, Katharine McCook Knox, came across it. So impressed was she by its sensitive delineation of character that she not only set about unraveling the tangled history behind it, but made plans to have the best possible color reproduction made of it, to sell for a nominal sum. After months of negotiations with a Dutch firm, there is now available an almost life-size full-color reproduction. It costs two dollars, and can never be priced higher. (One young father came here, studied the portrait, and bought the print, saying, "I have been looking for something to hang in my son's room—something that he can grow up with. I won't find anything better than this.")

The final moments of your Lincoln tour—and these will probably come in late evening—should find you at the beautiful Lincoln

Memorial (not far as you proceed south on Seventeenth Street and west on Constitution Avenue, toward Memorial Bridge).

The Lincoln Memorial is open from 9:00 A.M. to 9:00 P.M. daily, and is closed only on Christmas Day. But any time you walk or drive by you can look up and see the quiet figure seated inside,

Memorial Bridge Approach, Looking West

beneath a soft diffused light if it's between 9:00 P.M. and midnight, or stronger, more direct illumination if the hour is earlier.

This Memorial, one of the world's most beautiful, was many years coming. Two years after Lincoln's death, Congress approved the incorporation of the Lincoln Monument Association—but years slipped by with no results. Even after Congress in 1911 directed through legislation that a memorial to Lincoln be erected, there were many stumbling blocks. People proposed various kinds: some wanted a memorial highway from Gettysburg to Washington; others suggested a memorial hospital. But the Lincoln Memorial Commission felt that the memorial should be purely and simply that— quite without outside aspects. Finally, the newly conceived Commission of Fine Arts, working with the Commission, recommended that the memorial take the form of a monumental building.

The question of site came up. When the present site was recommended, it was just a low-lying marsh. Joe Cannon, Speaker of the House and a member of the Commission, said he would never agree to placing a memorial to such a great man in the middle of a swamp. It took an artist's presentation of the finished memorial and its surroundings finally to convince Uncle Joe. (It was on or near the spot that Dr. William Thornton planted saplings and bushes about 1800, convinced that deposits from the Potomac would more speedily fill up this "flat." Later called the "Kidwell flats," the area figured in a celebrated legal dispute which the Government won.)

In order to ensure that the heavy Memorial would never sink through the filled-in ground, concrete pillars were put down to rest firmly on the bedrock which engineers had found forty-four to sixty-five feet below the original ground level.

The approved plan included not only the Memorial building, but the gracious approach to the Memorial Bridge (then not yet constructed) and the Reflecting Pool stretching out to capture the Washington Monument's image. Henry Bacon was the architect. Daniel Chester French was the sculptor of the famous seated figure of Lincoln.

Ground was broken February 12, 1914, and the completed Memorial was dedicated eight years later.

Each of the thirty-six Doric columns you see around the exterior walls represents a State in the Union at the time of Lincoln's death; the frieze above the colonnade names those States.

Twenty-eight blocks of white Georgia marble were used in the nineteen-foot statue. Yet beneath the misty lighting in the inner quiet, the stone mysteriously loses its cold reality. Gazing at Lincoln, you almost expect the hands to relax, the brooding, intent face to soften. This is a hallowed place; many come again and again to stand here, read the Gettysburg Address engraved on the south wall, and reflect again on this man's greatness.

On February 12, 1954, a little girl posted a letter in Chicago. It was addressed to "Former President A. Lincoln, Lincoln Tomb, Washington, D.C."—one of many so addressed that reach the Capital each year around Lincoln's birthday. It read:

> DEAR ABE LINCOLN:
> I admire you very much. I
> have studied about you in school.
> I watch your programs on television.
> I know you are dead, but you still
> dwell in my heart.
>
> > Sincerely yours,
> > LINDA RAE BOCK

Tour V

Supreme Court, Capitol, Library of Congress, Folger Shakespeare Library

SUPREME COURT, First Street and Maryland Avenue, NE. Open 9:00 A.M. to 4:30 P.M. Monday through Friday, 9:00 A.M. to noon Saturday. Conducted tours every 15 minutes except when court is in session. Last tour week days at 3:45 P.M. Last tour Saturday at 11:45 A.M. Closed Sunday and holidays.

At eleven o'clock on a Monday during the months in which the Supreme Court of the United States is in session is the time to schedule this visit, if possible. Then you will see opinions being handed down by this famous tribunal—and it is one of the Capital's most unforgettable scenes. It is the more memorable because photographs of the sessions are prohibited, and your "eye view" is the only record you can take away with you.

The term of the Court begins on the first Monday in October, the day fixed by law, and closes about the first of June. Those eight months are usually fairly well divided between hearing of cases and periodic recesses. Sittings last about two weeks, in which time twenty-five or thirty cases are either argued or submitted on briefs; during alternate intervening recess periods (generally of two-week duration) the Court is occupied in study and writing of opinions. Thus, there are Mondays during the term when the Court is not sitting, and often on other weekdays the Court may not sit, so be sure to call or drop a card to the Clerk of the Court for schedule information. The schedule for the new term is usually available before October 1.

This white marble building was especially designed on lines of noble scale as indeed a symbol of "the national ideal of justice." Dignity and beauty are expressed in the Greek style of architecture, Corinthian order; marble—Vermont almost exclusively for the exterior—was considered the most suitable material.

Cass Gilbert, Cass Gilbert Jr., and John R. Rockart designed the building, and David Lynn, Chief Architect of the Capitol, aided in its successful completion in 1935. (Not the least remarkable fact about this structure is that not only did building costs stay within the appropriation made by Congress for this purpose, but furnishings as well came out of the sum, with money left over.)

Before you go inside to view the nine chairs behind the long mahogany dais known as The Bench, take a moment to observe the nine figures sculptured in the pediment above the main entrance. Liberty Enthroned is in the center, guarded by Order on her right and Authority on her left. The remaining figures represent Council and Research, and here the sculptor, Robert Aitken, is believed to have drawn on historical and living subjects for his symbolic types. There are Chief Justice Charles Evans Hughes and the sculptor himself as Council figures on the right. On the left is the designer, Cass Gilbert, with the statesman Elihu Root. Representing Research are John Marshall, our first Chief Justice, and William Howard Taft, the only President of the United States to serve as Chief Justice of the Supreme Court.

You will be in the audience before the impressive entrance of the black-robed Justices, with time to notice the rich red velour hangings blending with twenty-four columns of tinted Siena marble.

At 11:55 A.M. two page boys emerge from behind the hangings and pull back the Justices' chairs. One at the left is left in place, but angled so that it faces the Chief Justice's central spot.

Two minutes later, the Clerk of the Court sits down at his desk just to the right of The Bench.

On the stroke of noon, a gavel bangs and the Court Crier calls out sonorously, "The Honorable Chief Justice and the Associate Justices of the Supreme Court of the United States!"

Kicking up their long black robes behind them, the Justices in order of their seniority file into the room as the audience stands.

"Oyez, oyez, oyez!" The Crier raises his voice again. "All persons having business before the Honorable, the Supreme Court of the United States, are admonished to draw near and give their attention, for the Court is now sitting. God save the United States and this Honorable Court."

If this is the opening of the new term on the first Monday of October, the business includes the formal admission of lawyers to practice before the high bench. Tradition guards every move—and almost never are there innovations. However, at the start of the 165th term in 1955, there were several concessions to modernity. A tape recorder had been installed to give the Justices a record of oral arguments. Important to reporters and visitors both, a loudspeaker system has enabled everyone in the room to hear the arguments. Individual microphones are available to each Justice as well as to the attorneys at the lectern in front of The Bench.

The October opening session is brief but usually brings out many prominent political figures as well as their wives, and you may find yourself standing in the corridor craning for a view of the proceedings. But should your visit come when the Court is in summer recess, there is an advantage, too. You can walk through the deserted Court Chamber and listen to the guide cover in minute detail the Court procedure. The guide also elaborates on the rich appointments of this beautiful building.

During sessions the Justices enjoy unusual privacy. Convenient to the Court but out of sight are the suites of the Chief Justice and Associate Justices, their Conference and Robing Rooms. On the second floor is their private dining room. The Justices arrive in automobiles which follow a special ramp to the basement, ignoring the steep front entrance, and a private elevator carries them to their rooms above, off corridors the public never sees.

Although the Supreme Court has occupied this site since 1935, the location is famous for an earlier structure. During the restoration of the Capitol following the War of 1812, a building was hastily thrown up here to forestall any action to remove the Capitol and Federal City. It came to be known as "the old Brick Capitol." Congress met in the small building until its permanent fire-scarred rooms in the Capitol were rebuilt under direction of Benjamin H. Latrobe.

CAPITOL OF THE UNITED STATES, on Capitol Hill. Open 9:00 A.M. to 4:30 P.M. daily and Sunday. Open after 4:30 P.M. if Congress is in session, until one-half hour after adjournment. Tours 9:00 A.M. to 3:55 P.M.; groups form every 15 minutes. Guide service: 25 cents.

If you have but one day in Washington and spend it all in the United States Capitol, seeing nothing else, you still will have a most valuable capsule of history that will expand in retrospect.

Your tour may start or finish with the Rotunda, churning with people. You'll study the mural frescoes of Constantino Brumidi, whose single masterpiece, *Apotheosis of Washington,* in the "eye" of the dome is reason enough for his being called the Michelangelo of the Capitol. Just above eye level are John Trumbull's famous historical paintings which he enlarged from 30″ x 20″ originals to help restore the Rotunda after the British partially destroyed the Capitol in 1814. (Trumbull painted the miniatures as a young man— when he dreamed of being the historical painter of the American Revolution.) The four paintings on the east wall represent the pre-Revolutionary period.

Off to the left in Statuary Hall you'll find all is dignity today except for a few persistent echoes, as compared with an earlier scene. For more than fifty years the House of Representatives met here, but when it moved in 1857 to its present large south chamber, for a brief time all was bedlam as peddlers hawked their wares at "apple stands," even hauling over worn wooden floors their carts loaded with gingerbread, oranges, and root beer.

All four great stairways have fine canvases, but in the House west wing stairway to the galleries hangs the panorama, *Westward the Course of Empire Takes Its Way,* by Emanuel Leutze. It shows an emigrant wagon train struggling over a high Rocky Mountain pass.

It was painted during the Civil War, under contract, in an effort to increase public confidence in the Government.

Soon you will visit the Senate or House to watch legislators of television and newspaper familiarity grow very real. Just above and behind the rostrum in either chamber you will recognize the press gallery, and perhaps some of your favorite by-liners will drop into a seat, listen for a while, and hustle out. You might treat yourself to a bowl of the Capitol's famous bean soup in the dining room. More memories of the day may include a ride on the monorail subway from the Capitol to the Senate Office Building, and a visit to the office of your Senator or Congressman.

Now you may seek a quiet corner where you can sit down and sort out your impressions, to savor again the anecdotes and human-interest touches your guide adroitly wove into his talk. Crossing to the little park opposite the east entrance, you'll have an opportunity to do this as well as study the silhouette cherished by those who never saw it finished, yet whose minds and hands went into its building.

Those United States flags whipping in the breeze are both symbolic and informative. Flags flying over the House and Senate wings (extreme left and right extensions as you face the east front) signify that each body is in session. Colors at the west and east entrances fly at night also—two of a very few United States flags permitted to fly at night in peacetime.

A fifty-two foot lantern built between the dome and the lofty Statue of Freedom sends out a powerful beam when Congress goes into night session. You are pretty sure to see its gleam in July when the lawmakers begin to push toward adjournment.

As you face this east front, look for a small round window high in the old north wing, the first unit ready for Congress to move into from Philadelphia in 1800. One long-time Washingtonian, who came here as a child, recalls how she used to sit up in that little lookout to watch the Presidential inaugurations just below.

"I was a big girl before I knew it wasn't Papa's Capitol," she said.

Her father for many years was superintendent of the Senate Document Room.

It was in this old north wing that Congress met and John Adams, second President, addressed the first joint session. Here in that same year Washington's first important political deadlock was resolved. That was the contested Presidential election in which Thomas Jefferson and Aaron Burr received equal votes, and the House had to decide which man would be President and which Vice President.

After the Senate moved in 1810 to occupy the completed Senate Chamber above, with the House of Representatives already occupying the south wing, heated differences grew over the Missouri Compromise. The question was whether Missouri should be admitted into the Union as a pro-slavery State.

In 1830 Senator Daniel Webster of Massachusetts and Senator Robert Hayne of South Carolina had their famous clash over the "nullification" question, and on one historic day Webster cried out his deathless "Liberty *and* union, now and forever, one and inseparable!"

Those were some of the forensic fireworks of the day. The deep red draperies, Greek-amphitheater style of the room, and gray-green Potomac marble columns made a dramatic setting for the great oratory, the finger-wagging, the floor-pacing.

In the old room today there is a picture showing it as it was in 1850, with each Senator's place marked on a chart near by. That was twenty-four years after Secretary of State Henry Clay challenged John Randolph of Roanoke to a duel, for accusing the Secretary of forgery on the floor of the Senate. (The two gentlemen fought it out near the west end of Chain Bridge, and both came out of the encounter whole.) The Chamber held the Supreme Court of the United States from 1860 to 1935, when the Court moved to its own great building.

The Capitol's physical history started one Wednesday morning, September 18, 1793, with the laying of the cornerstone in the southeast corner of that same north wing. The Masonic ceremony attending it was one of great solemnity, as carefully reported a week later in the *Columbian Mirror and Alexandria Gazette.*

The official march began after ten o'clock when Masonic officials and members congregated and "there appeared on the southern banks of the Grand River, Potomack, one of the finest companies of Volunteer Artillery that has been lately seen, parading to receive the President of the United States who shortly came in sight with his suite." Saluted and met on the shores of Maryland, the party proceeded to the President's park and from that point "the procession marched two-abreast, in the greatest solemn dignity with music playing, drums beating, colours flying, and spectators rejoicing . . . to the Capitol in the City of Washington where the Grand Marshall ordered a halt."

The ceremony, with George Washington officiating and the Volunteer Artillery frequently punctuating the speechmaking with booming salutes, then got under way. The official party included, among many, the Surveying Department, the Mayor and Corporation of Georgetown, Commissioners, stonecutters, mechanics, and Masonic leaders. Afterward the whole company retired to an extensive booth "where an ox of 500 lbs. weight was barbacued, of which the company generally partook. . . . The festival concluded with 15 successive volleys from the Artillery."

On paper the Capitol was already very real. A competition had been announced and advertised offering "a lot in the city, to be designated by impartial judges, and $500, or a medal of that value," to anyone who before July 15, 1792, could produce "the most approved plan for a Capitol" to be erected, "and $250 or a medal for the plan deemed next in merit." A similar competition was arranged for a plan for the President's house.

While the gifted Irishman James Hoban won the latter with his plan for the Executive Mansion, the numerous drawings submitted for the Capitol fell sadly short of Jefferson's and Washington's hopes. The only contestant to make a favorable impression was a Frenchman named Étienne Hallet; he was asked to come to Washington and discuss his designs, with a view to improving them for possible use.

Then, about three months after it officially closed, a young physician entered the competition. He was William Thornton, born in the Virgin Islands and educated in the British Isles, where he received a degree in medicine. He was no scientist, yet by the time he was thirty he had joined in John Fitch's experiments in propelling steamboats with a paddle device. By his own offhand confession Dr. Thornton was no architect, yet he had won a prize with his design for a building for the Library Company of Philadelphia. Explaining his successful technique, he said: "I got some books and worked a few days, then gave a plan in the ancient Ionic order, which carried the day."

Just as the young Federal City had attracted Pierre Charles L'Enfant with his great talents, so did it continue to draw to it others with genius and great versatility. In Dr. Thornton's design for the Capitol, to quote the President's words, "Grandeur, simplicity, and convenience appear to be so well combined" that there would be no difficulty in getting official approval from the Commissioners.

Dr. Thornton went on to design many other Washington landmarks, including The Octagon and Tudor Place. In 1802 Jefferson placed him in charge of patents over which he functioned as superintendent until his death in 1828. (A small group of Washingtonians interested in the early Federal City call themselves the Thornton Society, and meet periodically to listen to speakers reveal more of the city's past.)

Hallet was awarded a kind of consolation prize, the same sum and a lot in Washington that Thornton received, but he was still second best, a circumstance that made him extremely critical of the winning plan. He was finally discharged from his position as superintendent of construction by the Commissioners; yet he had been the ablest contestant. Before connections were severed, however, Hallet had left his own mark forever on the Capitol. The great dome, and wings extending from the central portion, are much as shown on Hallet's drawing.

The parade of promising architects and engineers upon the scene was well under way. Young George Hadfield (whose beautiful sister, Maria Cosway, had been found to be so charming by Thomas Jefferson while in Paris in 1786) came as Superintendent of the Capitol in 1795. He was dismissed three years later for failing to follow Thornton's plan; yet he, too, contributed.

Despite labor shortages and personality clashes, the small rectangular building which is the old north wing was ready in 1800 for the two bodies of Congress.

The work continued (with Thornton in charge until 1802) as others, including the White House architect James Hoban, contributed skill and knowledge. Benjamin H. Latrobe, second Architect of the Capitol, was responsible for carrying to completion the two wings of the original building; after several years of private endeavors, he went on to rebuild the Capitol after the War of 1812. He resigned in 1817 as Architect of the Capitol. The unusual "cornstalk columns" and "corncob capitals" in the ground floor vestibule of this old north wing are by Latrobe. He wrote to Thomas Jefferson on August 28, 1809, that "these capitals during the summer session obtained me more applause from Members of Congress than all the works of magnitude that surround them." Above, in the small Rotunda, is a similar Latrobe design of two rows of tobacco leaves forming classic crownlike capitals.

To Charles Bulfinch, third Architect of the Capitol, is given credit for constructing the central portion, the Rotunda and the dome, a small wooden one covered with copper. This low dome in the mid 1820's was an important step toward the Capitol's completion.

Even so, it was a slow business. In the House proceedings of February 23, 1827, one Member rose to his feet and said: "It is a curious fact, sir, I occasionally meet, in my district, old men who worked upon this building in their youth, who are utterly astonished to learn that the Capitol is still unfinished. Why is it that this

Nation, with all its resources, has been unable to finish this house in a period of thirty years?"

In 1855 Congress authorized replacement of the low dome with a larger one according to the plans of Architect of the Capitol Thomas U. Walter, who was already working on sizable extensions to provide more space for the House and Senate. Photographs of Lincoln's inauguration in 1861 show the unfinished dome—and, despite wartime shortages, work continued.

The bronze Statue of Freedom created by Thomas Crawford, on a scale of three times life size, would take position at the very pinnacle above the lantern. (The figure in five sections was hoisted up by derricks in the middle of the Rotunda, straight through the eye of the dome and the lantern by way of inside scaffolding, then bolted in place.)

A fitting tribute to the Capitol's completion took place at exactly high noon on December 2, 1863. Dramatically the great helmeted headpiece was hoisted up and slipped into place. An ear-splitting thirty-five gun salute was fired. Cannon boomed from twelve of the forts circling wartime Washington and the American flag floated over Freedom's head.

From the beginning there were those who for public or private reasons disliked the Potomac site and seized every opportunity to promote other localities. A prominent source of irritation was that large numbers of livestock seemed to roam the city with greater freedom than in other metropolitan centers. One Senator was so enraged when he viewed the destruction wrought upon his Massachusetts Avenue lawn by a rooting old sow that he declared publicly, "I am going to introduce a bill to have the Capitol removed!"

Similar intentions have been declared by other lawmakers, but there on its modest hill the Capitol of the United States still stands.

LIBRARY OF CONGRESS, First Street between East Capitol and B Streets, SE. Exhibit halls open 9:00 A.M. to 10:00 P.M. Monday through Saturday; 11:30 A.M. to 10:00 P.M. Sunday. Tours begin Monday through Friday, at 9:15, 10:00, and 11:00 A.M., and 1:00, 2:00, 3:00, and 4:00 P.M.

City planner L'Enfant must have slept uneasily in the 1890's when the massive main building of the Library of Congress was going up. There it was, practically nudging the Capitol—and the Frenchman had been very firm in his plan that Congress House should hold pre-eminence on the city skyline. Architecturally, though, its gray sandstone Italian Renaissance grandeur now blends in more happily with the Capitol dome than with the chaste lines of its modern white marble Annex across the street.

(Library of Congress facilities were different in 1852. This public notice appeared concerning the space given to the Library in the Capitol: "The old Library-room has been cleared, an iron-framed roof replacing the old wooden one; the alcoves and shelving for books are entirely of ornamental cast-iron, leaving nothing for fire to operate on.")

As you climb the steps or enter at ground level of the main building, consider the magnitude of a mythical newsboy's job, dropping papers at this big door. Each day more than fifteen hundred newspapers come in here. Some fifteen thousand books arrive in the mail room in any day.

The best way to see the Library is to join one of its free guided tours, taking about forty minutes. Available long-time employees are channeled into the business of showing off their Library, for there is no commercial guide service. You come away with a sense of learning, plus the feeling that it must be a privilege to work in the Nation's Library.

One day when I was there about twenty green-clad Girl Scouts, all ten- and twelve-year-olds, came up the steps with their two mother-sponsors. They had eaten lunch on the lawn outside, and now in a body they yielded the remnants of brown paper bags, Coke bottles, and candy wrappers to the wastebasket at the guard's desk. Then off they went, ebbing and flowing around the tall, white-haired guide like a bubbling green wave. When the guide pointed to the twenty-two-carat gold ceiling in the Great Hall, they were awed, and they exclaimed aloud when he said, "This is probably the world's largest library."

Among the permanent exhibits on the second floor are those you have long heard about. Here is the first draft of Lincoln's Gettysburg Address—and the second draft, from which he read during those hushed few moments at the battlefield.

Here is Thomas Jefferson's "rough draft" of the Declaration of Independence, bearing small changes by Benjamin Franklin and John Adams. (The engrossed and signed copy is on display in the National Archives, along with the Constitution of the United States.)

You'll probably be surprised, too, to discover that the renowned Gutenberg Bible—first major book to be printed from movable metal type—is in three volumes. Special guard protection is provided this exhibit, day and night. This is one of the three perfect vellum copies known to exist; aside from these, all others on vellum have been found imperfect.

This copy—printed about 1450–55—belonged to the Order of the Benedictines. On the flyleaf of each volume is the bookplate of the Benedictines of Saint Blasius in the Black Forest. During the Napoleonic Wars the monks removed the Bible and prized books to other houses of the order in Switzerland and Austria. The Bible remained in the Abbey of Saint Paul in Austria until 1930, when it came to the Library of Congress.

Mystery still surrounds its beginnings. The name Johannes Gutenberg appears nowhere in the Bible. Yet bibliographers all agree that the city of Mainz was where it was produced, that Gutenberg was the acknowledged inventor of the process of printing from such type. Other contemporary evidence added to that has prompted the name Gutenberg Bible.

The rich detail of the hand-written Giant Bible of Mainz near by is equally fascinating. Your guide will tell you that "hides of 250 goats were used to complete it." You'll notice that the book is open to a page not yet finished. The hand illumination of one corner in gold was interrupted, and waits, unmindful that centuries are slipping away.

Among the Library's priceless possessions not on exhibition is

Pierre Charles L'Enfant's famous plan of Washington. It is in the Map Division—with 2,300,000 other maps and views.

As you go from one floor to the next, you may discover that there are study rooms available for those doing advanced research. There are 270 such rooms, each in great demand. Those I saw were sunny, glassed-in cubicles, with doors to shut scholars off from the sounds of traffic along distant corridors or conversation at tables in the open areas.

Several steps are necessary to obtain any kind of study space. If you are a graduate student doing serious research on a master's degree, your approved request may bring you a shelf. There your books will be held undisturbed thirty days as you come and go. This is a great convenience, but only the beginning of the Library's special research facilities.

With your master's degree or an equivalent behind you, it may now be your intention to do research on your doctoral dissertation. (Or you may be a historian working on a book.) Your application will acquaint the Chief of the Stack and Reader Division with your plans and, too, persuade him that you can finish your research within a reasonable and stated length of time. If approved, this finds you lined up, often desk-to-desk in an open room, or along a wall, set apart from readers by screens. For this privilege there is often a long waiting list.

But suppose you are working on an official research project for a Congressman or a Congressional committee. Your application for space will probaby get you the first study room to become available. For this is, primarily, the Library *of Congress*. It was started in 1800 with an appropriation of five thousand dollars and allocation of space in the unfinished Capitol, to provide library facilities for the members of Congress.

Applications for special working space may mention such topics for advanced study as the history of Southern Asia, Buddhistic influence on German thought, or the impact of American agriculture on modern France.

Available for students, and popular too, are a number of coin-operated typewriters. Drop a dime in the little slot and the keys will operate for thirty minutes. Then, no matter how lucid your prose or how heavy your touch, the machine won't write another word without a dime to encourage it.

Your tour will take you down to the Control Room, where books are consigned for distribution. Through pneumatic tubes books whoosh to the Capitol or to the Annex. It takes about thirty seconds for a metal container bearing six or eight medium-sized volumes to cover two blocks in the air-powered tube, from station to station.

Your tour will probably skirt some desks where, year in, year out, thousands of inquiries are read and answered. Letters ask for all sorts of help, such as figures on population or a quiz book on Presidents. Some come from misinformed high school students who think this is a circulating library, which it decidedly is not. (Only members of Congress and Government agencies are privileged to "withdraw" books—that is, to take them out of the Library.) One little girl wanted "everything you have on Yosemite," for a term paper; a sculptor in St. Louis wanted two good pictures of Will Rogers; a bartender in Canada wanted books on his trade, plus wine lists from "the best places in the USA."

Somewhere along the tour your guide may correct another popular misconception—that "the Library of Congress has every book that was ever published in this country." Rather, it has a *selection* of all books printed here—a selection the Library largely makes itself. It results from the copyright law's requirements that two copies of each new book published (plus four dollars) must be deposited with the Library to obtain a copyright certificate. Some of this great number are retained. But this has been one of the great sources of material, for it includes not only books but maps, photographs, prints, motion pictures, etc. Gifts and exchange bring in between three and four million items each year, but not all are added to the permanent collections.

Stand on the Visitors' Gallery and look down upon the magnificent Reading Room, with its lighted reading lamps tracing circu-

lar patterns. All those people, so absorbed, so intent, as they sit at
the long desks, quietly reading and turning pages—who are they?

A librarian answered the question:

"Retired people, who get the habit of reading; students; scholars,
who hope to contribute to knowledge. Then there are business
people—and many foreigners, since the war."

Not long ago a Mexican family of six came in; three girls, one boy,
and the parents. The father was in the air-conditioning business and
could speak no English. His son and one of the girls acted as in-
terpreters. He was looking for a Spanish text on air conditioning.

Some come from the Philippines, from India, from Indonesia.
Some come wanting to examine treaties between nations, hoping for
ways to improve their relations with other countries.

A European carpet manufacturer's representative came in looking
for new markets for his products.

Each one in his search for knowledge and truth was welcome,
just as you are. There is no question of *why* you want the material—
the librarian only asks *what* you want. So it has been since the
Library and the City of Washington began, more than 155 years ago.

FOLGER SHAKESPEARE LIBRARY, East Capitol Street, beside Library of Congress Annex. (No admission charge.) Open
11:00 A.M. to 4:30 P.M. every day except Sunday and holidays.
Exhibition Hall only open to the public.

Folger Shakespeare Library is a series of stimulating paradoxes.
The exterior of the building, modern yet classic in its great simplicity, prepares you not at all for the Elizabethan interior. The
Exhibition Hall which you will see is a long room, oak-paneled and
imposing, somber but comfortable, and filled with treasures.

Folger belies its name. It is much more than the greatest collection of Shakespeareana in the world—as if that were not enough. It
is dedicated to the accumulation of every significant book that
illuminated life in the sixteenth and seventeenth centuries.

Louis B. Wright, Director, explained that goal: "The background
of our own American civilization goes back to those two centuries.
The New World was explored and colonized then. Our fundamental

laws, customs, and religious feeling are deeply influenced by the thought and writing of those times. Folger provides the serious scholar with background material to reconstruct that history."

Folger's great store of knowledge—its collections—is primarily for the scholar. Anyone interested in study here can apply for a reader's card and expect to get it if his purpose is serious examination of those times or of Shakespeare materials.

For those who wish merely to sample the rare offerings in the Exhibition Hall, the lighted cases are rich indeed. Most of the exhibits are permanent. They include the first edition of Shakespeare's first printed play, *Titus Andronicus* (1594), the rarest item in the Library's possession; the great seals of Queen Elizabeth and King James I, and Henry VIII's privy seal of 1542.

The day I examined the cases there was on display an exhibit of early printing in London and the outlying provinces.

One book particularly caught my eye. It was called *New Englands Prospect,* by William Wood, a smallish volume of aged, ivory-toned pages, with a map, a short list of Indian words, and a tabulation of miscellaneous information about Indian culture. It might well have been one of the earliest guidebooks, designed to assist colonists in getting about America in the year 1635.

The book was open to a page bearing a group of words and their translation, with the note, "Because many have desired to heare some of the Natives Language, I have here inserted a small Nomenclator, with the Names of their Chiefe Kings, Rivers, Moneths, and dayes, whereby such as have in-sight into the Tongues, may know to what Language it is most inclining; and in such as desire it as an unknowne Language onely, may reape delight, if they can get no profit."

As serviceable as any list in today's guide for foreign travel are short helpful Indian phrases and sentences in this "unknowne Language," such as "Who lives here?" "faint with hunger," "Lend me monie," "Will you not trade?" and "I love you."

This forerunner of today's guide was published only a few years after another famous adventure story. This one, also in the case, must have made compelling reading. It is *The Generall Historie of Virginia, New-England, and the Summer Isles . . . From their first beginning Ano 1584 to this present 1624,* by Captain John Smith.

The exhibits in some of the cases change, but the model of the Globe Playhouse is permanently on display for you to study. It is built to a scale of one-half inch to the foot and is octagonal in shape, allowing no spectator to be more than sixty feet from any central stage action. Tiny bricks in the inner court are made of ink-eraser rubber, and plaster between the beams was laid with a spoon and a medicine dropper.

You may want to compare the Globe with the full-size theater which occupies the building's east wing and is open to the public. It does not reproduce any particular playhouse, but merely attempts to give an impression of a characteristic theater of Shakespeare's time. A rosy light focuses on the two-level stage. Lanterns along side walls shed a dim light, lending an atmosphere of another time.

While this Library has been called a bit of old England on Capitol Hill, the story of the man whose dream it symbolizes is typically American. Henry Clay Folger began life as a poor boy, but later became president and chairman of the board of directors of the Standard Oil Company of New York. At Amherst College he heard Ralph Waldo Emerson and discovered Emerson's eulogy marking the tercentenary of Shakespeare's birth. Thus began his life-long interest in the Bard. After his marriage his wife joined him in searching out rare folios and other pieces of Shakespeareana—play-bills, scrapbooks, contemporary literature. Nearly fifty years of successful collecting culminated in the building of Folger Library on Capitol Hill.

Scholars from all over the world come here to study, while the Library sends its staff to far corners to search for more rare and significant works.

The Folger is an oddity among Washington sight-seeing attractions, in that it has no connection with the Federal Government. In a sense it is an institute of advanced study conducted in Washington by Amherst College. The founder vested complete control of the Library and endowment in the trustees of Amherst.

Tour VI

Waterfront, Tidal Basin, Hains Point, Jefferson Memorial, National Zoological Park

THE WATERFRONT

Just south of the railroad bridge that spans the Potomac, the Washington waterfront begins. It is not extensive, as waterfronts go, but it is one of the city's most colorful areas. Yacht anchorages are filled with sleek pleasure craft, mostly power boats but with a few sailing craft lifting proud masts. There is a whole row of seafood restaurants, some with outdoor balconies from which diners may gaze across Washington Channel to East Potomac Park and Hains Point. The other side of the street is given over largely to wholesale produce houses.

Stroll along Maine Avenue (formerly Water Street), watching for salty shop-window signs like "shad guts," or one with a faintly musical ring, "porgy and bass." This is Seafood Row, where sturdy Chesapeake Bay boats put in filled with fish, oysters, or crabs, depending upon the season. The boats arrive early in the morning with their fresh cargo from down the Potomac or the Bay. You can see watermelons, too, piled high on decks with one or two sliced cleanly through for sampling. Take time to explore the broad paved seafood market place.

Reminiscing old-timers, with moist eye and dry mouth, like to recall an old saloon that stood just opposite the wharf of the Norfolk and Washington Steamship Line on Maine Avenue. In front, they say, was painted a magnificent portrait of a stein, fully three feet tall, foaming up to a creamy froth. In large letters were the words "WANTED! 10,000 Men to Unload Schooners—5c Each."

From the Wilson Line's Pier 4, at Maine Avenue and N Street, the steamer for Mount Vernon sails daily at 10:00 A.M. and 2:00 P.M., from early in April to early in September. Nightly in summertime, moonlight rides down the river, with dancing and other entertainment aboard the steamer, start from the same pier. There are also frequent excursions to Marshall Hall, an amusement park on the Maryland side of the river. Occasionally, on irregular dates, there are trips all the way down the Potomac and up the Bay to Baltimore, with the voyagers returning from the latter city to Washington by bus.

If you suddenly find the sun warm you might like to stop in at one of the restaurants—like Cy Ellis's—and get up on a stool at the raw bar. Half a dozen clams thus consumed are bound to revive you. Or you may want to lunch or dine outdoors on a balcony overlooking the fishermen's craft and the yacht basin; try Herzog's or the New England Raw Bar and Restaurant.

These are fitting surroundings for remembering how it used to be. Thirty years ago a Southwest Washington native told a Columbia Historical Society meeting: "In the long ago it was not unusual to see fifty or a hundred sailing vessels in the harbor at one time, and the hungry but jolly Jack Tars would rush ashore to John McKinney's old restaurant for chowder, beef, crabs, and beer, or they would go farther up the street to the restaurants of John Branson or Joe Gordon or John Kenny. Those were great old days with wonderful appetizing meals, served for a song, to as quaint a clientele as ever graced our city."

Walk past the graceful auxiliaries and cabin cruisers near the Capital Yacht Club. Many of these are permanent homes of Government workers and others, equipped with such refinements as shower stalls, television sets, and window boxes. One beamy craft, a venerable Chesapeake Bay bugeye named *Colonel R. Johnson Colton*, has housed a whole series of large families. Built in 1886, the *Colonel Colton* is one of the last of her type and one of the oldest vessels listed in *Lloyd's Register of American Yachts*. Some of the people you see living aboard these boats were driven here by Washington's wartime housing shortage, and just stayed on. Others simply prefer to live in quarters that rise and fall with the tide and

The Waterfront

rock gently in the wash of passing vessels—and that can go cruising in summertime.

Leaving the waterfront and retracing your steps northward, you again pass under the railroad bridge and find yourself close to the famous TIDAL BASIN, setting for the crowning of the Cherry Blossom Queen at the Thomas Jefferson Memorial, in the annual springtime festival.

An unforgettable way to see the clouds of Japanese cherry blossoms is by moonlight or under the brilliant searchlights that circle the Tidal Basin after dark when the trees are in bloom.

The path around the Tidal Basin is a year-round favorite for strolling, and is frequented by fishermen at all hours. The pool is occasionally stocked with large-mouth bass, and other species wander in through the tide gates that admit water from the Potomac. One noon hour I saw a taxi driver drop a passenger at the Jefferson Memorial, park his cab, and then stare thoughtfully at the water. Having made his decision, he burrowed into his car trunk, jointed up a long rod, mounted a reel and ran line through the guides, attached a lure, and began to cast expertly.

A concessionaire sells tickets for swan-boat rides and has pedal boats for rent at a landing platform on the east side of the Tidal Basin, just opposite the Jefferson Memorial.

West Potomac Park is the start of the famous drive when the cherry blossoms are out. The route leads along Riverside Drive and around HAINS POINT (East Potomac Park). Also in East Potomac Park, besides the cherry trees, are a swimming pool, miniature and regular-size golf courses, tennis courts, a bridle path, teahouse, tourist camp, and picnic tables. During the summer a ferry runs between Maine Avenue and East Potomac Park; speedboat rides also are available. Opposite East Potomac Park, on Greenleaf Point, stands Fort Lesley J. McNair, site of the National War College and the Industrial College of the Armed Forces. The general public is barred from this reservation.

The THOMAS JEFFERSON MEMORIAL with its effective setting on the Tidal Basin (and in line with the cross-axis of the White House and Washington Monument) is a favorite of many sight-seers. It follows the classic feeling of architect John Russell Pope, and it is altogether fitting that the low dome and pedimented portico are reminiscent of Jefferson's own Monticello.

The statesman's specific wish was for a modest monument "of a plain die or cube of 3 f., without any moldings, surmounted by an obelisk of 6 f. height, each a single stone." But almost a decade before the two-hundredth anniversary of his birth the Thomas Jefferson Memorial Commission was created by act of Congress. In 1936 Congress authorized the expenditure of three million dollars for a suitable memorial to the third President of the United States.

The cornerstone was laid in 1939 by President Franklin D. Roosevelt, and the memorial building was substantially finished in four years, but it was not until 1947 that the ten thousand-pound, nineteen-foot bronze statue was installed. It had been hoped that scuptor and foundry would have it finished by April 13, 1943, the anniversary date, but wartime shortages made that impossible. Ceremonies went off as planned, however, for a temporary bronze-painted plaster model had been erected and dedicated.

The story of the statue is one beset with problems. A nation-wide competition was held to select a fitting design. Of the 101 sculptors who presented credentials, 6 were asked to submit models. When all these models were rejected, the judges asked three competitors to furnish new ones. Again they were rejected, and again the three were asked to try. One of the three, Rudulph Evans, was discouraged to the point of withdrawing; besides, his money was getting low. His model was rejected and criticized by the judges for the ankle-length greatcoat he used on Jefferson. It was not authentic, they felt. Evans pointed out that Thomas Sully had painted Jefferson wearing just such a garment, but it was not until the Sully painting was finally traced to West Point that official papers gave necessary clues. The greatcoat had been a gift from General Thaddeus Kosciusko, the Polish patriot of the American Revolution.

Evans received the commission and spent months studying paintings and descriptions of his subject. He studied Jefferson's philosophy, his writings and speeches, until he knew he had every detail authentic. And the finished statue included the greatcoat.

Inside the Memorial, a frieze bears in letters two feet high a quotation from a letter written by Jefferson to Dr. Benjamin Rush in 1800: "I have sworn on the altar of God eternal hostility to every form of tyranny over the mind of man." Other excerpts from Jefferson's writings are inscribed on interior walls.

The Memorial is open from 9:00 A.M. to 9:00 P.M. daily.

NATIONAL ZOOLOGICAL PARK of the Smithsonian Institution, Rock Creek Park (main entrance in 3000 block Connecticut Avenue NW). (No admission charge.) Grounds open from daylight to dark year round. Buildings open 9:00 A.M. to 4:30 P.M. in winter;

9.00 A.M. to 5:00 P.M. in summer; and to 5:30 P.M. on Sunday in May, June, July, and August. Excellent cafeteria.

All year round, but particularly in Washington's warm months, the Zoo is a leafy green magnet drawing men and boys, mothers trundling infants in carriages, and picnicking families to join the three thousand birds and beasts in the cool shadows of Rock Creek Park.

Some folks head at once for the Reptile House to watch the slow movement of incredibly large pythons or the ceaseless darting and writhing of slim, sinister cobras, or to catch a motionless crocodile flickering an eyelid. Dr. William Mann, colorful director for the past three decades, knows some thirty boys in the Capital who keep coming back. "They all want to be Zoo directors when they grow up, and particularly to run the Reptile House." The house is a beautifully lighted modern building of one hundred cages and many decorative designs—lizards carved on capitals, stone turtles supporting twisted columns.

Those visitors who have developed a special affection for pigmy hippopotamuses speed toward the Large Mammal House, anxious to welcome the latest in the famed Gumdrop line. These baby hippos look exactly like shiny licorice when they are born; Gumdrop XVI weighed in at fourteen pounds two ounces, and got her picture in the *Evening Star* in January, 1955.

Or you may be a mere parent and be taken forcibly to admire Smokey, the brown bear which is the symbol of the highly successful forest fire prevention campaign conducted by State foresters and the United States Forest Service. Smokey is in the hillside bear pits; he was brought here when about six months old, after being found badly singed in a New Mexico fire in which his mother was killed. Along with Smokey are grizzlies, hybrid brown bears, and others. Smokey gets most of the mail sent to the Zoo—letters addressed to him personally by boys and girls who want to join the fire-fighting organization (the mail is turned over to the Forest Service, where from five hundred to a thousand similar applications a day pour in).

If you come early or late you'll be able to look in on feeding time

in some of the buildings and paddocks which take up a little less
than one hundred acres of the park. The Zoo's denizens are fed on
a strict schedule: animals in the Antelope House at 8:00 and 2:30;
deer, bison, and zebras in paddocks near the Connecticut Avenue
entrance at 8:00 and 2:30; bears at 8:00 and 3:00; seals and sea
lions in the pools at 8:30 and 3:15; Large Mammal House animals
at 8:00 and 3:00; reptiles (except snakes and amphibians) at 9:00
and from 1:00 to 2:30; monkeys in the Monkey House at 9:00 and
2:30; chimpanzees and gibbons in the Small Mammal House at 8:00
and 3:00; wolves and coyotes in dens at 1:00; lions and tigers in the
Lion House at 1:30 (not fed on Sundays); penguins at 2:00; other
birds at 9:00 and again from 1:00 to 2:00.

The big Flight Cage is a major exhibit in itself, with hundreds of
birds ranging in size from gulls to flamingos. Wild birds often build
nests near by, attracted by their own species in the enclosure. Flocks
of wild black-crowned night herons have nested in great bare trees
near the Zoo; during the mating season a caged male bird may be
seen slipping a tasty fish through the wire to an attractive female on
the outside. Once a bald eagle hung around for several weeks to
be near other eagles which have their own quarters near the
Flight Cage.

A typical Zoo menu may not exactly make your mouth water, but
it is welcomed with roars, pacing, stamping, drooling, and all manner of appreciative sounds and actions as feeding time rolls around.

Hors d'Oeuvres
Green Grass, Fresh Leaves, and Cod-Liver Oil
Entree
Mealworms   Eggs—Raw and Boiled
Roast Horse Meat, Small Portion
Sweet Potatoes, Carrots, Onions, Beets, Potatoes, Cabbage
Salad of Lettuce and Kale
Dessert
Rice Custard—Baked Custard—Oranges, Apples, Bananas
Raisins   Sunflower Seeds   Milk

Going to the Zoo is an old Washington habit; oldsters today watching their grandchildren race down the Lion House Hill can see themselves playing there fifty years before. Then, of course, there were fewer buildings, animals, and visitors.

Oddly enough, Zoo beginnings took shape rather incidentally in the Smithsonian's own backyard down on The Mall. The National Museum in the 1880's was assembling a collection of mounted animals for public exhibition, and many kinds of living creatures were shipped here to aid the taxidermists. Some were kept fenced in on the grounds, and live beasts in sight of the Capitol stirred great public interest. William F. Cody (Buffalo Bill) personally sent three American elk.

By the time the menagerie numbered some two hundred, a Department of Living Animals had been created with William T. Hornaday, a noted taxidermist and conservationist, in charge.

At that time the beautiful valley of Rock Creek was a pleasant carriage ride "out in the country." But when a suitable tract of land was sought for the future home not only of these animals but as sanctuary for such disappearing American mammals as the bison or buffalo, Rock Creek was chosen. In the heart of the wooded, rolling wilderness 175 acres were selected by a special commission for purchase. The famous landscape architect who planned the Capitol grounds, Frederick Law Olmsted, was retained to draw up a comprehensive plan, foreseeing the National Zoological Park very nearly as you see it today. Behind the planning, the man who was most responsible was probably Samuel Langley, Secretary of the Smithsonian; the Zoo was conceived as another arm of the great institution for the diffusion of knowledge.

The 185 animals were moved in a borrowed wagon from behind the Smithsonian to their new home. Clearings had already been made, roads built, and a single animal house was ready. W. H. Blackburne, a showman with the Barnum and Bailey Circus, became head keeper.

Out of the Zoo's annual report for that first year, 1890, come two incidents: a heroic nursemaid diverted an irritated buffalo cow

from charging the baby she was tending after the beast broke
through the fence, and "a brave spirit spat in a bear's eye and was
fined $5." That was about the time two elephants named Dunk and
Gold Dust were presented to the Zoo; Mr. Blackburne tied them to
a tree until a shelter could be built. Dunk lived more than twenty-
five years, a well-loved Zoo figure.

Since then steady growth has brought the Zoo to its present collection of three thousand animals and eight hundred different
species. The collection represents many gifts—from people in many
parts of the world, from children just a few blocks away, from
Presidents and foreign potentates. Exchange, purchase, and, of
course, just plain reproduction have accounted for many other ac-
cessions.

One early gift was a rare monkey-eating eagle, also known as a
harpy eagle. It was brought to the Zoo by the captain of the U.S.S.
Wilmington, with eighteen other animals and birds from Brazil. The
ship's cat had accompanied the party ashore, and the eagle dived
through a window onto the cat; snared under a blanket, the bird
was brought back and put on exhibition—a valuable accession. A
number of expeditions also aided the growing Zoo.

When the President of the United States takes an interest in an
animal or a pet, the Zoo immediately feels a bounteous reaction.
President Coolidge had a pet raccoon named Rebecca. Gifts of
great and small animals poured into the White House as Rebecca
caught the public's fancy. They were all turned over to the Zoo.
One was a cinnamon bear, and another was the first of the famous
pigmy hippos, a gift from the Firestone rubber plantation. (Another
pigmy hippo named Hannah was purchased as a companion and
was still living to a memorable old age in early 1956.)

A few years ago Prime Minister Nehru of India presented two
young Asiatic elephants as a gift to the children of America. They
were called Shanti and Ashok. They now live at the Zoo.

An urgent local telephone call may result in a sudden gift to the
Zoo: "There's a strange animal on my window sill." Many opossums
and raccoons as well as other wild local fauna are inherited in this

way as the Washington metropolitan area extends farther into "country."

The annual reports list donors and depositors (some people prefer to place their pets on loan, rather than give them outright, which is agreeable to the Zoo). Many bequests are from children whose pets become too big for bathtub or back porch. Among the 1954 gifts were a spotted salamander, a great horned owl, 71 rabbits, 127 Peking ducks, 33 hamsters, a cedar waxwing, a dozen skunks, and 6 robins. A grocery clerk gave the Zoo a beautifully marked necklace snake he had found in a food shipment from the tropics. That year, too, President Syngman Rhee gave President Eisenhower his own pets, two Korean bear cubs, now in the Zoo. The Government of New Zealand sent along a tuatara, a lizard-like reptile of a primitive type that in early stages possesses three or four eyes, but in adult form has only two.

A zoo is ever-changing: eggs are hatching, young things are opening their eyes for a first look around, new animals are coming and going on a purchase, exchange, deposit, or gift basis. (Someone may be mixing up a pablum-and-bamboo-leaf mixture for the lesser panda, which is a "specialized feeder" but thrives on this concoction.) When too many young come along to be accommodated, they are exchanged with other zoos for other desired animals.

But occasionally a mother will have her litter and then cast the youngsters out, refusing to feed or attend them in any way. Not so with the African porcupines, however. These parents and older brothers and sisters stand almost constant watch around the babies, their long, sharp spines forming an unbroken line of protection.

To save the rejected young, Director Mann and his wife Lucile often adopt them. A lion cub, Susan, was the first of a long list of animals the Manns have taken home to their apartment in a co-operative building on the edge of the Park. "We weren't allowed to keep pets in the apartment," Dr. Mann recalled. "You know—dogs, cats, parrots, and the like, so I wrote a letter to the board of directors asking for permission to keep a lion. Almost immediately the directors turned up. When they began talking baby talk to the little cub—well, that was just the beginning."

Since then the Manns have nursed baby tigers, monkeys, wart hogs, a brown bear, and many others. Susan the lion thrived on a formula of dried milk, and grew from three pounds to twenty in three months.

The question put most often to a zoo director is: "What is the most exciting moment you ever had?"—asked no doubt with visions of the man grappling with an enraged lion.

Dr. Mann's quick answer: "The time the Secretary of Interior's office called up to say the Zoo was getting $870,000 for new buildings!"

The Zoo Director's office is housed in the former Holt Mansion, built in 1805, on a hilltop in the Park near the Adams Mill Road entrance. Scratched on a second-floor windowpane are the words, "Huzza for Adams, Down with Old Hickory's enemies!" and the date, December, 1827. It was one of three estates bought by the Smithsonian for the Zoo about 1889.

Tour VII

Federal Bureau of Investigation, National Archives, National Gallery of Art, Botanic Garden

The FBI, in the Department of Justice Building, Ninth Street and Pennsylvania Avenue, NW. (No admission charge.) Open Monday through Friday, 9:30 A.M. to 4:00 P.M.; closed Saturday, Sunday, and all holidays. Tours start every half-hour and last approximately one hour. Advance reservations advisable for group tours.

Here you can spend a full hour or so in what ranks as one of the most carefully thought-out guided tours in the city. And you go forth again confident and proud. Through your young guide, who is a selected, trained man dedicated to this work, you get the certain feeling that this vast organization, by tracking down lawbreakers, is contributing mightily toward the building of communities where understanding and peace exist between men and women.

The Bureau was founded in 1908. Sixteen years later a young man not yet thirty, named J. Edgar Hoover, was appointed Director. In the years under his leadership the initials FBI have come to stand for law and order. The organization itself has become a career service in which ability and good character are required qualifications for appointment, and performance and achievement the sole basis for promotion.

Thus, when your tour has been under way only five minutes, you understand quite readily why the small boys break out in a constant barrage of "Wow!" and must almost literally be scraped away from the glass cases holding memorabilia of gunfights. As you go from room to room, each seems to hold more exciting exhibits than the last.

The tour is highlighted with daring episodes, complete with stark evidence. Among the first is the important and strange case of the two men who resembled each other so closely that it was impossible to tell them apart. (The two enlarged prison photographs hang side by side; you are invited to look for yourself.) The circumstances suggested a case of mistaken identity. The case proved to the FBI beyond a doubt that a more accurate, precise method of identification than one based on appearance must be adopted.

Fingerprinting was the answer. Today this technique is regarded as offering the only known means of positive identification. (Useful not only in crime detection, it is credited with bringing broken families together and with correctly naming amnesia and accident victims.) In 1955 the Identification Division contained some 138,-000,000 sets of fingerprints. Each day about twenty thousand prints are received for processing. Quite separate and filed under a special system are the fingerprints of more than ten million lawbreakers and their arrest records, and each month some one thousand wanted criminals are identified as their fingerprints are checked through these files. To the Division's experts the tented arches, loops, and plain whorls of fingerprints speak clearly in terms of guilt and innocence. (A nickname file, of particular value in sorting out aliases, contains such picturesque monickers as Big Meatball, Battin' Eye Charlie, Ash Street Slim.)

The huge clerical force required, as well as the space for the records, made it necessary to erect a building in Southwest Washington, as large as the Department of Justice Building itself, where the Identification Division has been housed since 1947.

A celebrated case illustrated in the tour is that of the criminal who outsmarted himself by undergoing a painful skin-grafting operation. Skin from his chest was used to erase his prints. His success boomeranged. His set of completely smooth fingertips proved unique; he is the one criminal the FBI has in its tremendous files who needs no looking up.

Every bit of sleuthing instinct in you stirs as you hear the story of "the woman in the red dress" who identified gangster John Dillinger as he left a Chicago movie theater. In the glass case are his straw hat (slightly soiled as it flew in the gunfire), his guns, and a death mask revealing the bullet scar on his right cheek.

You'll see souvenirs of Machine Gun Kelly, who when he surrendered tagged FBI agents with a name they never lost, as he pleaded, "Don't shoot, G Men!"

Perhaps your favorite exhibit will be the story of the fly speck that wouldn't rub off, the fascinating, suspenseful case of the microdot that turned out to be a hundred-word spy message, and how the FBI cracked it.

Upstairs, you watch the actual laboratory work going on. Here you will see a photograph of a hair magnified 17,500 times, and find out, among other things, whether the hair is of human or animal origin. Up here, too, are the valuable reference collections of heel prints, paper watermarks, dynamite wrappers, animal hairs, rope samples, automobile paint samples in every shade, and a catalogue of tire treads which has tripped up many a hit-and-run driver.

One thief who stole automobile tires hoped to escape detection by cutting off the numbers and thus any reference to the rightful owner. FBI laboratory experts treated the tires in such a way that the numbers could still be read, and proved that the tires had belonged to a particular man. These scientists can examine a broken lock and tell whether a jimmy pried it open; or whether a certain pair of pliers cut the wires of a burglar alarm; or identify the markings on a bullet.

The FBI laboratory was established in 1932 as a scientific aid in criminal investigation. It has grown to be the largest in the world— a clearinghouse for crime problems and evidence submitted by law enforcement officers all over the country. Scientists who work here are skilled in the use of the laboratory's precision equipment, which includes an electron microscope, cameras, analytical balances, and spectographs. It is the scientific way to findings that not only trap the murderer, thief, or spy, but remove the threat of circumstantial evidence hanging over the innocent. These facilities are also available to local law enforcement agencies.

In one case FBI scientists, at the request of an officer, made tests of scrapings taken from the fender of a blood-stained automobile and compared them with blood samples on the shoulder of the road. The two boys who had been in the car refused to explain the presence of blood; a hit-and-run death was suspected, but as yet no body had been found.

The tests shortly showed the stains to be beef blood. The car had struck a cow. The boys, still frightened, were absolved of the suspicion of killing a person.

The tour usually ends up in the basement firing range with a demonstration of marksmanship with a .38-caliber revolver and a Thompson submachine gun. Young visitors particularly enjoy this climax, for a handful of empty shells and the battered paper target are prized souvenirs to the lads who get them.

A group of boys from a Kentucky orphanage made the tour in 1955, and received these trophies after the actual practice demonstration had finished. The lucky eleven-year-old who lugged the target home with him wrote a letter back thanking the guide and closed with the wistful hope, "Would you write to me?" It was an occasion he wanted never to forget.

THE NATIONAL ARCHIVES, on Constitution Avenue between Seventh and Ninth streets, NW. (No admission charge.) Open 9:00 A.M. to 10:00 P.M. weekdays; 1:00 P.M. to 10:00 P.M. Sundays and holidays. Pennsylvania Avenue entrance open until 5:00 P.M. Monday through Friday; Constitution Avenue entrance open during all scheduled hours mentioned above.

If you come in from Pennsylvania Avenue, which is the building's fortress-like side, you'll see two pedestaled figures, the work of Robert Aitken, flanking the entrance. One represents the past, with the words of Confucius, "Study The Past"; the other speaks for the future with a quotation from Shakespeare's *The Tempest*, "What Is Past Is Prologue." It took a taxi driver to translate this to a passenger as "You ain't seen nothin' yet."

Once inside, turn left to climb to the main level on a broad marble stairway. It rises in the east stair well, where hangs the mammoth map which General Dwight D. Eisenhower used at his SHAEF headquarters during World War II. (Then, members of his staff plotted on it Allied troop movements from day to day.) Originally, it was composed of many sections; you now see it assembled and laminated for preservation.

If, however, you approach by the Constitution Avenue entrance, you'll doubtless link the pure classic architecture with, say, the National Gallery of Art just down the street. Both buildings were designed by John Russell Pope, foremost architect of the 1920's. Night lighting lends this view beautiful accents.

Inside you will find yourself in the foyer facing the very entrance to the great Exhibition Hall, where are kept the famous originals of the Declaration of Independence, the Constitution of the United States, and the Bill of Rights.

Look back to the doors through which you entered and notice that the tremendous window above is darkened. Shortly after the building was finished in 1937, sunlight streamed through the cathedral-like grillework, lighting up the great Hall and glancing briefly on some of the display cases. But sunlight fades ink and eats away at parchment, so this was stopped—one precaution in many that a belatedly alert Government has taken in the last thirty years to preserve the Nation's most cherished documents.

Should your visit be very early or very late in the year, after crowds have thinned out, you will be able to go up to the center cases first, and feel for a long unforgettable moment the impact of seeing for the first time these precious charters. Then, beginning at the far left, move leisurely from case to case as the development of the Union unfolds. The climax, of course, is the dramatic central display; following are historic documents, many dealing with the growth of the western country. There is so much here not only to see, but to muse over.

As a valuable memento of your visit, you may wish to buy *Charters of Freedom,* a handsome twenty-five-cent booklet containing reproductions of the Declaration, Constitution, and Bill of Rights. These and other reasonably priced facsimiles of historic documents are displayed at the sales desk in the foyer.

If you are shocked at the faded ink on the Declaration of Independence—even more pronounced in the signatures—there is ample reason for this one parchment to show its age more than the others. (You may look, almost at once, for what has become a symbol of all signature, as in the phrase, "Put your John Hancock here. . . ." It, too, is barely legible.)

It's also very plain that John Adams was premature when he wrote his "dearest friend" (his wife, Abigail) that July 2, 1776, the day the Lee resolution for independence was adopted by Congress, would be a day remembered around the world. The Declaration is dated July 4, of course; it took two days to get Thomas Jefferson's draft debated and adopted. The engrossed, signed Declaration you see today, however, was not in existence on July 4, 1776. It was August 2 before the text, inscribed on parchment, was ready for signing. (It's interesting that some signatures are those of men who, not being in Congress on July 4, 1776, were allowed to sign later in the year.)

During the document's first forty-seven years it must have had little real care. Along with the Constitution, the Bill of Rights, and other Government records, it was sent from Philadelphia down the Delaware River and by sea to the new Federal City in 1800. About twenty-three years later John Quincy Adams, then Secretary of State, commissioned "a respectable Engraver," William J. Stone, to make a facsimile. It is believed that Adams felt the Declaration already showed such deterioration from handling and exposure as to make some permanent facsimile necessary. Stone produced an exact copperplate engraving. His method probably involved transferring some of the ink from the document to the plate and then etching the image thus revealed. This is believed to have had the effect of permanently reducing the legibility of the document. But if the Stone facsimile had not been made we might not know today what the Declaration originally looked like. (Most of the reproductions you see, not only in the National Archives' publications but elsewhere, are based on the Stone plate of 1823. The historic copper etching is now in the National Archives.) Stone's work was done about nine years after the emergency evacuation in which the three documents with other records were carted to Virginia shortly before the burning of the public buildings by the British.

In 1841 the precious old document began another crucial period that nearly ended disastrously. It was hung in the old Patent Office Building at Eighth and F streets, NW, on a wall recommended no doubt by some well-meaning person for its good direct light. By miraculous good fortune, a few months before parts of the Patent Office Building went up in flames, the Declaration of Independence was removed. The occasion was the Centennial Exposition in 1876 when President Grant lent the document as an exhibit to the city of Philadelphia. Then followed almost a decade and a half in the library of the State Department. In 1896 the Declaration was finally taken from public view, wrapped carefully, and placed in a flat steel case, where it remained until its transfer to the Library of Congress in 1921.

Thus we approach the present. In 1933, when President Herbert Hoover laid the cornerstone of the National Archives Building, he said, "Further, there will be aggregated here the most sacred documents of our history, the originals of the Declaration of Independence and of the Constitution of the United States." But they were not actually transferred there until 1952.

During this period of waiting, while the famous originals were under guard in display cases at the Library of Congress, Washington columnists played on a piquant rumor that the two great agencies were feuding. Even now you may find a long-time Archives employee who will smile knowingly and say, "It took seventeen years to get 'em away from the Library." But Dr. R. D. W. Connor, first Archivist, mentioned specifically that no feud had ever existed between the two institutions.

However that may be, in the National Archives are official papers showing that the State Department was loath to part with the Declaration and Constitution at a time when the Library all but frankly asked for them. In 1906, with the Library occupying its new home on Capitol Hill, the Librarian, after a number of unsuccessful tries, pointed out that records could be protected from fire in a way not possible in the Departments (this, just after the awful loss to fire of San Francisco's old Spanish records). The Department of State sent over the Continental Congress papers, from which the precious documents were notably absent.

Following World War I, a committee appointed by the Secretary of State recommended that papers "purely historical in their nature" should be in one place, the Library of Congress. By Executive Order in 1921 the Declaration of Independence and the Constitution were transferred to the Library of Congress.

Of course, all this happened before the erection of a National Archives Building—and it was indeed a great day when, amid fanfare and in the presence of the President of the United States, the historic parchments were brought to the prepared place in December, 1952.

Today, as you stand on the platform between the shrine and the velvet rope, what hold the documents may look to be simply softly lighted, well-constructed glass cases.

What you are really seeing is a man-made "keeping place" which probably has no superior anywhere. The cases themselves are scientifically engineered to hold back time's heavy hand. The inert helium gas in which the documents are sealed has no ill effect on ink or parchment. Amber-toned filters let only the harmless rays of light through—never any ultraviolet. (That's why photography with flashbulb is generally forbidden. The filters are able to handle the normal amount of ultraviolet; more than that, as in flash photography, may have a damaging effect.)

A guard is always posted at the right of the shrine. At the flip of a switch the displays disappear, to be shielded by tons of steel and several thick walls in an unseen vault below.

"If the whole building should collapse on the vault holding the three documents, they would still be safe," an official told me.

"But suppose the electricity should fail at a critical moment."

"Well, there's another stand-by power system that would take over."

The small working model of this great mechanism, on view in the main floor corridor, shows you that it is like a bank vault standing on end. The push-button miniature, operating on schedule every five minutes, demonstrates how each morning and night the documents reach their appointed place. It was presented to the National Archives by the vault builders as a gift to the American people.

The part that private industry played in this bit of history is interesting, too. The cost to the Government of the remarkable vault was relatively small because the company—a hundred-year-old safe-construction concern—saw it as a truly once-in-a-lifetime project. That the organization was wide awake to the advertising potential is apparent, however, for on the day of the dedication a full-page advertisement proudly announced the event in nearly every large daily newspaper in the country.

But, at the same time, it was noted by many that the company's personnel and craftsmen became imbued with a sense of dedication summed up perhaps in the words of one, "I just want to tell my kids I helped create this safe place for the three greatest documents in American history."

The safe, or vault, itself weighs fifty tons. It is engineered to resist bombs, fire, burglars, and water. A hidden elevator mechanism lowers the charters undisturbed the slightly more than twenty-seven feet to settle into the waiting steel cavern. Immediately, the huge five-ton doors automatically swing shut and lock.

Elsewhere in this building the work of the National Archives goes on. For those who find it difficult to throw away old check stubs or dance programs, or have an attic full of magazines, the Archives has singular impact. The Federal Government creates about 3,400,000 feet of records each year. Of course, all this material cannot be kept permanently—indeed, probably no more than 5 to 10 per cent of it possesses enduring value. Nevertheless, the National Archives, in co-operation with all other agencies, must systematically review and evaluate the whole. The record-holding capacity of the National Archives Building is 1,000,000 cubic feet.

As the annual report of the agency for 1954 notes, "Holdings at the year's end were 788,700 cubic feet, a small decrease from the year before. More rigorous standards were applied to the papers accessioned and retained." (It was resolved that records lacking those elements necessary to render them of enduring value just wouldn't get even shelf room.)

Since 1949 the National Archives has been a division of the National Archives and Record Service of the General Services Administration. Many noncurrent records are held for a stated period of time in GSA's ten regional records centers and then destroyed. The National Archives, then, is the final resting place for permanent records of every agency of the Federal Government, including both Houses of Congress. Nothing received here, moreover, can be destroyed until it has had authoritative review in the light of the future as well as the past.

In the Archives' 196 stack areas of varying sizes and shapes are human stories—of military engagements, of diplomatic achievements, of road building, of ports and lighthouses, of land distribution, of exploration. In the central search room I opened a big book—an 1860 census account for the State of Kansas—and noticed that one family with two children (both born back East) emigrated from North Carolina to a homestead in Kansas. In fact, everyone listed down the page was from the East. Some lucky farmers were credited with land and money, but most were just waiting or working for a homestead.

Many literary figures have left behind in Government records bits of themselves. Ernest Thompson Seton, author of *Two Little Savages*, sometimes wrote to the old Biological Survey without signing his name; he just sketched some animal footprints at the bottom of the page. Clerks always recognized this signature. Some of these letters are part of the record. When Nathaniel Hawthorne lost his Government job, his many friends petitioned for his reinstatement. These letters are in the records, as are the documents showing the late Eugene O'Neill's service in the Merchant Marine.

Each year requests for information—whether in letters, personal visits, or by telephone—number in the hundreds of thousands. Some years ago a famous 1790 map of the District of Columbia held in the National Archives was introduced into court in a controversy over waterfront rights. In 1954, someone asked for data on the pensioning of bloodhounds serving in the United States Army, as set forth in a resolution introduced by John Quincy Adams in the House of Representatives in 1840. The motion picture and television industries frequently draw on the 60,000,000 feet of movie film and more than 250,000 sound recordings in the National Archives.

Among the Archives' 2,000,000 still pictures is the Mathew Brady collection of Civil War photographs. From them a scene captioned simply "Soldiers and Citizens" was studied inch by inch. Several prominent Civil War figures were recognized and the scene was identified as Gettysburg. One man in a high hat stands out in the crowd; he is now believed to be Abraham Lincoln, on the occasion of his Gettysburg address in 1863. Enlargements of this and other Brady photographs hang on the walls near the Pennsylvania Avenue west entrance to the Exhibition Hall.

Before you leave the building be sure to explore the semicircular corridor on the main floor where an exciting selection of early Federal documents associated with the history of the forty-eight States is on display. They are placed in the order of the States' entry into the Union and include primitive maps, treaties, battle plans, letters, and the like.

One display, for example, shows the first homestead application, entered in Nebraska in 1863 by one Daniel Freeman, a Civil War soldier home on leave.

Another displays the journal of that English astronomer, Charles Mason, showing the survey of the famous Pennsylvania-Maryland boundary line which he made jointly with Jeremiah Dixon from 1763 to 1767.

In the New York alcove is the deed of the gift of the Statue of Liberty to the American people from the French people. The illuminated parchment is inscribed with an interesting view of the statue.

Louisiana has, for part of its exhibit, the original "exchange" copy of the Louisiana Purchase Treaty, signed by Napoleon Bonaparte and Talleyrand—with the skippet (small box for preserving the great seal).

Montana's history is represented by General George Custer's last known notes to his superior officer telling his plans for the fatal Battle of the Little Big Horn in 1876 (with a striking Mathew Brady photograph of the handsome General).

As you look through these windows on history, one of the remarkable paradoxes of this great National Archives may occur to you. This is the safest, best constructed building in all Washington. Its invulnerability is aided by interior stretches where no light reaches, and thicknesses of steel and stone reinforce the whole—yet, your personal sense of reopening old doors that lead to America's great men and ideas is never stronger than here. Before you come away you may want to say the words softly to yourself, "When in the course of human events it becomes necessary for one people to dissolve the political bands which have connected them with another . . ." Even today, there are no more timely words around the world than these.

NATIONAL GALLERY OF ART, on The Mall, Constitution Avenue between Fourth and Seventh Streets, NW. (No admission charge.) Open every day in the year except Christmas Day and New Year's Day: 10:00 A.M. to 5:00 P.M. on weekdays; 2:00 P.M. to 10:00 P.M. on Sunday. Cafeteria on ground floor: open 11:00 A.M. to 4:00 P.M. Tuesday through Saturday; 4:00 to 7:00 P.M. Sunday. Cafeteria closed Monday. Tours: free guided tours scheduled. *Note:* On Monday just one tour given at 3:00 P.M.

Your first view of the exterior of this long, low classic building of rose-white Tennessee marble at once pleases. (It is even more lovely in the rain, for then the rosy shading, deepest at the base, is most distinct.) The architect was John Russell Pope, who gave it the same sort of low dome he placed on the Jefferson Memorial. With funds provided for the purpose by Andrew W. Mellon, the building, which cost more than fifteen million dollars, was opened in March, 1941. The National Gallery of Art is a bureau of the Smithsonian Institution, as established by Congress, and belongs to all the people of the country. Thus, its collections are assembled and maintained as national collections and represent the best in the great tradition of Western painting, sculpture, and graphic arts.

How to tell you of what is here to see? Perhaps the first thing to know and use is the year-round schedule of free tours. At 11:00 A.M. and 3:00 P.M. Tuesday through Saturday a tour called "Introduction to the Collection" is given; it runs forty-five to fifty minutes. Six different lecturers are ready to lead these groups; all speak on this same subject—highlights of art from the thirteenth century to the present day. (Each of these docents manages to make his tour different, so don't hesitate to take a second one.)

At one o'clock Tuesday through Saturday, a completely different type of tour gets under way. A broad trend or theme in art is examined each month; in each of the four weeks a different facet of the subject is emphasized. For example, under the general heading of the attitudes of the artist toward his subject, the tour may one week focus on realism in painting; another week it may trace classicism. For those staying in Washington for any length of time, weekly attendance at the one o'clock tour brings increased understanding and appreciation. At your request, notice of programs will be sent to you free. (On the Friday I took this tour, I was part of a group of twenty-five, mostly women, some of whom were picking up where a college art course had stopped years before, others just anxious to add to their knowledge of great art.)

Another side of the broad program offered here is the almost family type of Sunday evening. It may begin as a pleasant hour viewing your favorite paintings and discovering new ones, or attending the 4 o'clock lecture; followed by Sunday dinner in the very good cafeteria; the 6:30 lecture on the "Picture of the Week," and then a concert or recital in one of the Garden Courts.

Musical programs are presented in the Garden Courts each Sunday night, except from mid-July through mid-September. Flowers from the Gallery's own hothouses bank the fountains—brilliant red poinsettias in December, azaleas in spring. The plump little angels adorning the fountains were made for gardens at Versailles more than 250 years ago. (It is known that there were four such groups, and Gallery officials have long been on the lookout for the other two.) The music will follow you if you should prefer to wander back to a picture gallery and sit—or gaze up at El Greco's mystical *Saint Martin and the Beggar,* and then ponder the subtle differences in the artist's smaller version of that painting near by.

In "doing" the Gallery it is possible to begin at Gallery 1, just off the magnificent Rotunda, and follow the development of European art in painting and sculpture through the centuries. But there are ninety galleries on the main floor. With so much to see it is easy to miss not only some significant works, but the fine detail which so enlivens and enriches each artist's works—unless you have a guide at least for the first visit.

If you find yourself frankly confused by so many acres of masterpieces, then you are quite typical. Favorites grow out of such confusion, however. You may discover yourself lingering before the forceful figure of Gilbert Stuart's *The Skater,* going on to recall a nostalgic feeling for Renoir's *A Girl with a Watering Can,* and standing in rapt wonder as you gaze into *The Mill,* by Rembrandt. These are everybody's favorites.

Your guide will begin with early Italian painting and sculpture and ably introduce you to the first simple religious subjects intended for church decoration. Moving from the thirteenth century to the fifteenth, you'll see the Madonna and Child develop from a wooden pose with heavily swathed Child to a more human, natural group. The Child gradually sheds His clothing, and catches at His mother, as she becomes a lovely young woman. And symbolism carries the burden of religious meanings. Viewing Giotto's *Madonna and Child,* you'll learn that the Hebrew word for star is Miriam, represented by the little star on Mary's right shoulder.

After the tour, you may want to examine some of the great collections at your leisure. Italian paintings, found chiefly in the Kress and Mellon collections, are among the finest in the land. In sculpture, the collection in the National Gallery represents most of the major trends of the Italian Renaissance.

Then, too, you may turn to the early works of American artists. A charming study in Americana is Edward Savage's large portrait, *The Washington Family.* Although some wag has described the group as "having been struck by lightning and not yet fallen over," nevertheless it is the family on the steps of Mount Vernon. Off on the horizon is the soon-to-come Federal City site. The map on the table is L'Enfant's famous plan, and Martha with her fan may mark the place of the present-day Capitol. The young girl, Eleanor Parke (Nelly) Custis, became mistress of Woodlawn Plantation; her brother, George Washington Parke Custis, later built Arlington House and officiated at the cornerstone laying of the Monument in 1848. Behind Mrs. Washington stands Billy Lee, the General's faithful servant.

When Savage began his preliminary sketches for the portrait he interrupted further work on it to study abroad. There he learned some accepted techniques, and returned to complete the painting in 1796. (The red curtain hardly belongs on the steps, but he may have added that in a try for sophistication; the folds and details of Martha's dress are quite professional, but the awkwardness of her right arm shows how anatomy must have troubled Savage.)

An interesting footnote: In 1798 Savage published his celebrated print of this canvas, made from his own copper engraving. It is recorded that he made ten thousand dollars from the sale at a dollar a print—an example of Yankee ingenuity, no doubt. (He was born in Princeton, Massachusetts.) One copy hangs today in Mount Vernon, but the others are scattered far and wide.

You'll want to remember, too, that the National Gallery has the largest American collection of Gilbert Stuart paintings (in 1955 his two hundredth birthday was celebrated). Stuart's gifted portrayal of Mrs. Richard Yates eyeing you shrewdly, drawing her sewing thread taut in the eternal gesture of the careful needlewoman, will hold you. His portraits of Dr. and Mrs. William Thornton are worthy of special mention. Dr. Thornton was the talented and sensitive first architect of the Capitol, who found himself often misunderstood; his wife's personal diary has guided historians for over a hundred years. It, in great brevity, invariably noted the weather and what "Dr. T." was doing. When her husband died, she recorded wistfully that she wished she might have understood him better.

Gilbert Stuart himself was a personality of great precocity, charm, and extravagances. At twenty-one, as a student, he was often hungry, for he wrote his benefactor Benjamin West, "For some time I have been reduced to one miserable meal a day and frequently not even that."

But fame was soon to come. For although Stuart was born in what is now Washington County, Rhode Island, it was in England, where he spent over fifteen years, that his talents were acclaimed. His portrait *The Skater* was considered startlingly original, for this was a sharp departure from the conventional drawing room figure. (The story goes that William Grant of Congleton arrived for his first sitting during a bitter cold spell. The decision that it was "a better day for skating than painting" sent them off to St. James's Park at Grant's suggestion, and *The Skater* was the interesting result of this excursion.)

Money came quickly, but Stuart's debts piled up even faster. He moved with his young family to Ireland, but debts continued until he finally chose to return to America. He planned to make his fortune by painting portraits of Washington, and remarked on leaving, "I calculate upon making a plurality of his portraits, whole lengths which will enable me to realize a fortune."

His prophecy came true. Stuart painted three portraits of Washington from life.

The portrait known as the Vaughan Washington, named for its

owner, Samuel Vaughan of London, is believed to be the first of the General that Stuart painted from life. The portrait in the National Gallery is a "replica" of that type by the artist himself.

One "must" while you are at the Gallery is the collection of Edgar William and Bernice Chrysler Garbisch, the largest and most comprehensive collection of American primitive paintings yet assembled, about fifteen hundred works. They are in oil, tempera, pastel, and water color, and date from the early eighteenth century to the middle of the nineteenth. A study of those on display will add immeasurably to the sense of watching history unfold.

Usually in two galleries, the paintings are like a strangely familiar old family album. Stiff little figures in their best clothes, calm, rugged faces over clean white collars represent our folk art—with simplicity and directness, yet an inherent "artistic innocence." The words "artist unknown" often mark a painting, adding mystery to charm. Many of them undoubtedly were made by itinerants who were professional artists only in the sense that they earned their living by painting. They traveled from farm to farm, from village to village, recording portraits and landscapes. These latter, whether real or imaginary, substituted very well for the fashionable scenic panels found in some fine mansions of the day.

The collection is drawn mainly from the Eastern third of the country and was started in 1945 (although collectors generally began taking such pictures seriously about 1930). With fashion designers copying the big floppy hat from Romney's *Miss Willoughby,* and decorators borrowing ideas in furnishings from Federal Period paintings, certainly out of this broad American collection could come inspiration for china, fabrics, and much more.

As you move from one gallery to the next, you'll find students working at easels, copying old masters. Any art student can do this free of charge. Arrangements start with a visit to the Assistant Director's office, perhaps with picture in hand showing what you can do. Easel, dropcloth, and such are provided by the Gallery; the student must bring his own paints and canvas. This is a time-honored way for students to follow in the brush strokes of the masters.

This building, aside from its great beauty and its priceless contents, is remarkable in many ways. It is allergy-free, which is easy on the old masters, too. Its intricate air-conditioning system adjusts

United States Botanic Garden

and cleans moisture content to the proper degree, regulates temperature, and washes the air in such a way as to make the Gallery just about the cleanest building in the world. A large housekeeping brigade sets to work after the last visitor's footfall has echoed away at night. All the galleries have comfortable oak flooring, so that you can crisscross it in thousands of steps without suffering the aches of "museum feet."

Before you leave, stop at the main desk for one of the most beau-

tiful and least expensive souvenirs you can take home: a reproduction of a painting you yourself "discovered" on this trip. Prices
range from five cents for a colored postcard to $20 for a large-size
print suitable for framing.

U.S. BOTANIC GARDEN, at First and Canal streets, SW, at the
foot of the Capitol. (No admission charge.) Open 9:00 A.M. to 4:00
P.M. weekdays and Sunday; 9:00 A.M. to 11:30 A.M. Saturdays.

You'll recognize the domed top of the conservatories rising just
east of the National Gallery of Art. The Architect of the Capitol is
Acting Director of this agency. When flowers and plants are avail-
able, members of Congress have the privilege of drawing on the
Botanic Garden for free floral decorations for special occasions.
(Plants are supplied on a loan basis.)

The beauty high spot of the year is usually from March into April
when azaleas and lilies are in bloom. Orchids too thrive in the moist
tropic and subtropic atmosphere, along with palms and exotics. In
the fall the hardy chrysanthemums put on a showy display; then
poinsettias follow in time for Christmas.

The nearest good restaurant for lunch is the cafeteria in the National Gallery of Art which will work in well for you on this tour. It
offers variety and is not expensive.

A dinner suggestion: west on Pennsylvania Avenue between Thirteenth and Fourteenth, NW, is the Occidental Restaurant. It is
recommended not alone for excellent menus and good service, but
for its fascinating memorabilia of the great and near great. A collection of fifteen hundred photographs covers the walls (insured, they
say, for one million dollars). The Occidental's thick onion soup and
rum buns have been favorites for years. Two people can eat well for
five dollars, plus tip.

It's not improbable that later this evening you might like to escape to something completely sedentary. There's Cinerama at 8:30
P.M. at the Warner Theater only steps away at Thirteenth and E
streets, NW, for vicarious traveling and thrills that will have your
eyes literally popping. The Trans-Lux at Fourteenth and New York
Avenue, NW, and The Playhouse on Fifteenth near H, NW, are

recommended. Or you might like to try one of the several movie houses here where foreign films are shown exclusively. The Mac-Arthur on MacArthur Boulevard at Forty-eighth Street, NW (a neighborhood house especially popular with the young married set) schedules only British productions. It often features such lively favorites as Alec Guinness and sometimes interesting little chillers. The Dupont on Connecticut Avenue just south of Dupont Circle offers a variety of foreign pictures (and while the theater is small, the seats are very comfortable).

Most of these special movie theaters serve coffee before the feature begins and display the work of local artists in their corridors.

Tour VIII

A Visit to Mount Vernon; Georgetown

MOUNT VERNON. (50 cents admission charge.) Open every day from 9:00 A.M. Entrance gate closes from March 1 to October 1 at 5:00 P.M.; from October 1 to March 1 at 4:00 P.M. (Boat schedule: leaves Washington: 10:00 A.M. and 2:00 P.M., arrives Mount Vernon: 11:10 and 3:10; leaves Mount Vernon: 12:30 and 5:15, arrives Washington 1:40 and 6:40.) The Mount Vernon Memorial Highway passing through Alexandria is a direct route from Washington.

After you pass through the turnstile into the 475–acre estate your eye may catch this line in the excellent free leaflet you have just received: "Mount Vernon is one of the best remaining examples of the plantations around which centered the highly developed social and economic life of the South."

Then, if it's early March, your gaze will wander to crocuses—white, violet, and yellow—snug along the brick walkway. The day may be misty, thus holding agreeably in the air gentle smells of spring. Gardeners are poking about in their usual mysterious fashion, adding the truly authentic touch to anyone's, but particularly a Southerner's, picture of an eighteenth-century plantation. (After many visits in all seasons, I am convinced that weather changes to "atmosphere" while one is at Mount Vernon. Let it be December's most bleak day in town; out here this merely enables you to step "live" into a steel engraving which might be called *Winter Scene at Mount Vernon.*)

However you may have reached this historic spot, by car or boat, you must know that your pilgrimage is part of a ceaseless tribute since George Washington's passing on a snowy Saturday in December, 1799.

The *Star* for August 19, 1850, noted that a steamboat operator had consulted with John A. Washington, last owner of Mount Vernon, to establish regular service between Washington and the home of the first President. For although the mansion and grounds then showed neglect and disrepair, a steady stream of visitors made the carriage and boat trips to the plantation. Almost all furniture and memorabilia had long since gone to descendants or friends, or been sold by the executors; thus it was an especially cheerless sight to the many oldsters who knew personally of the mansion's happier days.

In one account of such a visit made before the restoration, a "gay party of idlers" are eating their lunch on the stone steps overlooking the river; inside the house is blank and dismal. A wire covering protects from vandals the marble mantel (still in the Banquet Hall); the library has been stripped of its books; and the bedroom in which General Washington drew his anguished last breath is without any furnishing, except for the mantel. "The only interesting object, save the interior of the mansion itself, is the key of the Bastile . . . hanging in a case on the wall."

Such contrast with Mount Vernon as we know it today only serves to make one doubly grateful to the Mount Vernon Ladies' Association. This organization, under the leadership of Ann Pamela Cunningham, of South Carolina, built up sufficient funds through a nation-wide campaign to snatch the "decayed homestead" from certain destruction.

Now, as you go about, there is reason to remember Miss Cunningham's straightforward admonition to the Association on the occasion of her farewell address in June, 1874: "Ladies, the home of Washington is in your charge—see to it that you keep it the home

of Washington. . . . Those who go to the home in which he lived
and died wish to see in what he lived and died. . . . Upon you rests
this duty."

The official tour through the mansion permits you to enter directly
into the Banquet Hall, looking in on the West Parlor and Music
Room, and gaining another view from the passage or Center Hall.

The Banquet Hall was called "the New Room" by Washington,
perhaps because it was part of the addition which progressed in his
absence during the Revolution; then a distant relative, Lund Washington, capably managed the farm. The two men exchanged many
letters (forty-seven of Lund's letters have proved invaluable in the
restoration work); even in the year 1776, with war cares heavy upon
him, the General found time to write that the mantel be placed in
the exact center of the room. "In short I would have the whole executed in a masterly manner," he wrote.

The true grace of the room, accented in the Palladian window,
the rich warm woods of the wide flooring, gains added charm from
Washington's great love of farming. His desire "to be the first farmer
in the country" is symbolized in the homespun implements of farming found in the stucco ceiling. The sculptured panels of simple farm
animals in the mantel again emphasize the pastoral—although the
whole was a gift sent to the General from a London friend. In his
note of acknowledgment, Washington wrote: "I have the honor to
inform you that the chimney-piece is arrived, and, by the number of
cases [ten] too elegant and costly by far, I fear for my own room
and republican style of living." (The donor was Samuel Vaughan,
who ten years later ordered a portrait of the General from the hand
of Gilbert Stuart; the resulting portrait thereafter was called the
Vaughan Washington.)

The portrait of Washington now hanging above the mantel is a
Gilbert Stuart, right enough, but not the original painting that hung
on that wall. The Mount Vernon Ladies, however, have traced that
original and dream that one day it may come back to this "home"
spot.

The colors used in the spacious room (as all through the house) are those believed chosen by Washington. That Martha was fond of dimity is beautifully noted in the window drapery. White dimity curtains follow the fashion of the day, even to the dark green satin overdrapes. (This is not the sheer dimity we know. Original curtains of a heavy enough texture to be mistaken for "white chintz" by a young English guest might have confused this research problem, except that Martha willed a pair of cherished "dimity" curtains to a granddaughter.)

Architecturally, the first room to the right is outstanding, and even the youngest, most modern of interior decorators admire the West Parlor as one of the finest examples of Colonial Virginia interiors to be seen today. Be sure to peer far enough into the room to see the old mirror hanging on the outside wall which has been mended so many times it resembles a wrinkled map. The Washington family coat-of-arms appears in the decorative panel at the top. Look for it again in the carved pediment over the mantel and in slightly different form in the iron fireback of the fireplace. (The flag of the District of Columbia is based on the shield of the Washington Coat-of-arms.)

The portrait of the General facing the Banquet Hall is one of several painted by Charles Willson Peale during the Revolution. The artist's signature and the dates 1780–1796 would indicate that this is a replica of the original done in 1780. Missing is the painting executed from life at Mount Vernon and to which the General referred in his *Virginia Almanac for the years of our Lord God 1772*, under the expresive heading, "Where and How my Time is Spent:"

> May 20—I sat to have my picture drawn.
> May 21—I sat again to take the drapery.
> May 22—Set to Mr. Peale to finish my face.

The portrait resulting from these sittings hung in Mount Vernon until Martha Washington's death; then it passed to descendants and now is owned by Washington and Lee University at Lexington, Virginia.

(A story is told of Washington sitting years later in a Philadelphia studio for four members of the painting Peale family. Finding them grouped in a semicircle around him, Washington could not resist observing that he would indeed be "well Peeled today.")

The rug in the West Parlor is an unusually fine example of eight-eenth-century English craftsmanship, and so valuable that when dignitaries see the rooms, and the cords barring the way come down, a protective runner is laid over the rug to save it from direct foot-prints.

The handsome harpsichord in the next-door Music Room is the same much traveled one for which General Washington sent to London and which went with him from Philadelphia to Mount Ver-non in 1797. It was for his foster daughter Nelly; when she moved with her husband Lawrence Lewis to Woodlawn after her grand-mother's death, the harpsichord went too.

The piece has added significance, for with the return of this instrument by Mrs. Lewis' daughter-in-law began the flow back to Mount Vernon, by gift, loan and purchase, of original Mount Vernon memorabilia. It has continued year after year for four generations. The scope of the collection may be measured in part by the change in General Washington's bedchamber—described by the 1850 visitor as bare but for the mantel. Today the room is not only well fur-nished, but all furniture is original.

Careful searching of old inventory lists, Washington's will, his diaries, account books, receipts of purchases both here and abroad, and the study of history books have all been valuable in guiding generations of Mount Vernon Ladies in their painstaking restoration. In the detailed account of Mount Vernon by the American historian-engraver Benson Lossing, he mentions that the 6½-foot bed on which Washington slept, and finally succumbed to a bad cold, was made in New York in 1789. With the breaking up of Mount Vernon in 1802, the bed went to Arlington House (now Custis-Lee Man-sion) where it was carefully preserved by G. W. P. Custis. Quite early the bed was returned on loan to the room, then, in 1908, was confirmed by deed of gift. As you look in on the scene now, there is the same intimate feeling here that marks all the upstairs rooms. The

General's trunk at the foot of the bed must have been dust-covered more often than not, for this he used for his personal belongings during the Revolution. (Martha Washington slept in the dormered chamber above during the 2½ years she survived her husband.)

As you linger in the library, or study, it's pleasant to visualize General Washington busy here arranging his "voluminous papers," making entries in his diary, writing letters, studying the newspapers of the day, or exploring some of the more than eight hundred volumes and pamphlets he owned. Almost a hundred of these books have now found their way back, and are grouped in the bookcases, together with duplicates of titles listed in the executor's inventory.

At the pantry door you can as readily imagine Martha Washington holding a glass to the light or examining the china. A letter written almost a hundred years ago by Mary Custis Lee, Martha's great granddaughter, describes the mistress of Mount Vernon:

She was remarkable for inspecting everything daily, giving out with her own hands the meals, going into her dairy, cellar, etc. I have heard my mother say she always wore a white dimity dress on those occasions; that it was spotless and served her for a morning dress the whole week. The one put on for dinner answered the same purpose the following week. Having well-trained servants, of course, it was not necessary that she should, with her own hands, perform any household duties, as in these times we do.

When you learn that there were some 90 people residing on the Mansion House Farm in 1786 and more than 150 others living on the four adjoining farms, the responsibility of servants and their needs looms large for Mrs. Washington indeed. Daily supervision of the spinning house, where ten or more women worked constantly, spinning and knitting, must have been especially important.

There is much for the modern farmer and car-owner (who today finds less call for ingenuity than in Washington's day) to enjoy in the outbuildings. In the coachhouse, for example, is a remarkable wheel jack which must have worked very well, and a coach, beautifully fitted-out, contemporary to General Washington's vehicle.

The Museum, adjacent to the Mansion, is a treasurehouse of

Washington belongings. Of prime importance is Mount Vernon Ladies' most valuable possession, the bust of General Washington from life which was modeled in clay at Mount Vernon (and remained there) by the French sculptor, Jean Antoine Houdon. It represents the General about 1785 in his best physical condition, and is regarded as the finest among many likenesses. (Houdon was commissioned by the State of Virginia to execute a full-length statue of the Commander in Chief—this now stands in Richmond, Virginia. The clay bust from which impressions were taken was modeled at this time.)

In Washington's diary under date of October 2, 1785 he wrote:

After we were in Bed (about eleven O'clock in the Evening) Mr. Houdon, sent from Paris by Doctr. Franklin and Mr. Jefferson to take my Bust, in behalf of the State of Virginia, with three young men assistants, introduced by a Mr. Peris, a French Gentleman of Alexandria, arrived by Water from the latter place.

Here, too, is Martha Washington's bathing costume, fashioned of blue and white checked homespun, which she wore at Berkeley Springs, and the General's long white stockings with "clocks." Also there is the "expense account" for Martha's eight war years spent with the General, which comes to the amount of 1,064 pounds and 1 shilling.

If the red cypress shingles on the buildings seem to look new, they *are* new, having been replaced in 1955. They are hand-made and in random widths, copying the originals, but modern to the extent that they are proof against both fire and insects.

The Washington Tomb lies in the family vault, a short walk down the slope to the south. Express directions in the General's will provided for the building of the present vault "at the foot of what is commonly called the Vineyard Inclosure." But it was not until after 1830 that Congress abandoned its plan to erect a marble monument within the Capitol to hold Washington's remains. (Hardly a week after his death, Martha Washington was petitioned to give her permission to the plan, which she did, although she was forced to add in her letter: "In doing this I need not . . . say what a sacrifice of individual feeling I make to a sense of public duty.")

But today you can read the simple inscription: "Within this Enclosure Rest the remains of Gen. George Washington." Martha Washington is by his side. Marble shafts honor the memory of those other proprietors of Mount Vernon, Bushrod Washington and his nephew, John Augustine Washington. The shafts at the side mark the graves of Martha's granddaughter, Nelly Custis Lewis, and her daughter.

As you stroll back up the hill, perhaps winding through the gardens, with their boxwood hedges, believed to date to 1798, you might like to cross over to the salesroom where the Mount Vernon Ladies' Association has an excellent handbook on sale for fifty cents, together with postcards and other official publications.

A last look back as you take the outbound road is always convincing that in the choice of its site, overlooking the Potomac, in pleasing plan of the grounds, and in the gracious mansion itself, the judgment of our First President was indeed sound. "No estate in United America is more pleasantly situated than this . . ." was the way he felt.

It is possible to get sandwiches and beverages at the snack bar a few steps outside the entrance to the grounds.

On the drive back to Washington through the City of Alexandria, you may want to have lunch at the Old Club, a good eating place with more than a little history about it. Reasonable prices. Or, just out of Alexandria to the north is a Hot Shoppe where you can eat in your car a magnificent mouthful known as a "mighty Mo" (two hamburgers, melted cheese and relish for fifty cents).

GEORGETOWN, reached by following Pennsylvania Avenue or K Street to M Street and Wisconsin Avenue, NW.

A well-rounded plan to see Georgetown might properly be called "little rambles through an old Colonial town."

On an early evening, as the lamplights are coming on, stroll up from N or P or Q street and into the bystreets. You'll tread brick sidewalks and narrow lanes where small clapboard houses sit with an air of perhaps listening to a chance greeting. On high terraced lawns are formal, aloof brick mansions, relieved in their dignity only by the intimate clasp of green ivy at graceful doorways.

Gaslight lanterns flicker at an entrance, and you catch the sparkle of chandeliers through an open window—and voices or the splashing of a swimming pool beyond garden walls.

This was about the hour when in times gone by a combination watchman and weatherman made his rounds and cried, "Nine o'clock, a fair bright night—all's well!"

Georgetown is the place in Washington where you can see houses of the Federal period, streets of them, renewed and kept in shining order. All manner of organizations work toward a "better Georgetown." Citizens, eyeing the big transit buses that rumble through, complain that they are shaking some of the old structures. The Commission of Fine Arts must pass on all plans for building or exterior improvements.

When a Georgetown house goes on the market for rent or sale, some who walk through are no strangers to the place. They are former tenants or owners and probably still Georgetowners, drawn back out of curiosity or affection for an earlier abode. "I never would have cut a door there," someone says in a surprised, hurt tone. Or, scarcely hiding shock, "This wallpaper! I always used Williamsburg blue. . . ." It's as though one can never quite sever the personal tie with one of these old dwellings.

You'll see many examples of fine Federal architecture. The skill of Dr. William Thornton, who designed the Capitol, is apparent in Tudor Place, on Q Street at Thirty-first. This private residence shows little sign of age, yet its associations go back to the Washington family a century and a half ago. Tudor Place, set in spacious grounds, was the home of Martha Parke Custis, granddaughter of Martha Washington, who married Thomas Peter, founder of Georgetown's first bank. From the early 1800's to this day, the home has remained in the hands of Peter descendants. The house is famous, too, for the guests it has welcomed—among them Lafayette and Robert E. Lee—and for a cherished collection of Washington relics.

When in 1791 the "ten miles square" outlined the boundaries of the soon-to-come Federal City, Georgetown was already a busy community forty years old. Its name "George Town," honored George II, then King of Great Britain. The old street names may be found today on many lamp posts—Fishing Lane, Cherry Alley, Wapping, and Gay. The town early took advantage of its site at the head of Potomac navigation, and built the first wharf in the area. In much earlier times the site is believed to have been used by the Analostan Indians for their village of Tahoga. Navigator Henry Fleete, in 1623, was the first European to look upon this Georgetown-Washington area (if you agree with those historians who are convinced that Captain John Smith didn't get up this far). Fleete was impressed and wrote, "This place without all question is the most pleasant and healthful place in all this country . . . the air temperate in summer and not violent in winter."

Under the charter of Lord Baltimore, numerous grants of land along the river were made. Historic names in Georgetown annals include Ninian Beall, who in 1703 received a patent of 795 acres from the Province of Maryland as a reward for valiant action against the Indians. He named it Rock of Dunbarton (later spelled Dumbarton), probably remembering the great rock above the Clyde in his native Scotland. George Gordon took up his grant near by and bought another, calling his land Rock Creek Plantation. (Gordon, being Sheriff for a time, set up stocks as a form of punishment.)

In those early days fairs were held each year in April and October, at which time by law the town gave its blessing to all and sundry persons within the bounds of the community. No one could be arrested except for a felony or breach of the peace, and all travelers to and from the fairs, on the day before and the day after, were equally free from arrest.

In the Georgetown Custom House old records of imports, exports, and vessels go back to those early times. They reveal the town as a thriving fish market in the early decades of the nineteenth century.

In 1820 the inspection of flour rose to 107,320 barrels. Conestoga wagons, drawn by four- and six-horse teams, lined up on what is now Wisconsin Avenue right down to the water, and along P Street. These wagons brought produce and animals and sometimes took back loads of shad and herring. Catches in the Potomac were enormous in those days.

Looking at Georgetown's tidy streets and homes today, it is difficult to place it as the dejected, run-down area of some decades ago. This downhill trend set in more than a century ago as the Potomac River became choked with silt and vessels gradually found the stream unnavigable to the port. Another great hope faded as the Chesapeake and Ohio Canal, much delayed, finally was finished to Cumberland, Maryland, in 1850, only to be overshadowed forever by the railroad. Then, as the City of Washington prospered, families moved away from Georgetown. Until February 11, 1895, the old town was within District boundaries but had its own laws and government. Then, by act of Congress Georgetown was consolidated with Washington.

It was not until after World War I that strangers began disturbing the settled dust of Georgetown, started buying the fine brick houses and restoring them. The saturation point has been very nearly reached, according to real estate experts who often consider the sale and purchase of a Georgetown property a matter of "whims and fancies." This viewpoint is based on a buyer's apparent willingness to pay high prices for history and atmosphere—and often a dwelling that must be rebuilt to the outer façade.

Georgetown in the old days was often likened to a big tavern. Suter's Tavern, perhaps the most famous, was the "Board of Trade, Chamber of Commerce, Civic Center, Town Hall, Banquet Hall, and even occasionally the Court House." It plainly had a substantial hold on the town, but the location has skipped about since then, with historians striving earnestly to pinpoint its exact site. In September, 1955, a National Park Service historian felt he had evidence to "prove conclusively" that Suter's Tavern, later called Fountain Inn, was located on the northwest corner of Thirty-first and K

Wisconsin Avenue, Georgetown

streets. If there are those who still prefer to keep turning over old and new clues, the important fact is that this old lost landmark gathered to it such notables as General Washington, Thomas Jefferson, the City Commissioners, Dr. William Thornton, and Pierre Charles L'Enfant. L'Enfant stayed here while working on his famous plan.

"Dined at Suter's Tavern at a public dinner given by the Mayor," noted General Washington on March 28, 1791. John Suter himself must have been a jovial personality. In his will, dated July 14, 1784, he directed that "my large Bible, my small gin case" go to his wife. Unpaid accounts were handled informally; they were chalked up on the door.

But even forty years ago the shops along Wisconsin Avenue were few and nondescript. Today, people from all over the metropolitan area delight in spending a morning exploring the dozens of small specialty shops, intimate art galleries, antique shops, and book nooks that are sprinkled along Wisconsin Avenue and adjacent streets.

You might pick a Saturday morning, starting at Wisconsin and R where the red-brick Georgetown branch of the District of Columbia Public Library crowns a hill just opposite distinguished homes. Walk leisurely downhill past shop windows; the difficult decision will be which side to follow. On both sides of Wisconsin Avenue are restaurants, some modest in size and menu; others, like Billy Martin's Carriage House, reflecting the charm and opulence of Southern tradition.

Along M Street west of Wisconsin Avenue are auction rooms and Stombock's, a deluxe saddlery and leather goods shop whose two sections are separated by a little barbershop. The home of Francis Scott Key once stood near the Key Bridge approach; it was razed several years ago to make way for the Whitehurst Freeway. Up ahead rise the gray spires of Georgetown University, the oldest Catholic college in the United States, founded in 1789. In the Healy Building of the University is a fine portrait of Archbishop Carroll, founder, painted by Gilbert Stuart. John Carroll's preference was for the Potomac bluffs rather than for Jenkins Hill as a site for the school. The Capitol Hill location he considered too remote—"in the country."

Walking eastward on M Street, you will come to Number 3049—the Stone House, with traditions dating to pre-Revolutionary days. In 1955 restoration by the National Park Service began. One legend says L'Enfant occupied the building while he planned the City of Washington. Actual proof points out that in 1808 the house was a tailor shop, and later it became the quarters of a house painter.

On down the street, perhaps turning soon into Thomas Jefferson Street to follow the old Chesapeake and Ohio Canal for a few blocks. Wherever you go, brass door knockers, coach lamps, and bright doors painted red, blue, or candy pink lend a special charm that's augmented many times by the affection the residents feel for their historic old town.

Tour IX

A Time for Photography

If a gentle rain settles over the city while you are here and you are tempted to pack your camera away, remember that mist plus Washington-after-dark equals beautiful photography. Sharp contrasts are lessened in the haze; soft tones and a velvety extra dimension are gained through time exposures and occasional use of flashbulbs for near highlights. (For sixteen striking black-and-white examples of what a photographer can do with his camera on such nights, look up the April, 1940, issue of the *National Geographic Magazine*. The series is called "Washington by Night," and in it staff photographer Volkmar Wentzel created memorable studies of after-dark landmarks.)

Try, for example, an early evening picture of the Capitol as the lighted dome reflects on the gleaming wet Pennsylvania Avenue.

If you are lucky enough to time your visit with a rare snowfall, you can expect to see local cameramen, amateurs as well as professionals, drop everything and strike out with camera and tripod to capture winter's touch on scenes usually seen through sunshine and cherry blossoms.

Armed with such equipment and fast film, you can try for impressive pictures of the lighted landmarks. The night view of the National Archives facing south is a beautiful one, as concealed beams outline the classic architecture. This can be a stark winter picture at early nightfall—five or five-thirty on a December evening.

Often visitors who come here to photograph the Capital's monuments and domes spend days observing the structures from different angles, noting the exact time when the light is best on those subjects they most want to record.

Local amateurs—and some are excellent photographers—have experimented with these problems and found such data as these:

The north portico of the White House, the Jefferson Memorial, and other structures similarly placed can often be photographed at their best during the months of June and July. Then the long slanting rays of either the early morning sun or the evening sun make for better pictures than at any other season. The rays strike the pillars of the White House's north façade, highlighting them and illuminating the inner area which usually is shadowed.

The same is true of the Jefferson Memorial; the very early or late light—say about 8:00 P.M. Daylight Saving Time—casts a shimmering full reflection of the Memorial on the Tidal Basin.

The morning hours are best for pictures of the Lincoln Memorial. Then the east light is at your back, highlighting steps, pillars, and even reaching into the interior where the figure of Lincoln sits. The black-and-white photograph of the Memorial used in this book was made by an amateur photographer in the forenoon when natural light added to artificial lighting. Exposure was one second at ƒ 11, with a K-2 filter.

The famous photograph of the Washington Monument and the Capitol lined up with and framed by pillars of the south colonnade of the Lincoln Memorial is an afternoon picture.

In midsummer you are sure to find the elements of good pictures around the Columbus Memorial in front of Union Station. Youngsters often splash in and out of the fountain, and the south entrance of the station offers many good architectural details.

While the Washington Monument often seems difficult because of its great height, taken from the Lincoln Memorial at sunset it offers interesting composition for a color picture. The late shadows gradually climb the Monument, and there is a moment when the top is touched with gold. Line up your picture with the marble tripod on either side of the Lincoln Memorial steps. This is also a good spot to try for a time exposure of after-dark fireworks on the Fourth of July. You can catch the reflection in the pool—and you will want a firm prop for your camera.

Another interesting sunset picture has been made in early December by shooting into the late sunlight between the two massive gold statues at the entrance to the Memorial Bridge. Then the sun is almost exactly centered between the two, and when snared through a shred or so of cloud, it is effective photography—often good enough to make a handsome Christmas card.

If you need special instructions or help in operating your equipment, the camera shops here are familiar with these problems and will be happy to help. Some downtown shops will accept your camera in trade on a new model, change your film, snap your picture, and develop your prints. Most shops also have cameras for rent.

Tour X

Custis-Lee Mansion, Arlington National Cemetery, United States Marine Corps War Memorial

CUSTIS-LEE MANSION, overlooking the Potomac River in Arlington National Cemetery. (25 cent admission charge, which is waived for children and educational groups.) Open 9:30 A.M. to 4:30 P.M. October through March; from 9:30 A.M. to 6:00 P.M. April through September. Guided tours conducted; recitals Sunday afternoons 3:00 to 4:00 o'clock.

Many times before you finally follow the hillside road through Arlington National Cemetery to the Custis-Lee Mansion you'll glance toward it from the District side of the Potomac. At nightfall this memorial to Robert E. Lee glows in classic miniature above the dark Virginia shore, marking the mansion which is famous, too, for long association with the Custis and Washington families. (Here again we must bow to the infallible good judgment of those first home builders.)

After parking your car your approach will be into the area of the servants' quarters and the refurbished smokehouse and summer kitchen. Hams and sides of bacon hang realistically from the smokehouse ceiling; corn is drying in the kitchen; and in the air is a sense of suspended time, a feeling that everyone will presently return to take up his task. (That dignified, aging Indian cedar, planted after the Lees left, receives special care from the National Park Service, which administers this Memorial.)

The mansion itself rises on land that came to the Custis family in 1778, when Martha Washington's son, John Parke Custis, purchased eleven hundred acres. But it was not until Martha Washington's death in 1802 that her grandson George Washington Parke Custis came into his inheritance and began building Arlington House. It was named for an older Eastern Shore homestead. The boy, now nineteen, must have looked out many times from his hilltop, as the north and south wings were building, on the fascinating scene spread out below. Georgetown was then a busy port, and sailing vessels laden with flour, corn, and tobacco slipped down the Potomac bound for Europe. The Capitol Building in the Federal City was a modest rectangular structure, and the few scattered houses were lost in the green.

Seven years earlier a gifted English architect, George Hadfield, had arrived with an introductory letter from John Trumbull, the artist, to take the job of superintendent of the Capitol at three hundred guineas a year, plus his ocean passage. His major work proved to be the old City Hall (now national headquarters of the Selective Service System, on Indiana Avenue between Fourth and Fifth streets, NW), but in his obituary notice the design for Arlington House was credited to Hadfield. His influence is said to be apparent in the graceful arches and high doorways, emphasizing the period of Greek Classic Revival.

The life patterns of two separate families were spun out here almost simultaneously. For George W. P. Custis shortly married Mary Lee Fitzhugh of Chatham, Virginia. They lived temporarily in the north wing where a three-room apartment was arranged for them. Bricks burned from native clay, local timbers and foundation stones went into the mansion. But the two wings waited more than a decade, as war curtailed building.

In 1817 much, if not all, of the portico was finished. The eight Doric columns supporting the massive pediment added a timeless elegance. And all about the rooms were many fine pieces from

Mount Vernon—furniture, portraits, plate and china, plus a precious collection of intimate Washington possessions. In the small family parlor on the first floor, Jackson and Pierce as well as other Presidents visited with Custis, in a fine tradition of honoring General Washington. The stream of distinguished guests seemed drawn there to exchange a personal anecdote or to admire and examine the relics that so recently had come from Mount Vernon. The tradition of hospitality that Custis learned while growing up at Mount Vernon was continued at Arlington House; friends and relatives found it a welcome break in the dusty ride from Alexandria or from distant points, for the estate was on a main north-south road.

George W. P. Custis was more dilettante than planter. His plays were produced from Boston to Charleston, and his recollections of both his foster father and of his visits with Lafayette made interesting reading.

A new tie was made when Mary Anne Custis, the only surviving child, became the bride of Robert E. Lee, a handsome lieutenant who had graduated second in his class at West Point. The wedding was held on a rainy June evening in 1831 in the same family parlor. (It is said that Lee proposed to Mary Anne in the cozy little dining room as she was about to offer him a bit of fruitcake.)

In due time, life at Arlington House became increasingly gay with the sounds of small children. Six of Mrs. Lee's seven children were born here. The wide plank flooring on the second floor hallway—still there today—must have clattered with their footsteps as they overflowed the tiny playroom.

Distant tours of duty often kept Lee absent from the mansion. With the death of George W. P. Custis in 1857 came the responsibility of making his wife's inheritance, the plantation, pay after years of gradual neglect. The land stretched from Rosslyn to the Pentagon in present-day terms, and required constant attention to both the produce and the slaves—which old Mr. Custis, more easygoing than efficient, had not given. On temporary leave from the Army, Robert E. Lee became a farmer and brought Arlington back to good productivity. But even this period at home was interrupted when, now a lieutenant colonel, he was called upon to capture John Brown and his raiders at Harpers Ferry.

But it was another turn of events that brought Colonel Lee anguish, took him from Arlington House and its pleasant acres, saw the mansion empty and the hillside a Yankee burying ground. The mansion has not lost the full distress of those hours, as you hear your guide describe the events that followed Colonel Lee's ride across the Potomac to Blair House, on April 18, 1861. There he was offered command of Union forces which he declined.

On the 19th it was known that the State of Virginia had adopted the Ordinance of Secession. Shortly thereafter, Lee wrote to Secretary of War Simon Cameron, resigning his commission in the United States Army. Robert E. Lee in civilian clothes took the train to Richmond on April 22, 1861. There he was placed in charge of the military and naval forces of Virginia and in the following year took command of the Army of Northern Virginia.

Thus ended the private, happy life of Arlington House. Mrs. Lee stayed on gathering together family heirlooms and valuable Washington relics, and when she left for a sanctuary near Fairfax, as much as she could take went with her. When Federal troops occupied lands between Washington and Alexandria, Arlington became a key position. In 1862, the occupying Union Commander at Arlington sent on to the Patent Office as many of the Mount Vernon keepsakes as were to be found in the house, but by then some had disappeared.

The Robert E. Lees never returned to live at Arlington. In 1864 the United States Government confiscated the property for nonpayment of taxes and set aside some two hundred acres for a national cemetery. It took a Supreme Court ruling to restore the property to George Washington Custis Lee, grandson of the builder. But it was no longer a homestead; it was revered by the North and the South alike. Lee consented to give the government the mansion and land for $150,000, and in 1883 Congress appropriated this amount.

As your guide, dressed in period costume, takes you about, she'll point out original pieces that have come back to the mansion since the restoration work began in 1925. Some are "association" pieces, valued because a member of the families used them at some time.

Here, as at Woodlawn Plantation and Stratford Hall, restoration of original pieces is difficult because for such a long period the precious first possessions became scattered or lost. But restorers have filled in the lack with authentic antiques before the date 1861, and a few fine reproductions.

The great central hallway divides the north side with its family dining room and intimate family parlor. The impressive drawing room on the south side was not completed until 1855. Colonel Lee, shortly to leave for Texas, decided his family should have the gracious room for musicals and entertaining. The piano you see there is an "association" piece from a near-by home, where Mrs. Robert E. Lee used to visit.

The formal drawing room was called the "big room" in the Custis days. The mantelpieces are original; the graceful chairs are reproductions of a Sheraton set of Martha Washington's.

On the small dresser in Colonel Lee's bedroom is his shaving stand, and just in front of it is a miniature lectern with the initials "MCL," which held Mrs. Lee's manicure set. The door at the right enters into the small room where the Lee children were born.

The playroom will charm you completely. Bows and arrows hang on the wall, and a pair of ice skates recall that friends used to skate over "from Christ Church in Alexandria." That perfect little secretary on the floor has a tradition linked to it—it first belonged to Nelly Custis, sister of Arlington's first proprietor. When she grew up she gave it to Mary Anne. The dolls in calico dresses, with cloth bodies and china faces, are of the type the children played with.

You'll see the bedroom where Agnes, Annie, and Mildred Lee slept. Don't miss the cheerful schoolroom, or morning room, where the youngsters received part of their education. The globe, with Old World travel routes traced on it, was made in England in about 1795. Workmen repairing the roof found it hidden in the attic under the eaves some years ago.

The Sunday afternoon piano recital, between three and four o'clock, is a pleasant way to recall other days. Costumed hostesses, candlelight, and music of the period add to the charm of the elegant rooms.

You'll be sure to find the view from the portico still living up to the words of a most famous visitor—General Lafayette. This, he felt, was the most beautiful view of Washington City one could find. His visit in 1824 and 1825 came years after his last sight of Mount Vernon, yet the iron lantern in the hall he remarked as coming from Mount Vernon.

But another Frenchman who by this time you know well, Pierre Charles L'Enfant, sleeps just on the crest of the hill, and the monument honoring him carries a replica of his famous plan.

ARLINGTON NATIONAL CEMETERY. Grounds open daily and Sunday: October through March: 7:30 A.M. to 5:00 P.M.; April through September: 7:30 A.M. to 7:00 P.M.;

Strolling about the Custis-Lee Mansion you can sometimes hear the distant, mournful bugling of "Taps." It is a reminder, perhaps, that some two hundred acres of the old Custis plantation formed the nucleus of present-day Arlington National Cemetery. (George Washington Parke Custis and Mary Lee Custis lie buried near the Civil War dead under three giant oak trees.)

Your drive through the beautiful grounds, where in spring great splashes of pink dogwood and redbud, white dogwood and new green make it especially lovely, may seem a labyrinth as you mount the rolling hills and choose this road and that. Actually shaped like a spreading semicircle, most roads in the reservation will lead you up within sight of the Arlington Memorial Amphitheater. The elliptical Amphitheater of dazzling white Vermont marble, completed in 1920, was the design of Carrère and Hastings, leading architects of their times. On Memorial Day, official services take place here no matter what the weather. On Easter Sunday, the crowds assembled for ceremonies of the Knights Templar of the Masonic Order fill the four thousand places.

Near by is the famed Maine Memorial. The mast of the U.S.S.

Maine, its crow's nest still intact, was raised from the sunken battle-ship in Havana Harbor in 1912. Not far away the World War I dead lie in regular and almost endless lines, marked by simple white inscribed headstones.

First established as a burial place for Civil War dead, the cemetery was made a military cemetery by Lincoln's Secretary of War in 1864. Now heroes from the Revolution to the Korean War rest here. Permission for burial in Arlington is granted to any member of the Armed Forces of the United States dying in active service, or former member whose last active service terminated honorably, together with his spouse and minor children, regardless of race, color, or creed. About seventy-five interments are made in Arlington each week.

THE TOMB OF THE UNKNOWN SOLDIER lies at the eastern entrance of the Amphitheater. You will not want to miss a sight of the touching yet solemn ceremony that takes place here each day, every hour on the hour. It is the changing of the guard, and even the small boys who, in curiosity, almost charge into his path, step back as the young, lance-straight sentry treads the path, turns, clicks his heels, and paces the thirty or more steps along the paved terrace.

While you wait for the corporal of the guard to escort the relief sentry into position, you have time to read the simple yet meaningful inscription on the tomb "Here rests in honored glory an American Soldier known but to God." Beneath the tomb lies a sarcophagus holding the unidentified body of a soldier which was brought back from France. Honored with the Congressional Medal of Honor by the United States, and the highest military decorations from Allied Powers, the body lay in state in the Rotunda of the Capitol before it was interred.

Although it is a memorial to all American soldiers and sailors who lost their lives in World War I, it pays tribute also to the boy who did not come back from Normandy or from Iwo Jima.

THE MARINE CORPS MEMORIAL, recreating in bronze the heroic flag-raising on Mount Suribachi, Iwo Jima, is located just north of Memorial Bridge in Virginia. A "Marine Parade" and park, adjacent to the Memorial, also provides ample parking space. Several spine-tingling ceremonies are held here. Every morning and evening, rain or shine, a Marine Corps color guard in dress uniform raises or lowers the colors. The other longer and more colorful ceremony held during Daylight Saving Time, usually on each Thursday, includes an honor guard. The Marine Band provides marching music, and the brilliant uniforms against the dark green Memorial make an event to remember. The ceremony starts about 5:00 P.M. and lasts some thirty minutes.

The one-hundred-ton bronze Memorial, depicting a group of Marines in combat garb as they struggle to raise the flag of the United States on an island wrested from the Japanese, was designed by Felix W. de Weldon. Inspired by the famous photograph by Joe Rosenthal, of the Associated Press, de Weldon went on to recreate the event in sculpture. The sculptor studied the dynamic grouping in official Marine Corps combat film sequences. The three survivors posed for him in their positions in the group. From thirty-two different models he evolved the final scale model.

The memorial was dedicated in November, 1954, which also marked the 179th anniversary of the founding of the Marine Corps. Sealed inside the cornerstone is a waterproof, airtight lead box containing such memorabilia as pictures of every Marine uniform since 1775, photostats of Continental Congress documents establishing the Corps, biographies of the first twenty Commandants, and a copy of "The Marines' Hymn" ("From the Halls of Montezuma, to the Shores of Tripoli . . .").

Carefully masked in a cartridge belt on one of the figures is a door, which permitted skilled artisans to go inside the statue and complete the big job of fitting together the three massive pieces by bolting and then welding the major joints. These sections, cast in a Brooklyn foundry, were trucked slowly into Washington by night to avoid heavy traffic. The black granite above the base is the color of volcanic ash on Iwo Jima. The greenish hue of the figures, achieved by use of a chemical compound, lends the uniforms realistic camouflage, which is heightened and preserved by a coating of wax.

The cost of the memorial and landscaping around its knoll came to approximately one million dollars, the full amount contributed by Marines, former Marines, their families, and friends. It honors Marines of all wars killed in defense of their country, and is a gift to the American people from the Corps.

For luncheon or dinner you might like to stay in Virginia, driving south to Allison's Little Tea House at 1301 South Arlington Ridge Road. From inside, or out on the terrace, you can dine well and take a long look at the Capital. It's a pleasant place from which to watch the lights come on in the Federal City across the Potomac, and to make plans for tomorrow.

BIBLIOGRAPHY

Aikman, Lonnelle, "U.S. Capitol, Citadel of Democracy," *National Geographic Magazine*, Vol. CII, No. 2, August, 1952, pp. 143–192.

Angle, Paul M., *The Lincoln Reader*. New Brunswick: Rutgers University Press, 1947.

Anthony, Katherine, *Dolly Madison, Her Life and Times*. New York: Doubleday & Company, 1949.

Brown, George Rothwell, *Washington, a Not Too Serious History*. Baltimore: Norman Publishing Co., Inc., 1930.

Bryan, Wilhelmus Bogart, *History of the National Capital, from its Foundation through the Period of the Adoption of the Organic Act*. 2 vols. New York: The Macmillan Company, 1914–16.

Carr, Martha S., *The District of Columbia, Its Rocks and Their Geologic History*, Washington: Government Printing Office, 1950.

Columbia Historical Society, Records of. Vol. I through Vols. 51–52, 1894–1897, 1951–1952.

Ecker, Grace Dunlop, *A Portrait of Old Georgetown*. Richmond: Garrett & Massie, 1933.

Evening Star files, Library of Congress, Year 1860, and miscellaneous.

Federal Writers' Project, *Washington, City and Capitol*. Washington: Government Printing Office, 1937.

Frary, I. T., *They Built the Capitol*. Richmond: Garrett & Massie, 1950.

Furman, Bess, *Washington By-Line*. New York: Alfred A. Knopf, 1949.

———, *White House Profile*. Indianapolis and New York: Bobbs Merrill, 1951.

Helm, Edith, *Captains and the Kings*. New York: G. P. Putnam's Sons, 1954.

Holloway, Laura C., *The Ladies of the White House*. Philadelphia: A. Gorton & Co., 1881.

Johnston, Elizabeth Bryant, *Original Portraits of Washington*. Boston: J. R. Osgood and Company, 1882.

271

Kite, Elizabeth S., *L'Enfant and Washington*. Baltimore: Johns Hopkins Press, 1929.

Latimer, Louise Payson, *Your Washington and Mine*. New York: Charles Scribner's Sons, 1924.

Leech, Margaret, *Reveille in Washington*. New York: Harper & Brothers, 1941.

Monroe, Harriet E., *Washington, Its Sights and Insights*. New York: Funk & Wagnalls Company, 1903.

Morgan, John Hill, and Fielding, Mantle, *The Life Portraits of Washington*. Philadelphia: Privately printed, 1931.

Mount Vernon Ladies' Association of the Union, *Mount Vernon, Virginia*. Mount Vernon: Photogravure and Color Company. 1953.

National Intelligencer files, Library of Congress; years 1801; 1814 and miscellaneous.

Sandburg, Carl, *Abraham Lincoln: the War Years*, Vols. III and IV. New York: Harcourt, Brace and Co., 1939.

Truett, Randle Bond, *The First Ladies in Fashion*. New York: Hastings House, 1954.

——, *The White House*. New York: Hastings House, 1953.

U.S. Department of State, *Blair House, Past and Present*. Washington: Government Printing Office, 1945.

Whitney, Janet, *Abigail Adams*. Boston: Little, Brown & Co., 1947.

Wilstach, Paul, *Potomac Landings*. New York: N. Nelson Doubleday, 1921.

INDEX

273